# Strategic Responses to Domestic Contestation

I0894624

How have EU-level actors responded to the increase in salience and contestation across the member states? This volume explores and explains the actors' strategic responses and emphasises that domestic pressure has triggered both depoliticisation and politicisation.

Long gone are the times when EU decisions left citizens indifferent, and when the supranational was largely irrelevant for public opinion and electoral politics across the member states. Instead, a string of existential crises has struck and unsettled the Union over more than a decade. These crises have politicised Europe, tested the endurance of the supranational system to its core, and put EU-level actors under unprecedented pressure. This volume explores how and why EU-level actors respond to the various, sometimes competing, 'bottom-up' demands, and challenges the view that domestic contestation necessarily limits EU-level room for manoeuvre. Instead, contributions show that domestic pressure can be perceived as either constraining or enabling, with responses, therefore, ranging from the restrained to the assertive. Driven by the survival of the Union, by the preservation of their own powers, and by different perceptions of domestic demands, actors will choose to politicise or depoliticise decision-making, behaviour, and policy outcomes at the supranational level. The volume concludes that whilst domestic pressure triggers supranational responses, such responses should not be assumed to be restraining; they may equally be empowering including for European integration itself.

The chapters in this book were originally published as a special issue of the *Journal of European Public Policy*.

**Edoardo Bressanelli** is 'Montalcini' Assistant Professor in the Institute of Law, Politics and Development at the Sant'Anna School of Advanced Studies in Pisa, Italy, and Senior Visiting Research Fellow at King's College London, United Kingdom.

**Christel Koop** is Senior Lecturer in the Department of Political Economy at King's College London, United Kingdom.

**Christine Reh** is Professor of European Politics and Dean of Graduate Programmes at the Hertie School in Berlin, Germany.

## Journal of European Public Policy Series

*Series Editors*

**Jeremy Richardson** *is Emeritus Fellow at Nuffield College, Oxford University, UK, and an Adjunct Professor in the National Centre for Research on Europe, University of Canterbury, New Zealand.*

**Berthold Rittberger** *is Professor and Chair of International Relations at the Geschwister-Scholl-Institute of Political Science at the University of Munich, Germany.*

This series seeks to bring together some of the finest edited works on European Public Policy. Reprinting from Special Issues of the *Journal of European Public Policy*, the focus is on using a wide range of social sciences approaches, both qualitative and quantitative, to gain a comprehensive and definitive understanding of Public Policy in Europe.

**The Future of the Social Investment State**
Policies, Outcomes and Politics
*Edited by Marius R. Busemeyer, Caroline de la Porte, Julian L. Garritzmann and Emmanuele Pavolini*

**The Politics and Economics of Brexit**
*Edited by Simon Bulmer and Lucia Quaglia*

**Free Movement and Non-discrimination in an Unequal Union**
*Edited by Susanne K. Schmidt, Michael Blauberger and Dorte Sindbjerg Martinsen*

**The Political Economy of Pension Financialisation**
*Edited by Anke Hassel and Tobias Wiß*

**The European Union Beyond the Polycrisis?**
Integration and Politicization in an Age of Shifting Cleavages
*Edited by Jonathan Zeitlin and Francesco Nicoli*

**Ideologies and the European Union**
*Edited by Carlo Invernizzi Accetti and Jonathan White*

**Strategic Responses to Domestic Contestation**
The EU Between Politicisation and Depoliticisation
*Edited by Edoardo Bressanelli, Christel Koop and Christine Reh*

For more information about this series, please visit: https://www.routledge.com/Journal-of-European-Public-Policy-Special-Issues-as-Books/book-series/JEPPSPIBS

# Strategic Responses to Domestic Contestation

## The EU Between Politicisation and Depoliticisation

***Edited by***
**Edoardo Bressanelli, Christel Koop and Christine Reh**

Routledge
Taylor & Francis Group
LONDON AND NEW YORK

First published 2021
by Routledge
2 Park Square, Milton Park, Abingdon, Oxon, OX14 4RN

and by Routledge
52 Vanderbilt Avenue, New York, NY 10017

*Routledge is an imprint of the Taylor & Francis Group, an informa business*



*British Library Cataloguing-in-Publication Data*
A catalogue record for this book is available from the British Library

ISBN13: 978-0-367-74078-8 (hbk)
ISBN13: 978-0-367-74080-1 (pbk)
ISBN13: 978-1-003-15600-0 (ebk)

Typeset in Myriad Pro
by codeMantra

**Publisher's Note**
The publisher accepts responsibility for any inconsistencies that may have arisen during the conversion of this book from journal articles to book chapters, namely the inclusion of journal terminology.

# Contents

# Citation Information

The chapters in this book were originally published in the *Journal of European Public Policy*, volume 27, issue 3 (March 2020). When citing this material, please use the original page numbering for each article, as follows:

**Chapter 1**
*EU Actors under pressure: politicisation and depoliticisation as strategic responses*
Edoardo Bressanelli, Christel Koop and Christine Reh
*Journal of European Public Policy*, volume 27, issue 3 (March 2020) pp. 329–341

**Chapter 2**
*Politicisation management in the European Union*
Frank Schimmelfennig
*Journal of European Public Policy*, volume 27, issue 3 (March 2020) pp. 342–361

**Chapter 3**
*Contestation and responsiveness in EU Council deliberations*
Sara B. Hobolt and Christopher Wratil
*Journal of European Public Policy*, volume 27, issue 3 (March 2020) pp. 362–381

**Chapter 4**
*The Court of Justice in times of politicisation: 'law as a mask and shield' revisited*
Michael Blauberger and Dorte Sindbjerg Martinsen
*Journal of European Public Policy*, volume 27, issue 3 (March 2020) pp. 382–399

**Chapter 5**
*Let's speak more? How the ECB responds to public contestation*
Manuela Moschella, Luca Pinto and Nicola Martocchia Diodati
*Journal of European Public Policy*, volume 27, issue 3 (March 2020) pp. 400–418

**Chapter 6**
*Responsive withdrawal? The politics of EU agenda-setting*
Christine Reh, Edoardo Bressanelli and Christel Koop
*Journal of European Public Policy*, volume 27, issue 3 (March 2020) pp. 419–438

**Chapter 7**

*Understanding the European Commission's use of politicisation in the negotiation of interinstitutional agreements: the role of consultations and issue framing*
Adriana Bunea
*Journal of European Public Policy*, volume 27, issue 3 (March 2020) pp. 439–459

**Chapter 8**

*Politicisation and economic governance design*
Fabio Franchino and Camilla Mariotto
*Journal of European Public Policy*, volume 27, issue 3 (March 2020) pp. 460–480

**Chapter 9**

*The European Union's authoritarian equilibrium*
R. Daniel Kelemen
*Journal of European Public Policy*, volume 27, issue 3 (March 2020) pp. 481–499

# Contributors

**Michael Blauberger** is Professor of European Union Politics at the University of Salzburg, Austria.

**Edoardo Bressanelli** is 'Montalcini' Assistant Professor at the Dirpolis Institute, Sant'Anna School, Pisa, Italy.

**Adriana Bunea** is Associate Professor at the University of Bergen, Department of Comparative Politics, Norway.

**Nicola Martocchia Diodati** is Data Scientist at IQVIA, Milan, Italy.

**Fabio Franchino** is Professor of Political Science at the Università degli Studi di Milano, Italy.

**Sara B. Hobolt** is the Sutherland Chair in European Institutions and Professor at the London School of Economics and Political Science, UK.

**R. Daniel Kelemen** is Professor of Political Science and Law at Rutgers University, USA.

**Christel Koop** is Senior Lecturer at the Department of Political Economy, King's College London, UK.

**Camilla Mariotto** is Postdoctoral Researcher at the Institute for Political Science of the University of Innsbruck, Austria.

**Dorte Sindbjerg Martinsen** is Professor of Political Science at the University of Copenhagen, Denmark.

**Manuela Moschella** is Associate Professor of International Political Economy at the Scuola Normale Superiore, Pisa, Italy.

**Luca Pinto** is Assistant Professor of Political Science at the University of Bologna, Italy.

**Christine Reh** is Professor of European Politics and Dean of Graduate Programmes at the Hertie School, Berlin, Germany.

**Frank Schimmelfennig** is Professor of European Politics, Center of Comparative and International Studies, ETH Zurich, Switzerland.

**Christopher Wratil** is Lecturer in European Politics at University College London, UK.

# EU actors under pressure: politicisation and depoliticisation as strategic responses

Edoardo Bressanelli*, Christel Koop * and Christine Reh*

**ABSTRACT**

This contribution conceptualises bottom-up politicisation in Europe's multi-level system. EU-level actors, we argue, respond strategically to the functional and political pressures 'travelling up' from the member states. Perceiving domestic dissensus as either constraining or enabling, actors display both self-restraint and assertiveness in their responses. Motivated by the survival of the EU as a system 'under attack', and by the preservation of their own substantive and procedural powers, actors choose to either politicise or depoliticise decision-making, behaviour and policy outcomes at the supranational level. As a collection, this Special Issue demonstrate that the choices actors make 'under stress' at the EU-level – ranging from 'restrained depoliticisation' to 'assertive politicisation' – are, indeed, conditional on how bottom-up pressures are perceived and processed.

## Introduction

Over the last decades, the European Union (EU) and the multi-level politics of Europe have seen major change. Gone are the times when EU decision-making resembled 'policy without politics' (Schmidt, 2006, p. ix); when EU policies were made under 'permissive consensus' (Lindberg & Scheingold, 1970); and when national (electoral) and party politics played out largely unaffected by supranational developments (Mair, 2001; Reif & Schmitt, 1980). The EU and its policies have become ever more relevant across the member states, and the concomitant functional and political pressures reverberate across Europe's multi-level system. This Special Issue explores, systematises and explains how and why EU-level actors have responded to these pressures.

Indeed, the EU has been hit by a string of crises in recent history: the Eurozone, migration, newly illiberal regimes and Brexit have kept the Union in

*The authors would like to acknowledge their equal contribution to the article.

continuous turmoil, with some scholars referring to a single 'polycrisis' (Zeitlin, Nicoli, & Laffan, 2019). This polycrisis has tested the endurance and survival of the EU polity to its limits; it has also put the Union under unprecedented pressure to manage these crises and to address their concomitant policy problems. In parallel, the contestation of the EU's policies and institutions became an ordinary fixture of domestic politics across the member states. The emphasis on the economic gains of transnational regulation – enjoying tacit support for decades – began to give way to the 'constraining dissensus' of post-functionalism (Hooghe & Marks, 2009). Standing for openness and lowered barriers of transnational exchange, 'the very existence of rule-based institutions' beyond the state became contested (Hooghe, Lenz, & Marks, 2019, p. 732; 731–3) – in public opinion, political discourse, party programmes, and at the ballot box. Its roots reaching back to the Maastricht referendums of the early 1990s, the new era saw the domestic politicisation of 'Europe' along three dimensions: (1) the Union and its policies have become more visible; (2) European integration has triggered increased contestation and polarisation; and (3) engagement with the EU has broadened beyond elite actors (De Wilde, Leupold, & Schmidtke, 2016).

This collection takes the domestic politicisation of Europe as its starting point. Domestic politicisation, we argue, translates into pressures that travel 'bottom-up'. *Functional pressures* confront EU-level actors with unprecedented expectations to manage and address the policy challenges of the 'polycrisis'; *political pressures* confront the Union with a new type of conflict, going well beyond the contained economic, regulatory or distributive conflicts of the first decades of integration. To be sure, European governance has never been free of controversy. Yet, for decades, conflict mainly played out at elite level; the Union, in turn, relied on elite-level mechanisms to accommodate heterogeneous interests. More recently, conflict has expanded into the public arena, comprising a novel range of policy-challenges, and putting the Union under the attack of Eurosceptic voters, political parties and public discourse. Under such pressure, EU-level actors have to respond, as maintaining the status quo is untenable. This Special Issue analyses these responses, which, we argue, are strategic choices to politicise or depoliticise decision-making, behaviour and outcomes at the supranational level. Our contributions systematically map and explain these choices, within and across EU-level actors, institutions, arenas and policies. In doing so, the collection makes three main contributions.

First, our focus on how EU-level actors respond and adapt to pressures 'travelling up' shifts attention from the 'top-down' to the 'bottom-up'. Top-down politicisation focuses on how Europe affects domestic politics, including societal cleavages, public opinion and political representation. This development is well-explored in the literature (e.g., Grande & Kriesi, 2005; Hutter, Grande, & Kriesi, 2016). Bottom-up politicisation focuses on how the growing visibility of, polarisation around and engagement with Europe at the domestic level impacts on actors at the EU-level. This is an increasingly relevant but under-studied dimension of supranational governance (for exceptions, see Börzel & Risse, 2018; Koop, Reh, & Bressanelli, 2018; Schmidt, 2019).

Against this backdrop, the Special Issue conceptualises bottom-up politicisation; theorises the mechanisms underlying EU-level responses (Schimmelfennig, 2020); and analyses the types of responses chosen. The contributions look at supranational actors, like the Court of Justice of the European Union (CJEU), the European Central Bank (ECB) and the European Commission (Blauberger & Martinsen, 2020; Moschella, Pinto, & Martocchia Diodati, 2020; Reh, Bressanelli, & Koop, 2020) as well as intergovernmental ones, like the Council of the EU (Hobolt & Wratil, 2020). Also, they zoom in on different decision-arenas, including law-making and inter-institutional relations (Bunea, 2020; Franchino & Mariotto, 2020), and explore a variety of governance challenges, including transparency and the rule of law (Hobolt & Wratil, 2020; Kelemen, 2020). Taking the EU's growing domestic relevance as analytical starting point, each contribution feeds into building an integrated actor-centred theoretical explanation of the conditions under which domestic pressures do (or do not) translate into EU-level responses.

Second, in doing so, the collection challenges the dominant view of domestic dissensus as necessarily constraining and, therefore, limiting the room for manoeuvre at the EU level. Instead, we propose that the post-functionalist Union has space, too, for '*enabling* dissensus', with actors displaying both self-restraint *and* assertiveness. Actors adapt strategically to the new environment; they can opt for restraint, or they can capitalise on pressures to advance their substantive goals, extend the scope of their competences, and bolster their long-term survival. As introduced in detail below, these strategic responses will either politicise or depoliticise decision-making, behaviour and outcomes at the supranational level. Neither strategy is *apolitical.* Each explicitly recognises and deliberately responds to bottom-up pressure – be this pressure functional (such as a crisis-related policy problem) or political (such as the EU's visible contestation). In doing so, each strategy reinforces or moderates one (or more) of the three dimensions of domestic politicisation: visibility, polarisation and engagement (see Figure 1). Our contributors show that the choices made by EU-level actors are not fixed, predetermined or constrained – as implied by most theories of integration – but conditional on how actors 'under stress' perceive and process bottom-up pressures.

Third, if EU-level actors – in particular non-majoritarian institutions like the Commission or the ECB, designed to be insulated from public opinion and domestic electoral cycles – respond to bottom-up functional *as well as* political pressures, then they are 'responsive' and not just 'responsible'. Indeed, several contributions in this collection show that institutions react to the signals sent by public opinion, party political competition and electoral

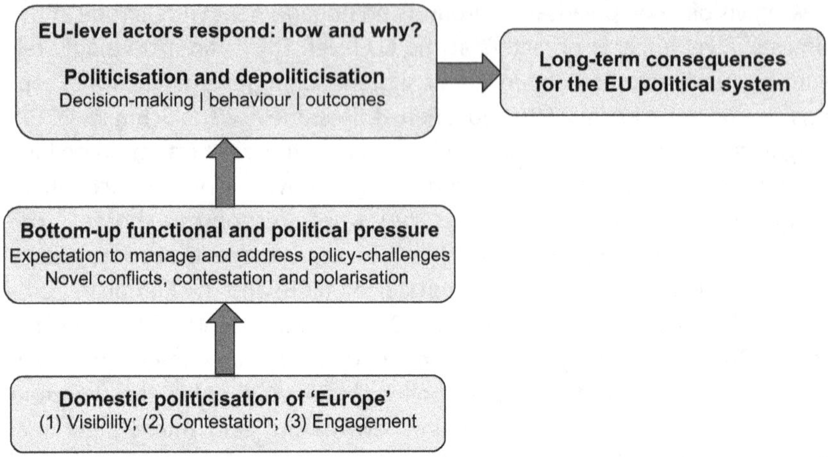


**Figure 1.** Bottom-up pressure and (de)politicisation as response.

politics across the member states (Blauberger & Martinsen, 2020; Hobolt & Wratil, 2020; Moschella *et al.*, 2020; Reh *et al.*, 2020). Contributing to a nascent research agenda on this aspect of EU and international governance (Hagemann, Hobolt, & Wratil, 2017; Rauh, 2016; Schneider, 2018; Wratil, 2018), the collection reflects on the responsiveness of individual actors and on the implications for the EU polity more broadly.

## Bottom-up pressure and the need to respond

The EU's growing relevance and its 'polycrisis' translate into functional and political pressures on Brussels as well as on Luxembourg and Frankfurt. Given the intensity of these pressures, the nature of the EU's political system, and the position and perception of actors in this system, the apolitical approach of the first decades of integration is viable no longer. Instead, EU-level actors will respond strategically to the challenges facing them from the bottom up.

First, since Maastricht, the Union's competences have been extended into the 'core state powers' of monetary policy and justice and home affairs (Genschel & Jachtenfuchs, 2018). Maastricht also deepened the Union's democratic and civic ambition, including provisions on European citizenship (Weiler, 1991). At the same time, electorally salient social and redistributive policies and resources remained national-level responsibilities (Moravcsik, 2002). When delegation to the supranational level was, in essence, seen as a response to functional pressure and economic interdependence, and when domestic elites, Europe-wide, subscribed to integration – if to varying degrees – this seemed a tenable status quo. Yet, in combination, these developments prepared the ground for pressures building up, until, in the early

2010s, 'Europe' hit the core of domestic electoral salience for the first time, and hit intensely as well as politically: budgets and redistribution, borders and belonging, protection and control. 'Opening up' and the accompanying economic, political and societal challenges led to loud calls for EU-level policy solutions, brought very visible change, and polarised through passionate endorsement *and* intense rejection at elite and mass level (De Wilde *et al.*, 2016; Hooghe *et al.*, 2019; Hutter *et al.*, 2016).

Under such conditions, the tried and tested supranational response – flanking Europe's market constitution with legal protections around free movement, building support through issue publics and organised interest, feeding on the legitimacy of national democracies (Cappelletti, Seccombe, & Weiler, 1986; European Commission, 2001; Scharpf, 2009) – became tenuous. Instead, when faced with intense and countervailing bottom-up pressures, simultaneously calling on the EU to act *and* to retreat, actors had to respond. These responses, we suggest, either politicise or depoliticise the supranational level; yet, no matter where exactly the responses fall, they invariably pertain to the newly political conflict around the EU and its policies.

Second, the European polity is, a priori, poorly equipped to respond. The EU is a political system whose competences are conferred by the member states. These competences have been 'in flux' since the outset, allowing flexibility, but limiting the Union's legal basis, financial resources and ability to tax and coerce. The EU's political system has traditionally been built on compromise, at the constitutional level and in everyday negotiation, accommodating competing interests, ideas and legitimating norms (Heisenberg, 2005; Moravcsik, 2005; Reh, 2012). When elites across Europe no longer share a basic preference for cooperation but clash openly and publicly, compromise becomes harder to reach and to communicate. More fundamentally, the EU is a system whose sheer existence polarises, and whose authority, institutions and outputs are fundamentally contested. Finally, the EU depends on its member states for effectiveness, legitimacy and stability (Scharpf, 2009); hence, when domestic elites are no longer trusted to deliver results, and when 'blaming Brussels' serves political point-scoring at home, the Union's ability to act and accommodate is directly affected. In sum, in a system whose very existence is contested, bottom-up pressures generate both opportunities to respond and constraints on how to respond.

Third, 'the EU' is under pressure, and our contributions explore and explain actors' responses at the supranational level. Like the system for which they were designed and in which they have evolved, these actors have never enjoyed an unquestioned existence, with diverse – and often competing – sources for their legitimacy debated. In developing their strategic responses to the new environment, EU-level actors will be driven by two motivations: (1) by the survival of the EU as a system 'under attack'; and (2) by the preservation of their own substantive and procedural powers. Under the stress of political contestation and visible conflict, actors need to fight for their own reputation as well as for the reputation of the system they serve and on whose continued existence they depend (cf. Carpenter, 2001).

We suggest that these motivations – if not the response routes taken – hold true for both non-majoritarian institutions like the Commission, the CJEU or the ECB, and for electorally more connected actors like the European Parliament (EP) and governments in Council. All these actors are under stress, and all need to take a stance on the newly political conflict of integration.

## Types of strategic responses

As discussed so far, the scope, nature and intensity of the changing attitudes towards Europe as well as the greater domestic relevance of the Union and its policies make it imperative to act at the supranational level. We assume that EU-level actors respond strategically; they will – through a variety of means – intentionally change the procedural, behavioural and substantive status quo at the supranational level so as to further their goals, taking other actors' expected behaviour and judgement into account (cf. Lake & Powell, 1999, p. 3). By its very nature, action is more prone to being strategic than inaction. Inaction, too, may be a strategic choice; yet, more often it is driven by habit, routine or the stickiness of standard practices. All these will continue to co-exist next to strategic responses, but they cannot remain the dominant route under intense pressure that puts the very survival of the system and its actors on the line.

Yet, perceiving pressure and recognising the need to act does not provide a blueprint for *how* to act. First, domestic politicisation may induce actors to increase their visibility, but may also incentivise them to keep a low profile and exercise self-restraint (Alon-Barkat & Gilad, 2016). Second, while domestic politicisation is primarily associated with Euroscepticism, it can also come as Europhilia (Turnbull-Dugarte, 2019). Moreover, attitudes towards Europe vary considerably across member states (De Vries, 2018). Hence, actors need to make choices between options, which often point into opposite directions and involve trade-offs. Indeed, zooming in on 'strategic politicisation management', Schimmelfennig (2020) argues that EU-level actors have agency in response to bottom-up pressure; the choices made, he theorises, are driven by actors' electoral accountability, mediated by issue salience, policy type, the degree of risk and election proximity.

We propose four types of EU-level responses to bottom-up pressure (see Table 1). Shifting the status quo at the supranational level, each response type is an explicit recognition of, and a deliberate attempt to impact on, domestic politicisation. Actors will choose the response most likely to further their main goal: survival of the Union, and/or preservation (and even expansion) of the actor's own powers. When making this choice, actors will consider two

**Table 1.** Types of responses by EU-level actors.

| | Strategy | |
|---|---|---|
| Perception of pressure | Politicisation | Depoliticisation |
| Enabling | Assertive politicisation | Assertive depoliticisation |
| Constraining | Restrained politicisation | Restrained depoliticisation |

questions: (1) Is the bottom-up pressure enabling or constraining? (2) Is a 'political response' to this opportunity or constraint likely to be acceptable? Actors will perceive a pressure as an opportunity (or constraint) if it enables (or constrains) their substantive or organisational (self-) empowerment through a broadly interpreted mandate, strengthened institutional competence, or an extended set of policy instruments. Actors will ask whether 'acting politically' – understood here as the explicit recognition of, and visible intervention into, political conflict – is or is not likely to be acceptable, and considered conform to the actor's mandate by elites and the public. If this is the case, an actor should attempt to actively politicise decision-making, behaviour or outcomes at the supranational level; if not, an actor should opt for a strategy that intervenes by depoliticising conflict. The answer to these questions – and, hence, the response type chosen – will not just differ across and within actors, but also vary with decision-arenas, issue-areas and specific constellations.

All four response types become options when the EU moves into the limelight of (domestic) politics (see Table 2). In this context, *depoliticisation strategies* aim to 'reclaim the shadow'; that is, while recognising the need to intervene, they are targeted at making the new conflict of integration deliberately and explicitly less visible, less polarising and less salient (cf. De Wilde & Zürn, 2012, p. 139). To do so, actors turn to decision-arenas that are secluded and reserved for narrow special interests and epistemic communities; when visible conflict occurs, negotiations display consensus-seeking behaviour, with wider communication conducted in technical terms; and actors produce outcomes that are problem-driven and presented as output-oriented and responsible. In their *assertive* form, depoliticisation strategies use the new opportunities from bottom-up pressure to actively expand or create secluded decision-arenas; to restrict participation; to shore up consensus-seeking when conflict occurs, including through formalisation and judicialisation; to use technical frames in public communication; and to put out messages of problem-solving responsibility. In their *restrained* form, depoliticisation strategies turn to existing spaces of secluded and restricted decision-making; actively move conflict out of the public eye; reduce outward-facing activity altogether; and justify outcomes as responsible expertise-based optimisation.

Contributors to the Special Issue show and explain the use of depoliticisation strategies by different EU-level actors. Revisiting Burley and Mattli's classic 'law as a mask and shield' argument (1993), Blauberger and Martinsen (2020) analyse the CJEU's recent jurisprudence, in particular on freedom of movement and citizens' rights. They demonstrate how the Court engages in assertive depoliticisation by using the law as both 'mask' and 'shield', while engaging in judicial self-restraint – a strategy of restrained depoliticisation – under high levels of contestation by both member state governments and public opinion. Focusing on the European Commission, Reh *et al.* (2020) show that this institution uses its power to withdraw legislative proposals when facing domestic contestation, particularly in sensitive policy areas for the member states. In doing so, the Commission assertively depoliticises contentious decisions. Finally, assessing reforms of the EU's economic governance, Franchino and Mariotto (2020) point to a shift in decision-arena, away from domestic and intergovernmental politics towards the (more technocratic and implementation-focused) supranational level. Importantly, these different contributions find more evidence of assertive than restrained depoliticisation.

Rather than chasing the 'lost shadow', EU-level actors can also move the status quo deliberately into the heart of politics. *politicisation strategies* at the supranational level do not shy away from visibility, polarisation and broad engagement (cf. De Wilde & Zürn, 2012, p. 139); instead, they are targeted precisely at reinforcing one or all of these dimensions. To do so, actors opt for more transparent decision-making, open arenas up to participation and scrutiny by the wider public, civil society and political parties; allow visible conflict in their negotiation behaviour; are more outward-oriented; and present outcomes as primarily responsive to salient public issues. *Assertive politicisation* strategies capitalise on the new bottom-up opportunities by actively expanding and creating transparent and inclusive decision-arenas; allowing – even promoting – visible conflict, including over ideology, redistribution and fundamental values; expanding public communication and engagement; and presenting outcomes as responding to public opinion. *Restrained politicisation* strategies rely on existing open decision-arenas and established channels of participation beyond issue-specific stakeholders; opt for formal conflict-resolution, even if allowing controversy to become visible; engage in public justification; and promote outcomes as policy-solutions that address issues of high domestic salience.

Our contributions show a variety of politicisation strategies in response to bottom-up pressure. Focusing on contestation in the Council, Hobolt and Wratil (2020) find that under domestic opposition, member state governments move away from the 'normal' consensus pattern, particularly when deciding on salient policies. Opposition enables member states to deviate from the consensual 'business as usual', thus empowering governments at the EU level; yet, it may equally reflect increased constraint imposed by domestic publics. Moschella *et al.* (2020) observe assertive politicisation in one of the most technocratic European bodies: the ECB. Analysing more than a decade-and-a-half of executive speeches, they point out that the Bank responds to negative public opinion by expanding the scope of its communication and by reducing the attention attributed to monetary policy only. Bunea (2020) offers a clear example of assertive politicisation by the European Commission in inter-institutional negotiations. Based on a perceived need to re-legitimise its role, the Commission actively expands openness and consultation beyond established stakeholders, makes conflict visible, and frames issues politically. Likewise, while Reh *et al.* (2020) depict a Commission that depoliticises through restraint, they also show an actor that assertively keeps domestically salient legislation on the agenda, even under visible adversity. Finally, Kelemen (2020) shows a paradoxical outcome in what he labels 'half-baked' politicisation of the Union. While the EU actively responded to political pressures strengthening EU-level parties and institutionalising the *Spitzenkandidaten* procedure, Europarties are not sufficiently known domestically to face any electoral consequence for what they (fail to) do in Brussels. The Hungarian leader Orban hugely benefitted from his membership in the European People's Party, whilst strengthening his illiberal regime undermining the EU's values. In short, on politicisation, too, our contributions find more responses that are assertive rather than restrained.

**Table 2.** Assertive and restrained (de)politicisation.

| | Politicisation | | Depoliticisation | |
|---|---|---|---|---|
| | Assertive | Restrained | Assertive | Restrained |
| **Decision-Making** (openness & participation) | **Transparency** | | **Seclusion** | |
| | Expand/create open arenas | Use existing open arenas | Expand/create secluded arenas | Use existing secluded arenas |
| | **Wider public, civil society & political parties** | | **Special interests & experts** | |
| | Seek/expand participation | Use established channels | Actively limit participation | Use established channels |
| **Behaviour** (negotiation & communication) | **Conflict & competition** | | **Consensus-seeking** | |
| | Allow or promote visible conflict | Formal conflict resolution | Consensus when conflict occurs | Active attempts to hide conflict |
| | **Outward-oriented** | | **Technical** | |
| | Increase public communication | Engage in public justification | Reframe controversy technically | Reduce outward-facing activities |
| **Outcomes** (drivers & frame) | **Public opinion** | | **Policy-problems** | |
| | Respond to public opinion | Respond to salient issues | Problem-solving responsibility | Expertise-based optimisation |
| | **Responsiveness** | | **Responsibility** | |
| | Focus on responsiveness as (re-) legitimation | | Focus on responsible output as (re-) legitimation | |

## Conclusion: Long-term consequences for the EU as a political system?

Much of the debate about the post-functionalist Union has focused on the 'constraining dissensus' across member states. We have argued, instead, that there is space, too, for *enabling* dissensus; that the strategic choices made by EU-level actors are conditional on how they perceive and process bottom-up pressure; and that dissensus has a differential impact. In a nutshell, we propose – and our contributions show – that domestic politicisation will not lead to 'the end of integration' but to a variety of supranational responses, ranging from restrained depoliticisation to assertive politicisation. Following up on our conceptualisation, Schimmelfennig theorises the conditions under which actors can be expected to adopt (de)politicisation strategies, while the individual contributions to the Special Issue showcase and explain such strategies across actors, arenas and issue-areas.

Turning to the EU's political system more generally, we suggest three tentative conclusions and future research routes. First, as a highly divided polity, the EU has, traditionally, been built on compromise and accommodation, in everyday negotiation and in constitutional choice. Indeed, several of the depoliticisation strategies shown here are geared at the possibility of consensus under contestation – be this through the exchange of arguments, the possibility of persuasion, or the extension of time to cope with complexity (e.g., Chambers, 2004). We would, therefore, caution against equating legitimisation too readily with politicisation and responsiveness. Second, all contributions analyse (de)politicisation as responses in an everyday context – be that legislative agenda-setting or decision-making, jurisprudence or public communication, macro-economic coordination or party-political interaction. In the long-run, we will observe whether any of these 'everyday responses' lead to formal institutional reform – as happened, for instance, with parliamentary empowerment that started in the interstices of EU decision-making before being translated into Treaty change (Héritier, 2007). Finally, and closely related, the Special Issue studies the (de)politicisation of decision-making, behaviour and outcomes. Yet, if our argument is correct, and if one response to bottom-up pressure is self-empowerment, we might also expect competence shifts – including in redistributive policies – to the supranational level.

In sum, the top-down impact of 'dissensus' on politics in the EU's member states is well-explored. This collection focuses, instead, on how political pressures 'travel' bottom-up, and conceptualises, theorises and analyses the strategic choices actors make 'under stress' at the EU-level.

## Acknowledgements

The authors would like to thank Harry Bauer, Berthold Rittberger and Frank Schimmelfennig for their constructive comments on an earlier version of the manuscript. The article also benefited greatly from the feedback and support of the contributors to this Special Issue, starting with a workshop on 'Politicising and De-Politicising the European Union' at King's College London in December 2017.

## Disclosure statement

No potential conflict of interest was reported by the authors.

## Funding

Research for this article was supported by a British Academy/Leverhulme Small Research Grant (SG160582; 'Politicising Europe') and a King's College London Faculty Research Fund Grant.

## ORCID

*Christel Koop* http://orcid.org/0000-0002-7125-6439

## References

Alon-Barkat, S., & Gilad, S. (2016). Political control or legitimacy deficit? Bureaucracies' symbolic responses to bottom-up public pressures. *Policy & Politics*, *44*(1), 41–58.

Blauberger, M., & Martinsen, D. S. (2020). The court of justice in times of politicisation: "law as a mask and shield" revisited. *Journal of European Public Policy*, *27*(3), 382–399.

Börzel, T. A., & Risse, T. (2018). From the euro to the Schengen crises: European integration theories, politicization, and identity politics. *Journal of European Public Policy*, *25*(1), 83–108.

Bunea, A. (2020). Understanding the European Commission's use of politicisation in the negotiation of interinstitutional agreements: The role of consultations and issue framing. *Journal of European Public Policy*, *27*(3), 439–459.

Burley, A.-M., & Mattli, W. (1993). Europe before the Court: A political theory of legal integration. *International Organization*, *47*(1), 41–76.

Cappelletti, M., Seccombe, M., & Weiler, J. (Eds.). (1986). *Integration through law. Europe and the American federal experience*. Vol. 1. Berlin & New York: De Gruyter.

Carpenter, D. P. (2001). *The forging of bureaucratic autonomy: Reputations, networks, and policy innovation in executive agencies, 1862–1928*. Princeton, NJ: Princeton University Press.

Chambers, S. (2004). Behind closed doors: Publicity, secrecy, and the quality of deliberation. *Journal of Political Philosophy, 12*(4), 389–410.

De Vries, C. E. (2018). *Euroscepticism and the future of European integration*. Oxford: Oxford University Press.

De Wilde, P., Leupold, A., & Schmidtke, H. (2016). Introduction: The differentiated politicisation of European governance. *West European Politics, 39*(1), 3–22.

De Wilde, P., & Zürn, M. (2012). Can the politicization of European integration be reversed? *JCMS: Journal of Common Market Studies, 50*(s1), 137–153.

European Commission. (2001). *European Governance—A white paper*. Brussels. COM (2001) 428 final.

Franchino, F., & Mariotto, C. (2020). Politicisation and economic governance design. *Journal of European Public Policy, 27*(3), 460–480.

Genschel, P., & Jachtenfuchs, M. (2018). From market integration to core state powers: The Eurozone crisis, the refugee crisis and integration theory. *JCMS: Journal of Common Market Studies, 56*(1), 178–196.

Grande, E., & Kriesi, H. (2005). The restructuring of political conflict in Europe and the politicization of European integration. In T. Risse (Ed.), *European public spheres: Politics is back* (pp. 190–223). Cambridge: Cambridge University Press.

Hagemann, S., Hobolt, S. B., & Wratil, C. (2017). Government responsiveness in the European Union: Evidence from council voting. *Comparative Political Studies, 50*(6), 850–876.

Heisenberg, D. (2005). The institution of 'consensus' in the European Union: Formal versus informal decision-making in the council. *European Journal of Political Research, 44*(1), 65–90.

Héritier, A. (2007). *Explaining institutional change in Europe*. Oxford: Oxford University Press.

Hobolt, S. B., & Wratil, C. (2020). Contestation and responsiveness in EU Council deliberations. *Journal of European Public Policy, 27*(3), 362–381.

Hooghe, L., Lenz, T., & Marks, G. (2019). Contested world order: The delegitimation of international governance. *The Review of International Organizations, 14*(4), 731–743.

Hooghe, L., & Marks, G. (2009). A postfunctionalist theory of European integration: From permissive consensus to constraining dissensus. *British Journal of Political Science, 39* (1), 1–23.

Hutter, S., Grande, E., & Kriesi, H.-P. (Eds.). (2016). *Politicising Europe: Integration and mass politics*. Cambridge: Cambridge University Press.

Kelemen, R. D. (2020). The European Union's authoritarian equilibrium. *Journal of European Public Policy, 27*(3), 481–499.

Koop, C., Reh, C., & Bressanelli, E. (2018). When politics prevails: Parties, elections and loyalty in the European Parliament. *European Journal of Political Research, 57*(3), 563–586.

Lake, D. A., & Powell, R. (1999). International relations: A strategic choice. In D. A. Lake & R. Powell (Eds.), *Strategic choice and international relations* (pp. 3–38). Princeton: Princeton University Press.

Lindberg, L. L., & Scheingold, S. A. (1970). *Europe's would-Be polity: Patterns of change in the European community*. Englewood Cliffs: Prentice-Hall.

Mair, P. (2001). The limited impact of Europe on national party systems. *West European Politics, 23*(4), 27–51.

Moravcsik, A. (2002). "In defence of the democratic deficit": Reassessing legitimacy in the European Union. *JCMS: Journal of Common Market Studies, 40*(4), 603–624.

Moravcsik, A. (2005). The European constitutional compromise and the neofunctionalist legacy. *Journal of European Public Policy, 12*(2), 349–386.
Moschella, M., Pinto, L., & Martocchia Diodati, N. (2020). Let's speak more? How the ECB responds to public contestation. *Journal of European Public Policy, 27*(3), 400–418.
Rauh, C. (2016). *A responsive technocracy? EU politicisation and the consumer policies of the European Commission*. ECPR Monographs Series. Colchester: ECPR Press.
Reh, C. (2012). European integration as compromise: Recognition, concessions and the limits of cooperation. *Government and Opposition, 47*(3), 414–440.
Reh, C., Bressanelli, E., & Koop, C. (2020). Responsive withdrawal? The politics of EU agenda-setting. *Journal of European Public Policy, 27*(3), 419–438.
Reif, K., & Schmitt, H. (1980). Nine second-order national elections: A conceptual framework for the analysis of European election results. *European Journal of Political Research, 8*(1), 3–44.
Scharpf, F. W. (2009). Legitimacy in the multilevel European polity. *European Political Science Review, 1*(2), 173–204.
Schimmelfennig, F. (2020). Politicisation management in the European Union. *Journal of European Public Policy, 27*(3), 342–361.
Schmidt, V. A. (2006). *Democracy in Europe: The EU and national polities*. Oxford: Oxford University Press.
Schmidt, V. A. (2019). Politicization in the EU: Between national politics and EU political dynamics. *Journal of European Public Policy, 26*(7), 1018–1036.
Schneider, C. (2018). *The responsive union national elections and European governance*. Cambridge: Cambridge University Press.
Turnbull-Dugarte, S. J. (2019). The impact of EU intervention on political parties' politicisation of Europe following the financial crisis. *West European Politics*, Online First.
Weiler, J. H. H. (1991). Problems of legitimacy in post 1992 Europe. *Aussenwirtschaft, 46* (3/4), 411–437.
Wratil, C. (2018). Modes of government responsiveness in the European Union: Evidence from Council negotiation position. *European Union Politics, 19*(1), 52–74.
Zeitlin, J., Nicoli, F., & Laffan, B. (2019). Introduction: The European Union beyond the polycrisis? Integration and politicization in an age of shifting cleavages. *Journal of European Public Policy, 26*(7), 963–979.

# Politicisation management in the European Union

Frank Schimmelfennig

**ABSTRACT**

Politicisation in the EU is mostly analysed as a domestic-level process constraining EU-level actors. Yet EU actors also engage in strategic politicisation management. This article theorises the conditions under which EU actors engage in either depoliticisation or politicisation strategies when they react to bottom-up pressures. It stipulates that politicisation management depends on the actors and issue context in question. Elected EU actors choose politicisation strategies, in particular if they represent challenger parties, deal with domestically salient and core state policies and are close to elections. By contrast, unelected EU actors prefer depoliticisation strategies except in the context of inter-institutional conflict. The politicisation of high-risk policies also produces depoliticisation. Recent empirical studies provide support to these conjectures and suggest that strategic politicisation management allows EU actors to maintain considerable room of manoeuvre.

## Introduction

Politicisation has become a key issue in scholarship on the European Union (EU). In postfunctionalist theory, it signifies a fundamental and game-changing process in European integration. Politicisation questions the traditional focus of integration theories and studies of EU policy-making on stakeholder lobbying, intergovernmental negotiations and inter-institutional bargaining operating under the condition of a 'permissive consensus' of citizens. Instead, in a politicised EU, public opinion, social identities and cleavages, party ideology and competition, national elections and referendums produce a 'constraining dissensus' on EU (government and supranational) actors and European governance (Hooghe & Marks, 2009).

Postfunctionalism has shaped the mainstream understanding of politicisation as a domestic-level process constraining EU actors. All three elements are important. First, politicisation is conceptualised as a (macro-level) process. The most widely shared definition of EU politicisation features the growing domestic salience of European governance, the polarisation of opinions and preferences on EU issues and the expansion of actors and audiences engaged in or attentive to EU affairs (De Wilde, Leupold, & Schmidtke, 2016, p. 4). Second, the politicisation of European integration originates in, and takes place predominantly at, the national level. National media generate and reflect the growing salience and contestation of EU issues; national (challenger) parties mobilise the Eurosceptic public opinion and vote; and national referendums on EU issues accelerate this process. Third, politicisation mainly affects European governance as a structural constraint. Politicisation pressures limit the room of manoeuvre of EU actors and generate downward pressure on the level and scope of European integration (Hooghe & Marks, 2009, p. 21).

It is a matter of debate whether the domestic politicisation of European integration really is a general and growing phenomenon across Europe (Grande & Kriesi, 2016; Rauh, 2016, pp. 22–5). Yet there is no doubt that it has become a powerful constraint on EU decisions on 'constitutive issues' such as 'widening' and 'deepening' (Grande & Hutter, 2016). Negative referendums from Maastricht to Brexit and the rise of Eurosceptic parties and governments are particularly visible events and developments. Even technocratic institutions such as the European Commission in 'low politics' areas such as consumer policy show responsiveness to bottom-up politicisation pressures (Rauh, 2016, 2019). Bottom-up politicisation pressures are, however, only one side of the politicisation of European integration. The other is top-down politicisation management.

Member state governments and supranational actors have strong incentives to overcome the constraints of domestic politicisation pressures or use these pressures to their advantage (Bressanelli, Koop, & Reh, 2020). Generally, they have an interest in maintaining the autonomy to pursue their preferred policies through the EU. Moreover, they are not only under domestic pressure but also face international challenges from inside and outside the EU. Inside the EU, they need to handle the deficiencies and crises of integrated policy regimes. They must negotiate intergovernmental conflicts, respect supranational rules and respond to inter-institutional demands by other EU actors. Externally, they need to react to challenges of globalisation and geopolitics.

Moreover, EU actors are not helpless 'victims' of domestic politicisation. They possess important material, political and institutional resources to manage bottom-up pressure through anticipatory and reactive measures. By (re-)framing and (re-)packaging policies, selecting and changing decision-making processes and (re-)designing institutions, EU actors can prevent or deflect politicisation that would limit their room to manoeuvre. Alternatively, they may choose to be responsive to domestic pressures or even 'ride the wave' by fuelling and exploiting politicisation pressures for their own purposes. In sum, EU actors have both the incentives and the capacity to engage in politicisation management.

The postfunctionalist and politicisation literature has only given scant attention to the agency of EU-level actors (De Wilde & Zürn, 2012, pp. 137–8; Grande & Kriesi, 2016, p. 291; Hooghe & Marks, 2009, p. 22). Traditional, functional integration theories have much to say about EU-level agency, but describe *anticipatory* depoliticisation strategies rather than reactions to manifest bottom-up pressures. Recent empirical work typically focuses on individual EU actors, issues, and stages of the policy-making process.

In the context of this special issue on politicisation and depoliticisation (Bressanelli *et al.*, 2020), this article therefore sets out to complement the dominant domestic-level 'politicisation as constraint' with an EU-level 'politicisation as agency' perspective. In contrast to the macro-level analysis of politicisation pressures as a domestic societal process, the analysis of politicisation management focuses on the strategies and instruments that EU actors have at their disposal. Going beyond the anticipatory depoliticisation discussed in integration theories and comparative politics approaches, it shifts the emphasis to reactive politicisation management. And in contrast to existing actor- or issue-specific studies, it aims at a more general account of politicisation management. The theoretical challenge of 'politicisation as agency' is to explain when and how governments and supranational actors choose between politicisation and depoliticisation strategies and whether and how these strategies enable them to preserve their policy-making autonomy.

The article briefly recapitulates the analysis of the EU as an 'anticipatory depoliticisation machine', which pervades both integration theory and comparative politics accounts of the EU. It then turns to theorising the motivations and capacities of governments and supranational actors for reactive politicisation management and the constraints and opportunities under which they act. My argument starts from the assumption that domestic politicisation constrains the policy and autonomy-seeking motivations of EU actors. How they respond to this constraint depends on the actors and the issue context. I hypothesise that elected EU actors have strong incentives and capacity to use reactive politicisation strategies in managing bottom-up pressure – especially if they represent challenger or GAL-TAN parties, domestic salience is high and elections are close. By contrast, unelected supranational actors focus on depoliticisation (except in the inter-institutional arena, in which they conflict with other EU actors). Moreover, policies that concern core state powers are more likely to be politicised, whereas high-risk policies are likely to be depoliticised. Finally, I point to pieces of evidence supporting these hypotheses and suggesting that EU actors have been able, indeed, to preserve considerable room of manoeuvre through strategic politicisation management.

## EU politicisation management: from anticipatory to reactive

### *The EU as an anticipatory depoliticisation machine*

In the EU literature, the term 'politicisation' generally denotes a societal process rather than an actor strategy. Yet the widely used three-dimensional conceptualisation based on salience, polarisation and expansion of actors and audiences (De Wilde *et al.*, 2016, p. 4) can be reformulated easily. 'Politicisation' and 'depoliticisation' then refer to responses of EU-level actors to bottom-up pressures (Bressanelli *et al.*, 2020). They denote strategies of increasing and decreasing salience or visibility, conflict or polarisation and responsiveness or participation. Together, politicisation and depoliticisation strategies constitute the two facets of what I propose to term 'politicisation management'.

In addition, we can distinguish anticipatory and reactive politicisation management (cf. Hinterleitner & Sager, 2017). Anticipatory politicisation management refers to a set of strategies that actors use before institutions and policies come under politicisation pressure. Typically, anticipatory management aims at depoliticisation, i.e., it designs and presents institutions and policies in a way that minimises salience and the risks of contestation and mobilisation. By contrast, reactive politicisation management responds to a situation in which anticipatory depoliticisation strategies have failed and an issue has become politicised against the will of policy-makers.

Theories of European integration and comparative politics approaches to the EU agree that EU institutions and policies were generally designed in a way that facilitates anticipatory depoliticisation (even though they do not use the term). They share the assumption that European integration has been a process driven by autonomy- and policy-seeking political elites who isolated EU institutions and policies from bottom-up pressure. This section establishes a theoretical baseline, from which we can start to theorise why and under which conditions EU actors shift from anticipatory to reactive politicisation management.

Integration theories assume that EU actors are motivated by a mix of autonomy and policy seeking. 'Autonomy seeking' refers to actors' motivation to increase their formal competencies and resources and to decrease their dependence on and accountability to other actors, whereas 'policy seeking' actors focus on attaining substantive policy goals.

Traditional intergovernmentalism assumes autonomy-seeking states, most fundamentally interested in using integration to secure state survival (Milward, 2000) and balance powerful member and non-member *states* (Grieco, 1996). By contrast, Wolf's 'new raison d'état' (Wolf, 1999, 2000) claims that states integrate to increase their autonomy vis-à-vis transnational and domestic *society*. By integrating small national markets and currencies, and by delegating regulatory authority to supranational organisations, states build capacity to tame globalised markets and rein in multinational corporations. At the same time, the transfer of authority to the EU frees national governments from domestic pressures and scrutiny.

By contrast, both neofunctionalism and liberal intergovernmentalism put the emphasis on states' policy-seeking motivation. Domestic groups and governments have a 'functional' motivation to engage in integration to increase the effectiveness and efficiency of policies. Preference formation and EU-level negotiation processes are policy-specific, too. Even though Moravcsik assumes that the integration process also increases states' autonomy (Moravcsik, 1994), this is best seen as a side effect of the policy-motivated creation of supranational organisations designed to enhance the credibility of state commitments to negotiated agreements. Supranational integration serves to remove common policies from the influence of domestic integration losers who might build up pressure for policy change or non-compliance. The degree to which governments pool and delegate their decision-making competences depends on the value they place on the issues and substantive outcomes in question and on their uncertainty about the future behaviour of domestic societies and other governments (Moravcsik, 1998, p. 9, 73).

Whereas states establish supranational organisations like the Commission and the Court with the aim of securing their agreed policies, these organisations also seek to increase their autonomy by expanding their competencies and resources. According to neofunctionalism, European integration has initially progressed because it was advanced by technocrats, pluralist interest groups and parties without sharp ideological conflict and because it proceeded incrementally based on 'covert economic choices with hidden political implications' (Haas, 1968, pp. xxiv–xxv). Moreover, neofunctionalists describe several ways in which supranational actors engage in anticipatory depoliticisation. 'Upgrading the common interest' refers to the expert-led design of supranational policies that maximise collective welfare and minimize bottom-up contestation (Haas, 1961). 'Actor socialisation' (Lindberg & Scheingold, 1970, p. 199) reduces contestation through the formation of common identities and beliefs. Finally, legal integration using the 'law as a mask and shield' (Burley & Mattli, 1993, p. 72) disguises judicial activism and deflects political criticism.

Analyses rooted in comparative-politics approaches and focusing on the study of public opinion, parties, elections and policies come to similar conclusions. For one, fragmented institutions and complex policy-making structures such as the EU with its multiple levels of governance and blurred separation of powers generally impede the attribution of political accountability (Hinterleitner & Sager, 2017, p. 598). The distance between 'Brussels' and the citizens, the lack of knowledge about the EU, the linguistic barriers and the relative scarcity of media coverage are additional obstacles to effective politicisation pressures. The absence of government-opposition dynamics and the prevalence of informal consensus-seeking even where formal rules allow for majority voting and inter-institutional conflict further promote depoliticisation. For instance, Novak (2013) explains the widespread absence of formal voting in the Council as a blame-avoidance strategy. Labels such as 'governance without opposition' (Neunreither, 1998) and 'policy without politics' (Schmidt, 2006) point to essential features of the EU succinctly. These features make it difficult for voters to identify the responsible actors and hold them to account (Hobolt & Tilley, 2014). In the words of Peter Mair, the 'sleeping giant', referring to the EU's citizens, 'has been deliberately sedated' (2007, p. 13). The traditional policy mix of the EU with its heavy focus on market-related regulatory policies and the marginal role of openly redistributive and coercive policies lends itself to depoliticisation, too. Moravcsik contends that 'EU legislative and regulatory activity is inversely correlated with the salience of issues in the minds of European voters' (2002, p. 616) and thereby discourages citizens from getting informed about and involved in EU politics.

In sum, the institutional set-up, the policy mix, and the decision-making behaviour of the EU is overwhelmingly located on the depoliticisation pole. Integration theories also agree, however, that anticipatory depoliticisation has its limits. Haas recognised that 'dramatic-political actors' like de Gaulle could disrupt the incremental and non-ideological integration process (1968, p. xv). Schmitter expected that 'spillover' would eventually give rise to controversy and actor expansion (1969, p. 166). Postfunctionalism detects a process of mass politicisation in the post-Maastricht era, resulting from the deepening of the EU and its expansion into the domain of 'core state powers' (Genschel & Jachtenfuchs, 2014) such as monetary and fiscal policy, internal and external security and border and migration policies, which mobilise national identities and heighten self-determination concerns (Hooghe & Marks, 2009, pp. 5–8).

The weakening of anticipatory depoliticisation requires EU actors as well as EU scholars to shift their attention towards reactive politicisation management. How does mass politicisation change the incentives and constraints of EU actors? When do they engage in reactive politicisation management and when do they choose depoliticisation vs. politicisation strategies in response to bottom-up pressures?

## *Reactive politicisation management: strategies of blame avoidance*

It follows from the assumption of integration theories and comparative-politics approaches that governments and supranational actors established and used the EU purposefully as a 'depoliticisation machine' to further their autonomy and policy preferences that they will in general perceive the growth of bottom-up politicisation as a threat or unwelcome constraint. Under certain circumstances, EU actors can safely ignore this constraint, e.g., if the policies they make have low salience or enjoy a broad consensus and to the extent that their offices and political careers are independent of domestic scrutiny and electoral support. Otherwise, they need to engage in (reactive) politicisation management. Under specific conditions, mass politicisation may even present EU actors with autonomy and policy-seeking opportunities they can exploit strategically in EU-level intergovernmental and inter-institutional conflicts.

Domestic politicisation has the effect of adding vote seeking to the traditional autonomy and policy-seeking motivations of EU actors. The more citizens are aware of, form structured preferences on, and orientate their vote towards EU issues, the more important it becomes for EU actors to consider voter reactions in EU policy-making. As EU policies affect policy-makers' chances of getting into and remaining in office, vote seeking is even likely to gain priority over policy and autonomy seeking.

To the extent that bottom-up politicisation pressures force EU actors to react and engage in vote seeking, the study of EU politicisation management converges with the literature on 'blame avoidance', which originated in the context of domestic policy-making (Weaver, 1986; Hood, 2011). The blame-avoidance literature describes the designs and strategies officeholders use to respond to accountability pressures and it starts from the assumption that electoral (vote-seeking) motivations take precedence over 'good policy' motivations in managing such pressures (Weaver, 1986, p. 372). In particular, this literature has developed rich typologies of blame-avoidance strategies, on which the analysis of EU politicisation management can draw (see Bressanelli *et al.*, 2020).

Hood (2011, p. 18) distinguishes agency, policy and presentational strategies. Agency strategies are directed at the design of institutions and the choice of institutional venues and arenas in policy-making. For instance, whereas majoritarian institutions with a partisan membership and public deliberations and voting maximise politicisation, the choice of non-majoritarian institutions deciding by consensus and behind closed doors constitutes a depoliticising agency strategy (De Wilde, 2011, p. 561). Weaver (1986, pp. 386–9) speaks of 'circling the wagons' when policy-makers diffuse blame by spreading responsibility among as many actors as possible and of 'passing the buck' when they delegate unpopular decisions to non-majoritarian institutions.

Policy strategies refer to the design of policies. Going back to Lowi's (1972) policy types, policies with redistributive implications, which create identifiable winners and losers, are more likely to be politicised. A policy design that emphasises or reinforces redistribution would therefore politicise the issue. By contrast, Weaver (1986, pp. 384–6) describes 'agenda limitation' as a strategy that keeps policy options with a high politicisation potential off the agenda and points to 'redefining the issue' as a strategy that diffuses and obfuscates losses or generates win-win situations. In addition, policy-makers can also move from discretionary to 'automatic' or 'self-executing' government (Weaver, 1986, p. 387). By contrast, subjecting policy implementation to discretionary decisions of partisan actors is a strategy of politicisation.

Finally, presentational strategies focus on how policy-making is communicated. Actors engaging in depoliticising communication typically use technical or legal language and hide behind collective decisions, factual constraints and functional necessities to deflect and diffuse blame. By contrast, in politicising communication, actors describe decisions as outcomes of political and personal conflict and struggle; they name winners and losers; they do not try to obfuscate responsibility but claim credit for themselves. In Weaver's (1986) classification, blame shifting is exemplified by 'finding a scapegoat' and by 'jumping the bandwagon' (i.e., criticising an unpopular policy and supporting a more popular alternative). In EU legislation, politicisation consists, for instance, in calling for an open vote rather than seeking consensus, registering disapproval through abstentions and 'no' votes rather than tacitly accepting the majority opinion, and using the formal reconciliation procedure rather than the informal inter-institutional trilogue in conflicts between the Council and the Parliament.

## Theorising reactive politicisation management

Whether and to what extent EU actors choose depoliticisation or politicisation strategies in response to the domestic politicisation of EU politics, depends on the actors, the policy and the domestic context. Figure 1 gives an overview of the factors that increase the likelihood that EU actors emphasise politicisation strategies in their reactive politicisation management. The opposite conditions hold for depoliticisation strategies.

I consider actor characteristics the most important set of conditions. The more EU actors are electorally accountable, the more they tend to engage in reactive politicisation management and to use politicisation strategies. In addition, challenger parties and governments, as well as those with a GAL-TAN partisan profile, focus on reactive politicisation. Policies and context are best understood as moderators of the relationship between actors and strategies. Electorally accountable actors are especially likely to use

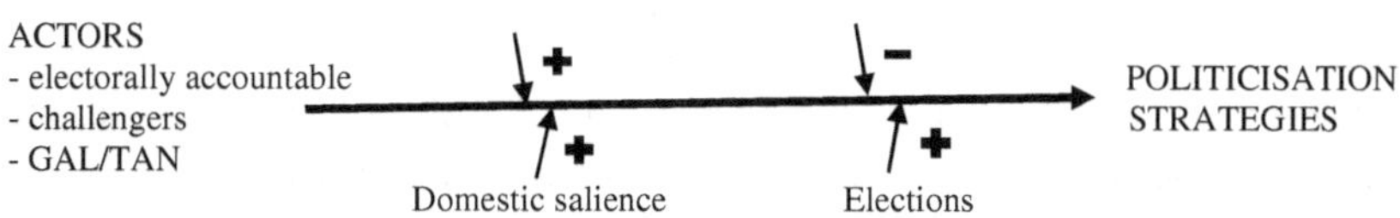


**Figure 1.** Conditions of politicisation strategies in politicisation management.

politicisation strategies in the context of high domestic salience and elections. And whereas they are especially likely to politicise policies related to core state powers, high-risk policies tend to be depoliticised.

### *Actors*

Whether EU actors typically manage bottom-up politicisation pressures by politicisation or depoliticisation strategies depends mainly on the extent to which they are subject to electoral pressures and capable of using them to their benefit. For one, EU actors comprise governments, parliamentarians and bureaucrats whose tenure depends to varying degrees on electoral support. Heads and cabinet members of national governments are under the strongest electoral pressure because their EU offices (in the European Council or the Council of the EU) depend entirely on national, first-order elections. Members of the European Parliament (MEPs) also owe their tenure to elections, but EP elections are typically second-order national elections and MEPs are less well-known and under less public scrutiny than members of national governments.

Bureaucrats are generally least motivated electorally because their tenure in the offices of the EU's supranational organisations is more weakly linked to electoral accountability. Moreover, the legitimacy of supranational agencies depends on expertise and political neutrality. The excessive pursuit of politicisation strategies would therefore undermine their authority. In contrast to, e.g., judges in the Court of Justice, heads of EU agencies or leading officials in the European Central Bank, top-level bureaucrats in the Commission or the Council, however, have an intermediate position, because their offices depend on the composition of the European Council and the EP and because they are often recruited from and sometimes plan to return to national politics.

In addition, EU actors possess unequal politicisation capacity, which depends primarily on their access to national parties and public spheres and on their media value. The ranking is roughly the same as for electoral accountability. Politicisation capacity is strongest for national governments, followed again by parliamentarians – to the extent they can mobilise their national parties and gain visibility – and by top-level Commission and Council bureaucrats. By contrast, other bureaucratic actors typically have weaker politicisation capacity. Moreover, governments and parliamentarians represent parties and voters, to which they can be responsive, whereas supranational actors represent the union and are responsible for its common good. They are therefore constrained in engaging in political conflict in general, and in taking an active role in domestic politicisation in particular.

In sum, the more electorally accountable EU actors are, the more they have to engage in reactive politicisation management and the more likely they will choose politicisation strategies in doing so. Governments and, to a lesser extent, parliamentarians and top-level Commission and Council bureaucrats have the strongest motivation and capacity to engage in reactive politicisation. By contrast, other supranational actors are expected to prefer reactive depoliticisation. Instead of pushing controversial or partisan issues and the expansion of supranational competencies, they focus on 'upgrading the common interest' and upholding common rules, and they seek to protect their core mandate, expertise and impartiality.

Yet governments and MEPs are not all alike. Both motivation and capacity depend on their partisan positions toward the EU and their position in the national party system. Mainstream parties of the centre-right and centre-left prefer to depoliticise European integration for three reasons (Hooghe & Marks, 2009, pp. 19–21). First, their voters tend to be more Eurosceptic than the party elites. Second, positions on European integration tend to be aligned along the cultural GAL-TAN or transnational cleavage and threaten to increase divides within parties traditionally organised along the left-right cleavage (Hooghe & Marks, 2018; Whitefield & Rohrschneider, 2019). Finally, parties that have been responsible for the current construction of the EU and supportive of European integration face credibility constraints in 'jumping on the bandwagon' of politicisation.

By contrast, challenger parties on the left and right are unconstrained in politicising the EU and thrive on winning over dissatisfied voters from the mainstream parties when EU policies become contested (Hobolt & Tilley, 2016). Not only when they are elected to the EP, but also when they form national governments, become members of the (European) Council and gain the right to nominate Commissioners, radical and challenger parties can be expected to continue riding the Eurosceptic wave and politicising EU policy-making to mobilise voters. According to the same logic, pro-integration, culturally liberal parties (such as the Greens) have an incentive to politicise integration, too, in order to mobilise their voters against the Eurosceptics. Thus, whereas elected EU actors are generally more motivated and able to engage in reactive politicisation than unelected EU actors, elected EU actors representing challenger or GAL-TAN parties have the strongest interest in the active use of politicisation strategies.

Finally, the domestic context shapes the choice of strategy. The more salient and contested a policy is in domestic politics, and the more mobilisation and protest it generates, the more EU actors engage in reactive politicisation management. In addition, national as well as European elections, which are also predominantly contested at the domestic level, produce challenges for politicisation management. Electorally accountable EU actors, and in particular those from challenger or GAL-TAN parties, have the highest motivation and capacity to engage in the politicisation of domestically and electorally salient issues, whereas depoliticisation should constitute the default reaction of unelected supranational actors. These theoretical considerations lead to the following hypotheses:

(1) The more EU actors are electorally accountable, the more likely they are likely to choose politicisation strategies.
(2) Challenger parties in the EP and in government are more likely to choose politicisation strategies.
(3) Parties aligned with the cultural (GAL-TAN) dimension of politics are more likely to choose politicisation strategies.
(4) Electorally accountable EU actors are more likely to choose politicisation strategies if domestic issue salience is high.
(5) Electorally accountable EU actors are more likely to choose politicisation strategies if elections are close.

Will electorally unaccountable actors ever choose politicisation strategies? I suggest that inter-institutional conflict about decision-making power and constitutional rules is the one issue context, in which all EU actors engage in politicisation strategies if they appear promising in strengthening their bargaining power vis-à-vis other EU actors. This is especially important for EU actors who are in a materially, politically or legally inferior position – such as the Parliament and the Commission in their competition with the (European) Council and individual governments. Denouncing institutional deficits and the behaviour of governments may mobilise European publics in support of these actors and their policies and shift the power balance in their favour. In inter-institutional conflicts, domestic publics and actors are not opponents of or constraints on EU-level policy-making, but serve EU actors as audiences granting legitimacy and political support to their competing competence claims. Politicisation management is proactive rather than reactive. Naturally, governments can also use politicisation strategies to block institutional changes and extract concessions in EU-level negotiations. Specifically, anticipated referendums strengthen the hand of governments and have moved the negotiating outcome closer to their preferences (König, 2018, p. 1254).

### *Issues*

Additionally, the choice between politicisation and depoliticisation depends on the issues at stake. For one, policies differ with regard to their (de)politicisation potential. Policies without tangible effects on citizens, their welfare, identity or rights, have low politicisation potential. They do not require reactive politicisation management or can be depoliticised easily by EU actors. By contrast, policies substantially affecting the state's core coercive and redistributive powers and the identity and self-determination of national communities have high politicisation potential, require strategic politicisation management and are more difficult to depoliticise. Thus, core state powers are more likely to be managed by politicisation strategies.

Moreover, politicisation management depends on issue risk. The blame avoidance literature expects that office holders seek to depoliticise the design and making of policies that impose substantial costs and losses on voters, in particular if losses are concentrated in groups with high capacity to organise, whereas benefits are diffuse (Weaver, 1986, p. 373 and 378) – as, for instance, when cutting back agricultural subsidies or welfare benefits. Under these conditions, policy-makers not only engage in depoliticisation to shield their decisions from public scrutiny and pressure, but also to avoid blame should policies fail or become unpopular (Hinterleitner & Sager, 2017, pp. 594–5).

Functional integration theories share this reasoning. According to liberal intergovernmentalism, states delegate policy enforcement to supranational organisations if the probability and costs of non-compliance due to the domestic mobilisation of integration losers are high (Moravcsik, 1998, p. 9, 486–7). According to the neofunctionalist mechanism of path-dependent integration, the management of badly performing or heavily contested integrated policies depends on the path-dependencies generated by the depth of international interdependence as well as sunk and exit costs (Pierson, 1996). If the risk of policy failure is low, or if the member states possess sufficient autonomy and capacity to manage the failure unilaterally, national governments have an incentive, or are at least not constrained, in politicising the policy failure, 'jumping on the bandwagon' of opposition against the policy, and shifting the blame to other EU actors. By contrast, if interdependence runs deep, the risk of disintegration is high, and national autonomy or capacity are weak, national governments are more likely to manage the policy failure by depoliticisation: delegation to supranational, technocratic agencies, engaging in blame diffusion and deflection, and emphasising threats, constraints and functional necessities in their policy communication.

Combining the conditions of core state powers and issue risk, the integration of core state powers is more likely to generate bottom-up contestation and mobilisation than the integration of other policies, and it is also more difficult for EU actors to depoliticise policies related to core state powers. EU actors are nonetheless more likely to engage in reactive depoliticisation if the functional and political risks of policy failure and disintegration are high. I thus propose the two following additional hypotheses.

(1) EU actors are more likely to choose politicisation strategies in core state policies.
(2) EU actors are more likely to choose depoliticisation strategies if issue risk is high.

## Politicisation management in action: initial evidence

Recent empirical research (including contributions to this collection) provides initial evidence in support of the actor and issue conditions of politicisation management – and for the considerable success of politicisation management in preserving the autonomous policy-making capacity of EU actors.

### *Conditions of politicisation management*

In line with the hypotheses, a growing number of studies show that electorally accountable EU actors politicise domestically salient issues, especially in the context of elections. Alexandrova, Rasmussen, and Toshkov (2016) observe an increasing alignment of the European Council agenda with the salience of policy issue in public opinion (even though they cannot exclude that both are driven by the severity of the underlying policy problem). Moving from agenda-setting to deliberations, Hobolt and Wratil (this issue) demonstrate that government representatives in the Council are responsive to domestic public opinion in formulating their positions on policies that are domestically salient. Moving from deliberations to voting, Hagemann, Hobolt, and Wratil (2017) find that governments are also more likely to oppose legislation when the issue is salient in domestic politics.

The effect of domestic issue salience is most pronounced in the context of national and European elections. Wratil (2018) finds that governments in the Council are particularly responsive to public opinion (on left-right issues) when elections are approaching. This also holds for the Parliament: MEPs are more likely to deviate from their party groups in legislative votes when legislation is salient and elections are close (Koop, Reh, & Bressanelli, 2018).

According to Christina Schneider's comprehensive analysis (Schneider, 2019), governments even show heightened responsiveness in the shadow of elections in the absence of domestic issue salience – presumably because they hedge against such issues becoming politicised during the election campaign. In order to appear competent and responsive to their electorate in the run-up to elections, governments take and defend positions, and seek to secure legislative and budgetary bargains that are in the interest of politically relevant voters.

Whereas negotiations at the EU level offer governments ample opportunities for position-taking and position-defending posturing, the actual realisation of favourable deals is more uncertain and more difficult, especially if they require major concessions by the other member states. If governments fear bargaining failure, they may yet resort to depoliticisation, e.g., by delaying decisions until after the elections (Schneider, 2019, p. 10, 14). Generally, legislative proposals are less likely to be adopted in the run-up to elections, especially in the case of close elections in large member states (Kleine & Minaudier, 2019).

This is not the only indication of strategic politicisation management. Whereas governments prove responsive to domestic politicisation and national elections at the deliberation stage of legislative proposals, they generally return to the consensus mode at the voting stage. Indeed, only two percent of the voting records show dissenting votes at all, and these dissenting (negative or abstention) votes do not prevent laws from passing (Hagemann *et al.*, 2017, p. 855). Therefore, Hagemann *et al.* (2017) and Schneider (2019) prefer to characterise this politicisation behaviour as 'signal responsiveness' rather than substantive responsiveness. In addition, Schneider's research suggests that governments help each other in 'hidden cooperation' to appear responsive to their citizens by making concessions or delaying decisions at election time.

By contrast, recent evidence suggests that unelected supranational actors tend to revert to depoliticisation strategies in managing bottom-up politicisation pressure. Several studies find that the Commission emphasises its mandate as guardian of the EU rules and the general Community interest when confronted with domestic politicisation. For instance, in a study of politically sensitive country-specific recommendations in the context of the European Semester, Van der Veer and Haverland (2018) show that the Commission focuses on those issues, for which it has the strongest mandate, and sends signals of resolve and political independence when dealing with relatively highly politicised countries. In his study of consumer policy legislation, Rauh (2016, 2019) finds that the Commission puts greater emphasis on safeguarding broader public interests and generating more widely dispersed policy benefits in the context of heightened bottom-up pressure. Finally, in their study of legislative withdrawals, a depoliticisation strategy, Reh, Bressanelli, and Koop (2020) observe that the Commission is more likely to withdraw controversial legislation if it is in the domain of core state powers and if Euroscepticism runs high. However, and in contrast with the expectations, they also find that higher domestic salience (measured as media attention) makes withdrawals *less* likely.

The initial evidence on the other non-majoritarian and unelected supranational actors is mixed as well. In line with the expectation that such actors choose depoliticisation strategies in the face of bottom-up pressure, Blauberger and Martinsen (2020) suggest that the Court becomes less activist when confronted by public and governmental opposition at the same time. By contrast, Moschella *et al.* (2020) find that the European Central Bank proactively expands its communication beyond its core mandate in reaction to decreasing public trust in the institution. As in the case of the Council, however, this expanded communication is best understood as signalling behaviour and an attempt to shield the Bank's core mandate and policy.

Moreover, both elected and unelected EU actors have engaged in politicisation strategies in inter-institutional conflicts. The EP has a long history of politicising the distribution of powers in the EU (Héritier, 2007; Rittberger, 2005; and most recently Meissner & Schoeller, 2019) – often by invoking its democratic legitimacy as the only directly elected body of the EU. Yet the Commission also seeks to (re)gain influence in the EU decision-making process by politicising the drafting process of legislative proposals and inter-institutional agreements (Bunea, 2020). And the Court might benefit from increasing communication efforts to publicise and justify its decisions in situations, in which governments are critical, but the wider public is favourably disposed toward its rulings (Blauberger & Martinsen, 2020).

Finally, the EU's recent crises provide evidence that EU actors orient their politicisation management towards the risks of EU policy failure. The substantive probability and the potentially prohibitive costs of disintegration in the Eurozone have motivated governments to agree on far-reaching steps of rule-tightening and supranational delegation in spite of unprecedented bottom-up pressure (Franchino & Mariotto, 2020). They accompanied this institutional agency strategy with a presentational strategy focusing on blame diffusion – rather than blame shifting to the EU – in the financial crisis (Hobolt & Tilley, 2014). This reactive depoliticisation stands in clear contrast to the migration crisis, in which comparatively low costs of non-integration and high national autonomy and capacity allowed countries – and in particular those governed by Eurosceptic parties – to engage in politicisation for electoral benefit (Schimmelfennig, 2018).

Thus, the bottom-up politicisation of European integration has not translated into a general politicisation of EU policy-making. Politicisation management offers EU actors both politicisation and depoliticisation strategies. Even though electorally accountable actors are more likely to engage in reactive politicisation than non-elected actors, they use politicisation management strategically depending on domestic salience, electoral pressures and policy risk. In inter-institutional conflicts, unelected actors also switch to politicisation strategies promising to increase their bargaining power.

### *Preserving the room to manoeuver*

EU actors retain important gatekeeping powers vis-à-vis in managing bottom-up pressures. Even if the politicisation of European integration is strong among voters and parties, it requires an institutional channel to affect EU-level decision-making. One channel is the formation of national governments that include Eurosceptic challenger parties. Another channel is the domestic ratification of EU-level agreements – in particular through national referendums. Closing or blocking these channels reduces the EU-level effect of domestic politicisation.

For instance, Winzen (2020) shows that popular, extra-parliamentary or opposition Euroscepticism alone does not undermine uniform integration in the EU. Eurosceptic parties only increase the probability of differentiated integration – one of the expected outcomes of domestic politicisation – if they enter the government. During the euro crisis, the consistent formation of Euro-friendly governments, grand coalitions and technocratic governments in the Eurozone was one of the recipes for shielding the rescue and consolidation process from the impact of domestic politicisation (Schimmelfennig, 2014, pp. 332–3).

Referendums have, indeed, turned into an increasingly disruptive force for European integration. According to Mendez and Mendez (2017, p. 32), the rate of 'referendum failure' has accelerated to nearly 40 percent since 2000, and over 60 percent since 2010. Yet, rather than stopping the integration agreements, negative EU referendums trigger further EU-level negotiations, in which governments most often find ways around the no vote, ranging from substitute agreements via minimal reinterpretations or revisions of the original agreement all the way to blunt disregard for the referendum as in the Greek bailout case (Schimmelfennig, 2019). Additionally, governments have designed agreements to minimise the chances that they are put to a referendum (as in the Lisbon Treaty) or that a failed referendum would invalidate the agreement (as in the ESM Treaty) (Schimmelfennig, 2014, pp. 333–4).

Finally, even if EU actors choose reactive politicisation strategies, they often do so strategically. Presentational strategies allow them to signal responsiveness to, or mobilise, domestic audiences in their deliberations, negotiations and public communication, all the while preserving or pursuing depoliticisation in their decision-making and their design of institutions and policies – especially if decision-making and policy failure entails high risks.

To conclude, the available evidence suggests that EU actors continue to enjoy considerable room to manoeuvre. The long chain of delegation from the citizen to the EU, the dispersion of power at the EU level and the complex and consensus-oriented negotiation and decision-making processes dampen and dilute the impact of bottom-up pressures in the EU multi-level system. Just as the gently ascending seaward slope of a dike is built to reduce wave loadings, these institutional features of the EU dissipate the energy of domestic politicisation pressures.

## Conclusions

This paper has made the case for the systematic study of EU politicisation management as a counterpart to the well-established research on domestic politicisation. The dominant perspective of politicisation as a constraint on EU actors remains incomplete without a complementary analysis of how EU actors manage – and potentially overcome – this constraint. I have sought to advance this research agenda by conceptualising politicisation management, theorising the motivations and capacities of EU actors, formulating basic hypotheses about the choice of politicisation and depoliticisation strategies and indicating initial evidence for strategic and effective EU-level politicisation management.

All these contributions point to the need for further research. First, the hypotheses do not go beyond the binary choice between politicisation and depoliticisation and do not detail the conditions under which actors choose specific (agency, policy or presentational) (de)politicisation strategies or act in an assertive or restrained manner (Bressanelli *et al.*, 2020). Moreover, there is evidence that EU actors mix strategies, e.g., politicisation in deliberation and communication with depoliticisation in voting and policy design. Second, existing studies focus on individual actors, issues and decision-making stages. In a next step, there is a need for comparative work on politicisation management, e.g., on how different EU actors manage the same issue, how they vary their behaviour across different issues and how they shift their strategies as they proceed through the policy-cycle from agenda-setting to implementation.

## Acknowledgment

I thank the special issue editors and anonymous reviewers for their valuable comments and suggestions.

## Disclosure statement

No potential conflict of interest was reported by the author.

## ORCID

*Frank Schimmelfennig* http://orcid.org/0000-0002-1638-1819

## References

Alexandrova, P., Rasmussen, A., & Toshkov, D. (2016). Agenda responsiveness in the European Council: Public priorities, policy problems and political attention. *West European Politics*, *39*(4), 605–627.

Blauberger, M., & Martinsen, D. (2020). The Court of Justice in times of politicisation: "law as a mask and shield" revisited. *Journal of European Public Policy*, *27*(3), 382–399.

Bressanelli, E., Koop, C., & Reh, C. (2020). Introduction. EU actors under pressure: Politicisation and depoliticisation as strategic responses. *Journal of European Public Policy, 27*(3), 329–349.

Bunea, A. (2020). Understanding the European Commission's use of politicisation in the negotiation of interinstitutional agreements: The role of consultations and issue framing. *Journal of European Public Policy, 27*(3), 439–459.

Burley, A., & Mattli, W. (1993). Europe before the court: A political theory of legal integration. *International Organization, 47*(1), 41–76.

De Wilde, P. (2011). No polity for old politics: A framework for analyzing the politicisation of European integration. *Journal of European Integration, 33*(5), 559–575.

De Wilde, P., Leupold, A., & Schmidtke, H. (2016). Introduction: The differentiated politicisation of European governance. *West European Politics, 39*(1), 3–22.

De Wilde, P., & Zürn, M. (2012). Can the politicisation of European integration be reversed? *JCMS: Journal of Common Market Studies, 50*(s1), 137–153.

Franchino, F., & Mariotto, C. (2020). Politicisation and economic governance design. *Journal of European Public Policy, 27*(3), 460–480.

Genschel, P., & Jachtenfuchs, M. (2014). Introduction: Beyond market regulation. Analysing the European integration of core state powers. In P. Genschel & M. Jachtenfuchs (Eds.), *Beyond the regulatory polity? The European integration of core state powers* (pp. 1–23). Oxford: Oxford University Press.

Grande, E., & Hutter, S. (2016). Beyond authority transfer: Explaining the politicisation of Europe. *West European Politics, 39*(1), 23–43.

Grande, E., & Kriesi, H. (2016). 'Conclusions: The postfunctionalists were (almost) right'. In S. Hutter, E. Grande, & H. Kriesi (Eds.), *Politicising Europe. integration and mass politics* (pp. 279–300). Cambridge: Cambridge University Press.

Grieco, J. (1996). State interests and international rule trajectories: A neorealist interpretation of the Maastricht Treaty and European economic and monetary Union. *Security Studies, 5*(3), 261–306.

Haas, E. (1961). International integration: The European and the universal process. *International Organization, 15*, 366–392.

Haas, E. B. (1968). *The uniting of Europe. Political, social, and economic forces 1950–1957* (2nd ed.). Stanford: Stanford University Press.

Hagemann, S., Hobolt, S. B., & Wratil, C. (2017). Government responsiveness in the European Union: Evidence from Council voting. *Comparative Political Studies, 50* (6), 850–876.

Héritier, A. (2007). *Explaining institutional change in Europe*. Oxford: Oxford University Press.

Hinterleitner, M., & Sager, F. (2017). Anticipatory and reactive forms of blame avoidance: Of foxes and lions. *European Political Science Review, 9*(4), 587–606.

Hobolt, S. B., & Tilley, J. (2014). *Blaming Europe? Responsibility Without accountability in the European Union*. Oxford: Oxford University Press.

Hobolt, S. B., & Tilley, J. (2016). Fleeing the centre: The rise of challenger parties in the aftermath of the euro crisis. *West European Politics, 39*(5), 971–991.

Hobolt, S. B., & Wratil, C. (2020). Contestation and responsiveness in EU Council deliberations. *Journal of European Public Policy, 27*(3), 362–381.

Hood, C. (2011). *The Blame Game: Spin, Bureaucracy and Self-Preservation in government*. Princeton: Princeton University Press.

Hooghe, L., & Marks, G. (2009). A postfunctionalist theory of European integration: From permissive consensus to constraining dissensus. *British Journal of Political Science, 39* (1), 1–23.

Hooghe, L., & Marks, G. (2018). Cleavage theory meets Europe's crisis: Lipset, Rokkan and the transnational cleavage. *Journal of European Public Policy, 25*(1), 109–135.

Kleine, M., & Minaudier, C. (2019). Negotiating under political uncertainty: National elections and the dynamics of international co-operation. *British Journal of Political Science, 49*(1), 315–337.

König, T. (2018). Still the century of intergovernmentalism? Partisan ideology, two-level bargains and technocratic governance in the post-Maastricht era. *JCMS: Journal of Common Market Studies, 56*(6), 1240–1262.

Koop, C., Reh, C., & Bressanelli, E. (2018). When politics prevails: Parties, elections and loyalty in the European Parliament. *European Journal of Political Research, 57*(3), 563–586.

Lindberg, L. N., & Scheingold, S. A. (1970). *Europe's would-Be polity: Patterns of change in the European community*. Englewood Cliffs: Prentice-Hall.

Lowi, T. (1972). Four systems of policy, politics and choice. *Public Administration Review, 32*(4), 298–310.

Mair, P. (2007). Political opposition and the European Union. *Government and Opposition, 42*(1), 1–17.

Meissner, K., & Schoeller, M. (2019). Rising despite the polycrisis? The European Parliament's strategies of self-empowerment after Lisbon. *Journal of European Public Policy*. doi:10.1080/13501763.2019.1619187

Mendez, F., & Mendez, M. (2017). *Referendums on EU Matters (PE 571.402)*. Brussels: European Parliament. http://www.europarl.europa.eu/RegData/etudes/STUD/2017/571402/IPOL_STU(2017)571402_EN.pdf

Milward, A. (2000). *The European rescue of the nation state* (2nd ed.). London: Routledge.

Moravcsik, A. (1994). *Why the European Union strengthens the state: Domestic politics and international cooperation* (CES Working Paper 52).

Moravcsik, A. (1998). *The Choice for Europe: Social purpose and state power From messina to Maastricht*. Ithaca: Cornell University Press.

Moravcsik, A. (2002). In defence of the "democratic deficit": Reassessing legitimacy in the European Union. *JCMS: Journal of Common Market Studies, 40*(4), 603–624.

Moschella et al. (2020). Let's speak more? How the ECB responds to public contestation. *Journal of European Public Policy, 27*(3), 400–418.

Neunreither, K. (1998). Governance without opposition: The case of the European Union. *Government and Opposition, 33*(4), 419–441.

Novak, S. (2013). The silence of ministers: Consensus and blame avoidance in the Council of the European Union. *JCMS: Journal of Common Market Studies, 51*(6), 1091–1107.

Pierson, P. (1996). The path to European integration. A historical institutionalist analysis. *Comparative Political Studies, 29*(2), 123–163.

Rauh, C. (2016). *A responsive technocracy? EU politicisation and the consumer policies of the European commission*. Colchester: ECPR Press.

Rauh, C. (2019). EU politicisation and policy initiatives of the European Commission: The case of consumer policy. *Journal of European Public Policy, 26*(3), 344–365.

Reh, C., Bressanelli, E., & Koop, C. (2020). Responsive withdrawal? The politics of EU agenda-setting. *Journal of European Public Policy, 27*(3), 419–438.

Rittberger, B. (2005). *Building Europe's parliament. Democratic representation beyond the nation-state*. Oxford: Oxford University Press.

Schimmelfennig, F. (2014). European integration in the euro crisis: The limits of post-functionalism. *Journal of European Integration, 36*(3), 321–337.

Schimmelfennig, F. (2018). European integration (theory) in times of crisis. A comparison of the euro and Schengen crises. *Journal of European Public Policy, 25*(7), 969–989.

Schimmelfennig, F. (2019). Getting around no: How governments react to negative EU referendums. *Journal of European Public Policy*, *26*(7), 1056–1074.
Schmidt, V. A. (2006). *Democracy in Europe: The EU and national polities*. Oxford: Oxford University Press.
Schmitter, P. C. (1969). Three neo-functional hypotheses about international integration. *International Organization*, *23*(1), 161–166.
Schneider, C. (2019). *The responsive Union. National elections and European governance*. Cambridge: Cambridge University Press.
Van der Veer, R. A., & Haverland, M. (2018). Bread and butter or bread and circuses? Politicisation and the European Commission in the European Semester. *European Union Politics*, *19*(3), 524–545.
Weaver, R. K. (1986). The politics of blame avoidance. *Journal of Public Policy*, *6*(4), 371–398.
Whitefield, S., & Rohrschneider, R. (2019). Embedding integration: How European integration splits mainstream parties. *Party Politics*, *25*(1), 25–35.
Winzen, T. (2020). Government Euroscepticism and differentiated integration. *Journal of European Public Policy*. doi:10.1080/13501763.2019.1703789
Wolf, K. D. (1999). The new raison d'état as a problem for democracy in world society. *European Journal of International Relations*, *5*(3), 333–363.
Wolf, K. D. (2000). *Die Neue Staatsräson – Zwischenstaatliche Kooperation als Demokratieproblem in der Weltgesellschaft*. Baden-Baden: Nomos.
Wratil, C. (2018). Modes of government responsiveness in the European Union: Evidence from Council negotiating positions. *European Union Politics*, *19*(1), 52–74.

# Contestation and responsiveness in EU Council deliberations

Sara B. Hobolt and Christopher Wratil

**ABSTRACT**

Decision-making in the Council of the European Union appears highly consensual at the voting stage. However, we focus on Council deliberations, where we find higher levels of contestation. What drives government opposition in the Council? Using a novel approach of studying the Council through video footage of its public deliberations (DICEU – *Debates in the Council of the European Union*), we demonstrate that contestation between governments is, at least in part, driven by their responsiveness to domestic public opinion. Analysing deliberations on legislative packages in the Economic and Financial Affairs Council between 2010 and 2015, we show that governments are responsive to public opinion when setting out their policy positions, but primarily when the policy issues are salient domestically. Our study thus contributes to our understanding of government responsiveness in the EU.

What drives the positions taken by governments in the Council of the European Union (henceforth, 'the Council')? Voting records suggest that Council decision-making is highly consensual with very little government opposition to legislative proposals (Hagemann *et al.* 2017; Heisenberg 2005; Hosli *et al.* 2011; Novak 2013). However, we know that European Union (EU) policies have become more contested in recent decades, not least in response to the Eurozone and refugee crises (Börzel and Risse 2018; Cramme and Hobolt 2014). The EU has also become more politicised in the domestic sphere, as the issue has been mobilised by issue entrepreneurs (De Wilde and Zürn 2012; Hobolt and De Vries 2015; Hooghe and Marks 2009). Studies point to considerable disagreement between governments at various stages of the EU negotiation process (Häge 2013; Kleine 2013; Thomson 2011). This raises the question of the degree and timing of

Supplemental data for this article can be accessed at https://doi.org/10.1080/13501763.2020.1712454

contestation between governments in the Council and, importantly, what drives such conflict?

To examine these questions, we adopt a novel empirical approach. Specifically, we analyse the negotiation positions of governments in the Council by coding the official video recordings of public deliberations in the Council, using the so-called *Debates in the Council of the European Union* (DICEU) database (see Wratil and Hobolt 2019). This database allows us to systematically measure conflict in the Council during the different stages of legislative negotiations and show that intergovernmental contestation is highest at the early stages of negotiations. We then examine the causes of this contestation. Several studies have examined the drivers of disagreement in the Council, using voting, policy statements, document or interview data. Much work focuses on diverging economic interests and geographical divisions (e.g., Bailer *et al.* 2015; Thomson 2011; Zimmer *et al.* 2005). While these factors are undoubtedly important in explaining conflict in the Council, we focus on the role of domestic electoral politics. Specifically, we argue that public opinion influences government positions in public deliberations, especially if issues are salient domestically. Recent work has shown that governments adjust their initial policy positions at the beginning of EU negotiations to the 'public mood' (Wratil 2018) and use opposition votes in the Council at the end of the legislative process to 'signal responsiveness' to Eurosceptic domestic electorates (Hagemann *et al.* 2017). Moreover, other research has demonstrated that the Council now pays more attention to issues that the public considers salient and that public opinion also influences how many and which policies are agreed at the EU level (Alexandrova *et al.* 2016; Schneider 2018; Toshkov 2011; Wratil 2019).

In this article, we build on this work to demonstrate the impact of public preferences during Council negotiations. Importantly, we present the first analysis of government responsiveness in the Council that measures public opinion not as a general 'public mood' for policy, but as the public support for concrete and specific legislative proposals. Empirically, we analyse 58 debates in the Economic and Financial Affairs Council (ECOFIN) from 2010 to 2015. We thus focus on a significant area of policy-making with considerable variation in the degree of politicisation across issues, ranging from technical discussions on specific taxation policies of companies to the more politicised issues of the financial transaction tax and the EU budget. As we expect that governments have greater incentives to be responsive on issues that are domestically salient, we can leverage this variation to examine the moderating effect of issue salience on government responsiveness.

Our findings show that governments are responsive to issue-specific public preferences, particularly when the policy issue is salient domestically. This paper thus contributes to the literature on EU policy-making by analysing an original dataset on Council negotiations and by showing how domestic politics and politicisation shape the positions taken by governments in the Council.

## Contestation and responsiveness in the Council

The Council is the EU's co-legislature (jointly with the European Parliament), where national ministers negotiate and subsequently vote on legislative proposals put forward by the European Commission. Legislative bargaining in the Council used to be highly secretive and has been described as characterised by an 'informal culture of consensus' (Heisenberg 2005: 68). As information on voting behaviour in the Council has become available, studies have shown that governments cast less than 2 per cent of all votes against legislative proposals (Hagemann *et al.* 2017; Hosli *et al.* 2011). At the pre-negotiation stages, however, studies have demonstrated that disagreement among member states on legislative proposals is far more pronounced than suggested by voting data. Most notably, the 'Decision Making in the European Union' (DEU) project has collected an impressive database of governments' initial negotiation positions in the Council based on interviews with officials on controversial issues (Thomson *et al.* 2006, 2012). While the DEU database documents high levels of disagreement among member states before negotiations start, we know less about contestation during the Council negotiations. The focus of this article is on the nature and causes of contestation during these negotiations.

A number of studies seek to explain voting behaviour, such as Bailer *et al.* (2015), who demonstrate that opposition votes can largely be attributed to economic explanations, notably domestic specialised interests. Some work has argued that governments' left-right ideology shapes their behaviour in the Council (Hagemann and Høyland 2008), while this has been disputed by other studies (Bailer *et al.* 2015; Hosli *et al.* 2011). Moreover, the DEU data has advanced our understanding of government positions in the Council, showing that geographically closer member states are more likely to vote together and that there is a cleavage between 'old' and 'new' member states (Thomson 2009), between the North and the South (Thomson 2011) and between net beneficiaries and net contributors to the EU budget (Zimmer *et al.* 2005).

These voting- and interview-based studies have thus generated important insights into the national interests that drive position-taking and opposition in the Council, yet they are largely silent on how domestic electoral politics may influence contestation in the Council. Indeed, the general assumption is that governments are largely insulated from electoral pressures when they legislate in the Council and that public preferences play a very limited role (see e.g., Bailer *et al.* 2015). Some recent work has challenged this assumption by showing that governments do respond to the 'public mood' on Europe when legislating in the Council. Using DEU data, Wratil (2018) shows that governments are responsive to public opinion on left-right issues in the run-up to national elections and on European integration issues when they are salient. Moreover, Hagemann *et al.*'s (2017) study of Council voting demonstrates that governments are more likely to oppose legislative proposals that expand the EU's authority when their domestic electorates are sceptical about the EU, especially when the issue of European integration is salient in domestic party politics. This suggests that governments use opposition in the Council to signal to Eurosceptic electorates that they are responsive to their concerns. Kleine (2013) has shown that member states in the EU use informal governance to accommodate governments under unexpectedly strong domestic pressure. Moreover, Kleine and Minaudier (2017) demonstrate that upcoming national elections in the large member states delay decision-making in the Council. These studies thus provide evidence that governments in the Council take domestic public opinion into account, especially when electoral sanctioning is more likely.

In this paper, we extend this work by exploring substantive government responsiveness on specific policies. We present the first study of whether the positions governments adopt in the Council are responsive not only to the general 'public mood', but also to public preferences on specific policies that are negotiated in the Council. For this purpose, we use cross-national public opinion data from the Eurobarometer on policy-specific items relating to five legislative packages. Moreover, we investigate a different stage in the legislative process by looking at the entire process of official intergovernmental negotiations at the ministerial level instead of pre- or post-negotiation stages. Specifically, we make use of an original dataset of the public deliberations of legislative packages in the ECOFIN Council between 2010 and 2015, which covers virtually all *official* deliberations between national ministers and their deputies (see also Wratil and Hobolt 2019).

Our theoretical expectations of government responsiveness in the Council build on the notion that government responsiveness to public preferences is driven by 'anticipatory representation', as governments focus on what they think voters will reward in the next election rather than what they promised during the campaign of the previous election (Erikson *et al.* 2002; Mansbridge 2003; Stimson *et al.* 1995). The reason is very simple: the fear of electoral sanction if they ignore public opinion. As a guide to what the electorates may want in the next election, governments are likely to pay attention to the current state of public preferences on an issue. Our expectation is therefore that governments in the Council are more likely to support a proposal that is supported by a majority of their domestic electorate and more likely to oppose it if most voters at home oppose it, just as they are when making policies domestically. Crucially, however, we primarily expect that governments will pay attention to domestic public opinion if doing so may influence their electoral fortunes, i.e., if there is a possibility that they will be held to account. In some systems, and on some policy issues, governments actions are much less likely to be consequential at the ballot box. Comparative studies of responsiveness at the national level have found that in systems of low clarity of responsibility and limited information, where it is difficult for voters to identify policy shirking, elected representatives are also less responsive to public preferences (see Carey 2008; Powell and Whitten 1993; Wlezien and Soroka 2012). That means that we would generally expect lower levels of responsiveness in systems with low clarity of responsibility, such as the EU.

However, as policy debates in the EU become more politicised and more salient to the domestic public, we also expect that governments will be more responsive when deliberating in the Council. When EU policy-making is salient in the domestic public debate, governments may be concerned that 'unpopular' positions in the Council, or subsequent policies, can potentially be electorally costly in the next national election, as the media, interest groups, or competitors may raise voters' attention to the government's unresponsive behaviour. We thus expect that responsiveness to public preferences in the Council will occur primarily when the legislative issues at stake are salient in the domestic public sphere.

One may argue that despite increased transparency in the Council, there is still not enough attention paid to deliberations in the Council to incentivise responsive behaviour by governments. In his work on accountability in the EU, Naurin (2006, p. 91) distinguishes between transparency and publicity, arguing that publicity is necessary for accountability, since it means that the information is not only available, but 'the content of this information has also become known among the voters'. Our argument is not that transparency of Council negotiations in and of itself guarantees publicity. Indeed, we are not expecting that ordinary voters watch videos of Council deliberations. But the fact that these negotiations are a matter of public record means that government positions *could* become known to voters, through the dissemination efforts of the media, other political parties or interest groups, and this means that there is a possibility that governments may be held to account for their stances in the Council. Governments may thus be concerned about the very possibility of publicity and its potential electoral consequences, which is likely greater in deliberations on issues that are salient domestically, and this encourages them to act more responsively. This leads to the following hypotheses:

> H1: Governments are more disapproving of EU legislative proposals in the Council, the more public opinion at the domestic level opposes the proposals.

> H2: The effect of public opinion on a government's policy positions in the Council is greater if the policy proposal is salient at the domestic level.

In the ensuing sections, we first describe our approach to measuring government positions and contestation in the Council and then we examine whether public preferences drive these positions.

### *Measuring government positions and contestation in the Council*

In order to measure government positions and contestation in the Council, we rely on the DICEU dataset (Wratil and Hobolt 2019). DICEU is based on the analysis of video footage of public deliberations of the Council and is the first dataset that systematically makes available data on these deliberations. In 2006, the Council for the first time made video recordings of its legislative deliberations public, and since the Lisbon Treaty, the Council must deliberate in public when negotiating legislative files or discussing questions of strategic relevance, and all debates are video-streamed on the Council's website. Videos of public deliberations of the Council, therefore, provide important first-hand evidence on legislative bargaining in the EU, more akin to intergovernmental bargaining than plenary debates in legislatures.[1] While a large part of these negotiations takes place outside the formal Council meetings (e.g., in COREPER and the working parties, or in informal settings), these deliberations constitute the highest level of the formal negotiation process.

In recent work, we have demonstrated the validity of DICEU data (Wratil and Hobolt 2019). In particular, we have shown that governments' ideal points scaled from videos yield meaningful and well-known conflict dimensions and that DICEU positions correlate highly with assessments of expert practitioners interviewed by the DEU project (e.g., staff from the permanent representations). The available DICEU data covers virtually all public legislative debates in the ECOFIN Council configuration between 2010 and 2015 (see Wratil and Hobolt 2019). This amounts to 89 debates. Human coders watched all debates and coded them according to a comprehensive codebook (see the Supplemental Material). As our main variable to measure contestation in the Council, we employ the 'General Approval' (V6) variable. This variable requires coders to identify a major dimension of approval versus disapproval within each debate. Typically, debates are structured and moderated by the Council presidency. Styles of presidents vary, but they will normally outline a topic for debate at the beginning of the meeting and in broad terms, this topic is almost without exception about approval or disapproval of either a legislative proposal presented by the Commission, the state of play on a proposal, or the state of negotiations with the European Parliament (EP).[2] In fact, many presidencies close their entry statement by asking whether delegations 'approve' of a proposal.

Coders used a 5-point Likert item to assess the degree of approval of each actor speaking in the debate from 'full approval' (1) to 'full disapproval' (5). The general *Disapproval* variable therefore always indicates the degree to which a government disapproves of the state of negotiations in each debate (either when a proposal is presented, amended later, or discussed with other institutions). The inter-coder reliability of this variable is high (Krippendorff's alpha = 0.82). Our data allow us to investigate the levels of contestation at different stages of the negotiation process. For this purpose, we compare the share of governments that express disapproval ('more disapproval than approval' and 'full disapproval') in public deliberations at three different stages: (1) debates on the presentation of legislative proposals ('initial presentations'), (2) exchanges of views about the content of proposals ('policy debates'), and (3) debates leading to political agreement ('debates on political agreement'). 11% of our debates are initial presentations, 38% are policy debates, and 51% are on political agreement. As a fourth and final stage, we also consider the share of governments that cast opposition votes ('no' or 'abstain') against proposals at the end of the negotiations.[3]

Table 1 compares the level of disapproval across negotiation stages as well as opposition votes for different packages of legislative proposals. Specifically, we allocate legislative proposals into six packages: 'Financial transaction tax' (FTT), 'EU budget'[4], 'Banking union', 'Tax issues', 'European Fund for Strategic Investments' (EFSI), and 'Other'.[5] The table shows that the most contested proposals during negotiations were on the FTT, with 34% of government interventions voicing disapproval. As a result, none of the FTT proposals was ever discussed in a debate on political agreement or put to a vote. Importantly, while there is substantial variation between legislative packages, on average, contestation diminishes over the course of negotiations, decreasing from 30% disapproving interventions in initial presentation debates to 17% in debates on political agreement. Nevertheless, even this figure of disapproval is more than four times higher than the 3.8% opposition votes observed at the voting stage.

This provides some novel quantitative evidence that governments resolve conflict over the course of negotiations. At the same time, it highlights that even towards the end of the negotiations some governments are still

**Table 1.** Comparing contestation during negotiations and in voting.

| Legislative packages | Disapproval in negotiations | | | | Opposition votes |
|---|---|---|---|---|---|
| | *Initial presentations* | *Policy debates* | *Debates on political agreement* | All stages | |
| FTT | 32% | 34% | No debate | 34% | No voting |
| EU budget | 41% | No debate | 25% | 30% | 5% |
| Banking union | 17% | 11% | 13% | 13% | 1% |
| Tax issues | No debate | 25% | 24% | 24% | 0% |
| EFSI | 15% | 30% | 0% | 12% | No voting |
| Other | 12% | 17% | 9% | 14% | 2% |
| All debates | 30% | 22% | 17% | 20% | 3.8% |

Note: Figures are shares of all government interventions/all votes cast by governments.

expressing disapproval about aspects of the proposal, but nonetheless cast a 'yes' vote on the act.

## Data and operationalisation

What drives this contestation in Council deliberations? To test whether government disapproval in the Council is shaped by public opinion, we use *Disapproval* (running from 1 to 5, with higher values indicating more disapproval) as our main dependent variable. Crucially, we also need a measure of policy-specific public opinion. The key challenge is to identify question items from public opinion surveys that ask respondents directly about their opposition to or support of EU policies that were discussed in the ECOFIN configuration, ideally at several time points. We use the Eurobarometer surveys as they regularly include questions on the legislative files the Commission prepares. We are able to identify suitable public opinion items for a total of five legislative packages (see Table 1), relating to 58 out of the 89 debates in the DICEU dataset. These five packages cover 72% of all legislative debates and 79% of all debating time in ECOFIN in our period of study.

First, for debates on the FTT we use a question that asks respondents: 'Thinking about reform global financial markets, please tell me whether you are in favour or opposed to the following measures to be taken by the EU'. One item to rate is 'The introduction of a tax on financial transactions'. The advantage of this question is that it clearly asks for a view on a FTT to be implemented by the EU. Second, for debates on cross-national tax issues (e.g., automatic exchange of information, common standards) we use the same question with the item 'Tougher rules on tax avoidance and tax havens'. This yields a measure of public opposition to tougher EU tax regulation, which was the main purpose of EU initiatives in this area. Third, for all public debates on the EU's banking union, we use the following item from the same battery: 'The introduction of a tax on profits made by banks'. While this item does not directly ask for opposition to the banking union, it taps into public attitudes on whether banks keep 'too much profit' for themselves. Since many of the legislative acts under the banking union umbrella (e.g., CRD IV, single resolution fund) ultimately impose costly regulation on banks with tax-like balance sheet effects, we use opposition to this item as a measure of opinion on the banking union.

Fourth, to measure public opposition to the EFSI we use disagreement with the following statement: 'Public money should be used to stimulate private sector investment at EU level'. Since the European Investment Bank itself defines the EFSI through its aim 'to mobilize private investment in projects which are strategically important for the EU' (http://www.eib.org/efsi/), the item should be an appropriate measure of public opposition to the EFSI.

Fifth, we measure public opinion on the annual EU budget amendments by a question asking respondents 'With which of the following two statements do you most agree?'. Respondents could either pick 'The EU should have greater financial means given its political objectives' or alternatively 'The EU's political objectives do not justify an increase in the Union's budget'. We operationalise public opposition to budget amendments (generally implying higher appropriations in our period of study) through the share of respondents choosing 'The EU's political objectives do not justify an increase in the Union's budget'.

We measure mean opinion on these Eurobarometer items in each country using post-stratification weights, with higher values indicating more opposition to (or *less* support for) the EU policy proposal. Specifically, we use estimates from the last survey (before the respective Council debate) in which the item was asked.[6] Using past opinion ensures that public preferences are measured prior to the governments' deliberations. Moreover, we use a *z*-score standardisation for each of the five different items, which corrects for the different response scales, and combine them in a single variable. This *Public opposition* variable indicates opposition in a country in terms of standard deviations from mean opposition to this legislative package across countries and debates (i.e., $z_{i,j,d} = \frac{PO_{i,j,d} - \overline{PO_j}}{\sigma(PO_j)}$, where $PO_{i,j,d}$ is public opposition in country *i* on package *j* at the time of debate *d*).

To test our second hypothesis of the conditioning effect of salience on responsiveness, we collect data on the national media coverage of the five legislative packages for which we have public opinion data. Dolezal *et al.* (2016: 43) convincingly argue that media coverage is the best indicator of EU politicisation in today's 'audience democracies', in which media 'play a central role of intermediation between citizens and the state'. Hence, we use media attention as a proxy measure for issue salience, and we expect that public opinion should matter more for governments' behaviour in Brussels when negotiating issues that are more salient. We are thus interested in capturing media attention to an issue as a general indicator of the public salience of that issue, rather than as a measure of media effects per se.[7] While media coverage is difficult to measure for each and every piece of EU legislation, we are able to measure the media coverage of the policy issues discussed in our five legislative packages. Specifically, we count the number of articles that refer to the legislative package and its contents in major newspapers in Austria, France, Germany, Ireland, Italy, Malta, Netherlands, Spain and the United Kingdom in the six-month period preceding a Council meeting. This is achieved by creating lists of search terms and patterns (e.g., distance between words) for each package that delineate articles referring to the topics of the legislative package from those dealing with adjacent issues (for a very similar approach, see Reh *et al.* 2013). Details are in the Supplemental Material.

Figure 1 plots media coverage (*z*-standardised within countries) over time and separately for each legislative package.[8] Most remarkably, the patterns of media coverage are very similar across countries for all packages. While media attention to tax issues and the EFSI is below average ('0'-line) in all countries at (almost) all times, there are temporal peaks of media attention at 1–2 standard deviations above the mean for the budget, the banking union, and the FTT in most countries. This is indicative of the higher domestic salience of these proposals that have the chance to be disproportionately covered in the media at times. Since media attention is a proxy for public salience and we were only able to obtain media data in nine out of 28 EU countries, we focus on a binary classification delineating more salient from less salient legislative packages. Specifically, we use a dummy variable *Salient legislative package* that is '1' for debates on the FTT, the budget and the banking union and '0' for debates on tax issues and the EFSI, which captures the contrast between 'high salience' and 'low salience' packages.[9]

We also control for several factors that have been found to influence government behaviour in the Council and that may also be correlated with public opinion. First, we include a measure of the government parties' positions on economic policy matters as well as European integration. This addresses findings that government ideology matters for Council politics (Hagemann and Høyland 2008). It also seeks to ensure that our estimates capture actual responsiveness to public opinion (i.e., anticipatory representation), and not simply changing government behaviour due to changes in

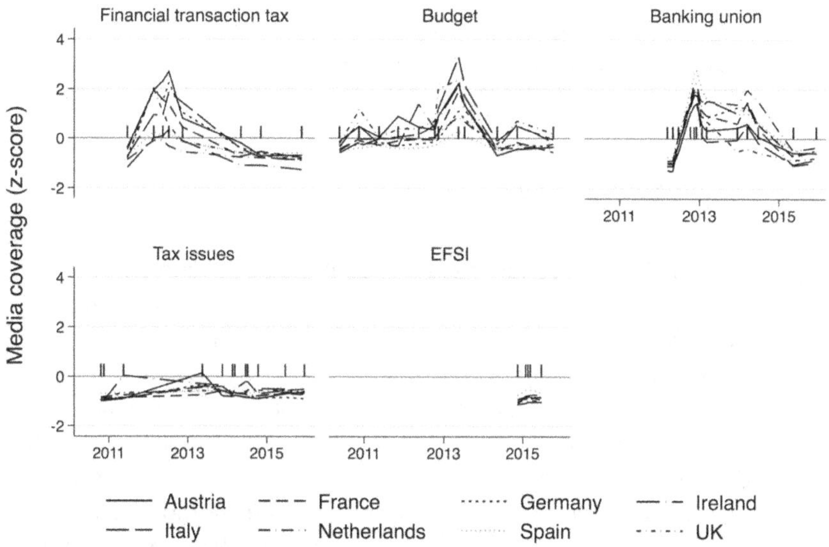


**Figure 1.** Media coverage by legislative package.

Notes: Vertical bars indicate dates of debates on the package.

government composition that may be correlated with fluctuations in opinion (see Stimson 1999). For economic matters, we use the Comparative Manifesto Project's (CMP) coding of the government parties' election manifestos on the planned economy scale ('planeco') (Volkens *et al.* 2018). This scale is constructed as the percentage of quasi-sentences that parties devote to the topics of 'Market Regulation' (per403), 'Economic Planning' (per404), and 'Controlled Economy' (per412). This relates most precisely to our legislative packages that deal with regulation (e.g., tax regulation) and states' intervention into the economic realm (e.g., banking union, FTT). In addition, we also use a pro-anti integration scale that is the percentage of positive quasi-sentences minus the percentage of negative quasi-sentences on European integration (per108 – per110). Where applicable we obtain aggregated positions of government parties by seat-weighting the manifesto estimates of the individual coalition partners.

In addition, we also control for governments' annual receipts from the EU budget (percentage of GDP) as well as for annual national unemployment and inflation rates. On the one hand, this takes account of findings on the decisive role of national economic interests for government behaviour in the Council (Bailer *et al.* 2015; Zimmer *et al.* 2005). On the other hand, it also ensures that our estimates on public opinion represent more than fluctuations in the economy that have the potential to move opinion (e.g., Stevenson 2001). We also control for differences between small and big countries with a measure of a country's population (in million inhabitants) (Schure and Verdun 2008; Thomson 2011).

Lastly, we control for the negotiation stage, since we have shown above that governmental disapproval is higher in initial presentations than in policy debates or debates on political agreement.

## Analysis and results

To analyse responsiveness in the Council we use mixed-effects linear regressions with *Disapproval* as the dependent variable (running from 1 to 5). We account for potential unobserved heterogeneity between countries and debates with different random and fixed effects specifications. Since we face non-trivial amounts of missing values (e.g., 9% of the public opinion data), mainly due to the incompleteness of the Eurobarometer and the CMP data, we multiply impute these values using chained equations with predictive mean matching, creating 30 multiple-imputed datasets (see the Supplemental Material). The results are reported in Table 2. Whereas Models 1 and 2 are specified with random effects for debates and countries, Model 3 uses fixed effects for countries, ruling out country-level time-invariant confounders.

**Table 2.** Models of governmental disapproval.

| | Model 1 | Model 2 | Model 3 |
|---|---|---|---|
| Public opposition | 0.342 | 0.112 | 0.107 |
| | (0.047)** | (0.080) | (0.080) |
| Salient legislative package | | 0.260 | 0.341 |
| | | (0.191) | (0.212) |
| Public opposition * Salient legislative package | | 0.321 | 0.326 |
| | | (0.094)** | (0.096)** |
| Government *planeco* position | −0.059 | −0.056 | −0.063 |
| | (0.015)** | (0.015)** | (0.020)** |
| Government EU position | −0.006 | −0.011 | −0.009 |
| | (0.022) | (0.022) | (0.026) |
| Receipts from EU budget | −0.076 | −0.070 | 0.049 |
| | (0.036)* | (0.036) | (0.078) |
| Unemployment rate | −0.031 | −0.029 | 0.013 |
| | (0.012)* | (0.012)* | (0.028) |
| Inflation rate | −0.062 | −0.080 | −0.049 |
| | (0.041) | (0.043) | (0.047) |
| Population | 0.004 | 0.005 | |
| | (0.003) | (0.003) | |
| Policy debates | −0.580 | −0.536 | |
| | (0.279)* | (0.277) | |
| Debates on political agreement | −0.907 | −0.874 | |
| | (0.249)** | (0.248)** | |
| Constant | 3.615 | 3.390 | 1.835 |
| | (0.290)** | (0.319)** | (0.387)** |
| *N* | 751 | 751 | 751 |
| Number of countries | 28 | 28 | 28 |
| Number of debates | 58 | 58 | 58 |
| Fixed effects | | | Countries |
| Random effects | Debates, Countries | Debates, Countries | Debates |

Notes: All are mixed effects regressions; standard errors in parentheses; multiple imputation estimates using chained equations with predictive mean matching ($m = 30$).
*$p < 0.05$.
**$p < 0.01$.

To test H1 we first include just the main term of public opinion in Model 1. This reveals that, on average, governments disapprove more strongly of legislative proposals if public opposition is greater. To test hypothesis H2 we include an interaction term between public opposition and salient legislative packages in Models 2 and 3. In both models, the interaction term is positive and statistically significant. This indicates that the effect of public opposition on governments' disapproval of EU policy proposals in the Council is stronger for those legislative packages that receive high domestic media attention at times. In fact, the effect of public opposition is not significant but still positive for packages with lower salience ($p = 0.16$).

In Figure 2 we plot the effect of public opposition for legislative packages with low (left panel) versus high (right panel) salience based on the results from Model 2. While public opposition at home is virtually irrelevant to governmental disapproval in the Council for legislative packages with comparatively low domestic salience, governments are very sensitive to the public if

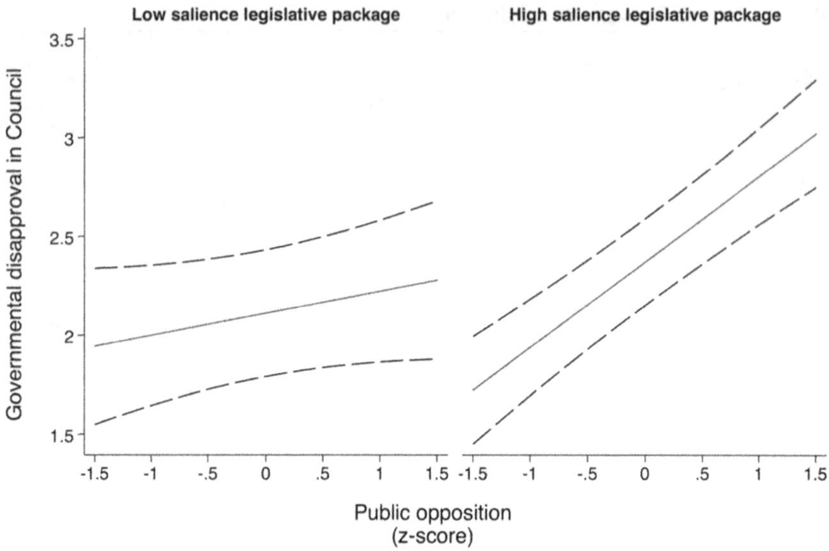


**Figure 2.** Effect of public opposition on governmental disapproval by issue salience.
Notes: 95% confidence intervals as dashed lines.

the package is highly salient. This is key evidence for H2. Note that due to our use of country fixed effects in Model 3, these results are not driven by cross-national differences but by changes in public opposition within countries over time and across legislative packages.

In terms of the control variables, the effect of the government's *planeco* position is most remarkable: government parties that have stressed a preference for more economic planning and economic regulation in their election manifestos are *more* approving of the major ECOFIN policy proposals in the period 2010–2015. While this finding is in line with our theoretical expectations, since projects like the FTT, tax issues, or the banking union are clearly targeted at more tightly regulating economic activities, it is important evidence for the idea that party politics matters in the Council (e.g., Hagemann and Høyland 2008), and parties are engaging in mandate fulfilment at the EU level (Franchino and Wratil 2019). In contrast, the evidence for economic explanations of governments' preferences is more mixed: governments with higher unemployment at home are more approving of the state of negotiations (at least in Models 1 and 2), but the EU budget position and inflation do not matter significantly. As expected, we find significantly less governmental disapproval in debates on political agreement.

One concern about our models is the pooling of different question items into a single public opposition variable. While this provides us with the statistical power to test our hypotheses (especially, H2), we would like to exclude the possibility that it drives any results. Hence, we also estimate

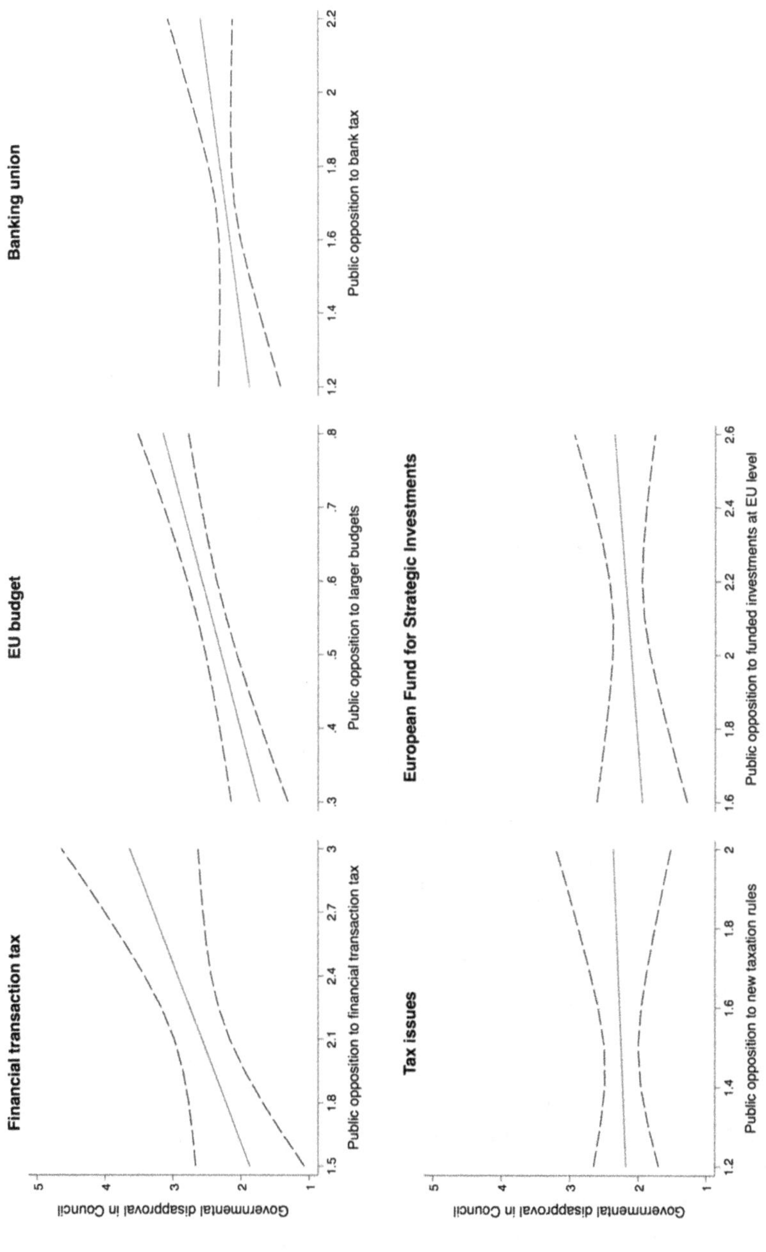


**Figure 3.** Effect of public opposition on governmental disapproval by legislative package.

Notes: 95% confidence intervals as dashed lines.

separate linear regression models for each of our five packages using the original public opinion items with varying scales. This also allows us to use varying sets of control variables that are more specific to each of the legislative packages. Moreover, the models do not include the fixed effects for the negotiation stage nor the random effect for debates, since only a few debates per package are held (see details in the Supplemental Material). In Figure 3 we plot the effect of public opposition for each package. This reveals that the effect of public opposition is strongest on the FTT and the EU budget. In these cases, the coefficients on public opposition are also statistically significant, for the banking union it is close to significance ($p = 0.11$). For the two other packages, the relationship between opposition and governmental disapproval is positive but far from statistical significance. Given that these three packages are also the packages that we classified with high domestic salience, these findings are in line with our hypotheses.

In the Supplemental Material, we perform several robustness and sensitivity analyses. In particular, we report results with different classifications of salient legislative packages, different operationalisations of opinion, using ordered instead of linear regression, and estimating the models without multiple imputation and control variables. We also address concerns about reversed causality in the relationship between governments' position-taking in the Council and public opposition. All these tests support our core results.

## Conclusion

The EU's primary legislative chamber, the Council, used to be highly secretive. But recent transparency reforms have created new avenues to examine the drivers of intergovernmental conflict. This paper takes advantage of a novel dataset on public televised deliberations in the Council to examine the nature and domestic drivers of contestation. We demonstrate that contestation is highest at the early stages of the negotiations and that it is partially shaped by domestic opposition when negotiating salient legislative issues. This paper thus makes several contributions to the literature on legislative behaviour in the Council.

First, we present results from an original database on governments' legislative positions (DICEU). While most of the existing literature has focused on government positions at either the pre-negotiation stage (e.g., Thomson *et al.* 2006, 2012) or the voting stage (e.g., Bailer *et al.* 2015; Hagemann et al 2017), we are able to analyse contestation over the whole course of formal Council deliberations. As expected, our findings show high levels of disagreement between governments at the initial stages of the negotiations and increasing consensus as the negotiations approach voting. This study thus provides an important bridge between the interview-based studies of pre-negotiation positions that have demonstrated high levels of conflict in the Council and studies focused on the final voting stage that have highlighted the high degree of consensus.

The second contribution of this paper is to examine how domestic electoral politics influences contestation in the Council. Specifically, we use DICEU data to present the first study of government responsiveness to policy-specific public opinion in the EU context. There is a growing literature examining responsiveness to public opinion in the Council using mostly general Euroscepticism as an indicator of public preferences. Our results provide the first evidence that governments in the Council are not only responsive to the general 'public mood' (e.g. Euroscepticism), but also to issue-specific public opinion.

This finding primarily applies to governments' behaviour on legislative packages that are salient domestically. This demonstrates that governments in the Council are aware of public preferences and responsive to them when they fear that where ignoring the public opposition could be electorally costly. In other words, it suggests that the Council resembles a normal legislative body where politicians are responsive to public opinion, more than it does an opaque international institution insulated from electoral pressures. It is worth noting, however, that as we are focusing on the ECOFIN Council during a period when economic and financial issues were generally highly politicised across Europe, due to the Eurozone crisis, we may not necessarily find the same levels of responsiveness across all Council configurations or in other timeframes (e.g., when the EU was less politicised). Nonetheless, ECOFIN is a useful case study due to the still considerable variation in the salience of the legislative packages covered in our data – ranging from a high salience banking union to lower salience EU taxation issues. This variation allows us to draw more general inferences about the conditions under which governments in the Council are likely to be responsive to public opinion. Indeed, our findings suggest that responsiveness may be absent when the Council is debating issues that are not salient domestically. This suggests that governments are not insulated from domestic electoral incentives when they negotiate in the EU on domestically more salient matters, while public opposition plays a far smaller role on issues that are less salient. More generally, this study suggests that even actors in international organisations can be responsive to public opinion, when issues debated internationally are politicised domestically.

## Notes

1. As an illustration, we have included several extracts from the debates in the Supplemental Material.
2. Note that the varying meanings of disapproval across debates and at different negotiation stages may lead to measurement error, which is why we control for the negotiation stage in all main models.

3. Eight debates were discussions of presidency work programmes, and hence no official votes on these matters are recorded, and 23 debates were on legislative files without an official vote or without reporting it. As a result, we lack voting data on 31 of our 89 (34%) DICEU debates. This highlights that voting data neglects a substantial part of intergovernmental politics in the Council. In fact, we have no official Council votes on some of the most significant ECOFIN proposals discussed during the last years, most prominently the Commission's proposal for a financial transaction tax – the most frequently debated legislative proposal in the DICEU dataset (8 debates).
4. Note that ECOFIN deals primarily with the annual budget and not the multiannual financial framework.
5. We chose these categories guided by the availability of public opinion data on each of them.
6. The number of survey waves available varies between the opinion measures (e.g. from only two waves for the EU budget to frequent half-yearly estimates of opinion for the FTT). In the Supplemental Material, we also show that our results hold when interpolating between opinion surveys and using a six-month lag or current opinion.
7. We acknowledge that media attention is a noisy indicator of public salience. In some instances, the very failure of governments to respond to public opinion may fuel media stories. In such cases, attention is more a consequence than a predictor of responsiveness.
8. Note that we omit data for Malta from Figure 1, since the Maltese media data are very noisy due to the fact that the average number of articles on a legislative package in the six-month period preceding a Council meeting is just 3.6, while it is above 39 for all other countries.
9. In the Supplemental Material, we show that when we only use our sample of nine countries for which we have media data, and classify each country-package dyad according to whether average media coverage of a package in a country was below or above the country mean (as dummy variable), we obtain substantively the same results as in our main analyses. The same is the case when using an alternative measure of salience based on 'don't know' responses in the Eurobarometer surveys.

## Acknowledgements

The authors would like to thank Isabelle Brusselmans and her team in the Council Secretariat for their support in obtaining video footage from the Council, including archival material that was re-digitized for this project. The authors are also grateful to Rebecca Brooks, Sarah Ciaglia, Rebecca Kittel, Carolyn Konopka, Jason Krstic, Lukas Lehner, Julia Leschke, Ida Popovski, Pit Rieger, and Tim Rogers for their excellent research assistance, and to Edoardo Bressanelli, Fabio Franchino, Christel Koop, Filip Kostelka, Christine Reh, Thomas Saalfeld and the late John Peterson for insightful comments on previous versions of the paper.

## Disclosure statement

No potential conflict of interest was reported by the authors

## Funding

This work was supported by the Fritz Thyssen Stiftung [grant number 20.16.0.045WW] and the Leverhulme Trust [grant number RF-2013-245].

## ORCID

*Sara B. Hobolt* http://orcid.org/0000-0002-9742-9502
*Christopher Wratil* http://orcid.org/0000-0002-7339-9628

## References

Alexandrova, P., Rasmussen, A., & Toshkov, D. (2016). Agenda responsiveness in the European Council: Public priorities, policy problems and political attention. *West European Politics*, *39*(4), 605–627.

Bailer, S., Mattila, M., & Schneider, G. (2015). Money makes the EU go round: The objective foundations of conflict in the Council of ministers. *Journal of Common Market Studies*, *53*(3), 437–456.

Börzel, T. A. & Risse, T. (2018). From the euro to the Schengen crises: European integration theories, politicization, and identity politics. *Journal of European Public Policy*, 25(1), 83–108.

Carey, J. M. (2008). *Legislative voting and accountability*. Cambridge: Cambridge University Press.

Cramme, O., & Hobolt, S. B. (2014). *Democratic politics in a European Union under stress*. Oxford: Oxford University Press.

De Wilde, P., & Zürn, M. (2012). Can the politicization of European integration be reversed? *Journal of Common Market Studies*, *50*(1), 137–153.

Dolezal, M., Grande, E. & Hutter, S. (2016). Exploring politicisation: Design and methods. In S. Hutter, E. Grande & H. Kriesi (Eds.), *Politicising Europe: Integration and mass politics* (pp. 32–60). Cambridge: Cambridge University Press.

Erikson, R. S., MacKuen, M. B. & Stimson, J. A. (2002). *The macro polity*. Cambridge: Cambridge University Press.

Franchino, F. & Wratil, C. (2019). Representing the compromise: How institutions serve government support coalitions in European Union policy-making. *European Journal of Political Research*, 58(4), 1129–1151.

Häge, F. M. (2013). Coalition Building and consensus in the Council of the European Union. *British Journal of Political Science*, *43*(3), 481–504.

Hagemann, S., Hobolt, S. B., & Wratil, C. (2017). Government responsiveness in the European Union: Evidence from Council voting. *Comparative Political Studies*, *50*(6), 850–876.

Hagemann, S., & Høyland, B. (2008). Parties in the Council? *Journal of European Public Policy*, *15*(8), 1205–1221.

Heisenberg, D. (2005). The institution of "consensus" in the European Union: Formal versus informal decision-making in the Council. *European Journal of Political Research*, *44*(1), 65–90.

Hobolt, S. B., & de Vries, C. E. (2015). Issue entrepreneurship and multiparty competition. *Comparative Political Studies*, *48*(9), 1159–1185.

Hooghe, L., & Marks, G. (2009). A postfunctionalist theory of European integration: From permissive consensus to constraining dissensus. *British Journal of Political Science*, *39* (1), 1–23.

Hosli, M. O., Mattila, M., & Uriot, M. (2011). Voting in the Council of the European Union after the 2004 Enlargement: A comparison of old and new member states. *Journal of Common Market Studies*, *49*(6), 1249–1270.

Kleine, M. (2013). *Informal governance in the European Union. How governments make international organizations work.* Ithaca: Cornell University Press.

Kleine, M. & Minaudier, C. (2017). Negotiating under political uncertainty: National elections and the dynamics of international co-operation. *British Journal of Political Science*, 49(1), 315–337.

Mansbridge, J. (2003). Rethinking representation. *American Political Science Review*, *97* (04), 515–528.

Naurin, D. (2006). Transparency, publicity, accountability – the missing links. *Swiss Political Science Review*, 12(3), 90–98.

Novak, S. (2013). The silence of ministers: Consensus and blame avoidance in the Council of the European Union. *Journal of Common Market Studies*, *51*(6), 1091–1107.

Powell, G. B., & Whitten, G. D. (1993). A cross-national analysis of economic voting: Taking account of the political context. *American Journal of Political Science*, *37*(2), 391–414.

Reh, C., Heritier, A., Bressanelli, E. & Koop, C. (2013). The informal politics of legislation: Explaining secluded decision making in the European Union. *Comparative Political Studies*, 46(9), 1112–1142.

Schneider, C. J. (2018). *The responsive union: National elections and European governance.* Cambridge: Cambridge University Press.

Schure, P., & Verdun, A. (2008). Legislative bargaining in the European Union: The divide between large and small member states. *European Union Politics*, *9*(4), 459–486.

Stevenson, R. T. (2001). The economy and policy mood: A fundamental dynamic of democratic politics? *American Journal of Political Science*, *45*(3), 620–633.

Stimson, J. A. (1999). Party government and responsiveness. In A. Przeworski, S. C. Stokes, & B. Manin (Eds.), *Democracy, accountability, and representation* (pp. 197–221). Cambridge: Cambridge University Press.

Stimson, J. A., MacKuen, M. B., & Erikson, R. S. (1995). Dynamic representation. *American Political Science Review*, *89*(3), 543–565.

Thomson, R. (2009). Actor alignments in the European Union before and after enlargement. *European Journal of Political Research*, 48(6), 756–781.

Thomson, R. (2011). *Resolving controversy in the European Union. Legislative decision-making before and after enlargement.* Cambridge: Cambridge University Press.

Thomson, R., Arregui, J., Leuffen, D., Costello, R., Cross, J., Hertz, R., & Jensen, T. (2012). A new dataset on decision-making in the European Union before and after the 2004 and 2007 enlargements (DEUII). *Journal of European Public Policy*, 19(4), 604–622.

Thomson, R., Stokman, F. N., Achen, C. H., & König, T. (2006). *The European Union decides.* Cambridge: Cambridge University Press.

Toshkov, D. (2011). Public opinion and policy output in the European Union: A lost relationship. *European Union Politics*, *12*(2), 169–191.

Volkens, A., Lehmann, P., Matthieß, T., Regel, S. & Weßels, B. (2018). *The manifesto data collection. Manifesto project (MRG/CMP/MARPOR)*. Version 2018a, Berlin.

Wlezien, C. & Soroka, S. N. (2012). Political institutions and the opinion–policy link. *West European Politics*, 35(6), 1407–1432.

Wratil, C. (2018). Modes of government responsiveness in the European Union: Evidence from Council negotiation positions. *European Union Politics*, *19*(1), 52–74.

Wratil, C. (2019). Territorial representation and the opinion-policy linkage: Evidence from the European Union. *American Journal of Political Science*, 63(1), 197–211.

Wratil, C. & Hobolt, S. B. (2019). Public deliberations in the Council of the European Union: Introducing and validating DICEU. *European Union Politics*, 20(3), 511–531.

Zimmer, C., Schneider, G., & Dobbins, M. (2005). The contested Council: Conflict dimensions of an intergovernmental EU institution. *Political Studies*, *53*(2), 403–422.

OPEN ACCESS

# The Court of Justice in times of politicisation: 'law as a mask and shield' revisited

Michael Blauberger and Dorte Sindbjerg Martinsen

**ABSTRACT**

This contribution analyses if and under what conditions bottom-up pressures constrain the Court of Justice of the European Union (CJEU). Neofunctionalists famously explained the power of the Court by its use of 'law as a mask and shield'. Due to its technical nature, the Court is able to mask the political substance of 'integration through law' and to shield it from political challenges. We revisit this argument in times of politicisation of the EU and develop a typology of four constellations depending on different kinds of bottom-up pressures. We argue that depoliticised integration through law still functions, to varying degrees, in face of *either* governmental contestation *or* public politicisation. By contrast, if member state governments and the public *jointly* oppose further integration through law, the Court is constrained as further expansive jurisprudence could even reinforce politicisation and risk political backlash. We illustrate our argument with case law on EU citizenship.

## Introduction

Among all major EU institutions, the Court of Justice of the EU (CJEU) is the least likely to be affected by the bottom-up politicisation of EU decision-making. The Court has been famously described as 'tucked away in the fairy-land Duchy of Luxembourg' (Stein, 1981, p. 1) to stress the remoteness of European judges from EU political battles, let alone broader public attention. As with any court, the CJEU's authority rests on its perception as a non-political actor, settling conflicts by technical-legal means, and hence, CJEU judges have no interest in becoming agents of politicisation. Rather, the Court's ability to depoliticise conflicts is a crucial precondition for its role as an engine of integration. Due to its technical-legal nature, neofunctionalists have argued, law serves as a 'mask and shield', which obscures the political substance of CJEU jurisprudence and protects it from political challenges.

And yet, the CJEU is not immune against bottom-up pressures. Escaping the 'dictate' from Luxembourg was a major issue during Brexit negotiations. More generally, research on courts and politics has shown that judges do not rule in a political vacuum, but are responsive to changes in the broader 'political mood'(McGuire & Stimson, 2004). Against the background of increasing EU politicisation, we therefore revisit Burley and Mattli's classical argument about 'law as a mask and shield'.

We develop a typology of four constellations depending on whether CJEU jurisprudence is subject to bottom-up pressures stemming from member state governments and/or politicisation. Based on our distinction of bottom-up pressures, we qualify the 'mask and shield' argument in two respects. First, even if 'shielded' against outright political attacks, CJEU jurisprudence remains vulnerable to governmental contestation by legal means. Integration through law scholars underestimated member states' ability to contain the *impact* of expansive CJEU jurisprudence through creative compliance at the domestic level and legislative corrections at the EU level. Second, we argue that the Court faces a 'constraining consensus' if further *expansive jurisprudence* is not only contested by member state governments but faces also public politicisation. Under these circumstances, judges have to choose between self-restraint and the risk of political backlash (Madsen, Cebulak, & Wiebusch, 2018).

The following theoretical section briefly summarises the original neofunctionalist account, before we develop our own argument and typology of different constellations of CJEU contestation. Subsequently, we illustrate these four ideal-typical constellations with empirical evidence from the area of EU ideal-typical complemented with examples from other policy areas. The concluding section discusses the prospects of further Court-driven integration through law in times of politicisation.

## Law as a mask and shield revisited

### *The original argument*

In their seminal article 'Europe before the Court' from 1993, Anne-Marie Burley and Walter Mattli applied neofunctionalist theory to explain the CJEU's strength as an engine of integration (Burley & Mattli, 1993). The Court, they argued, often ruled in favor of further integration to an extent that goes significantly beyond what could be reached by the political agreement of governments alone. Crucially, this integration through law depends on the distinctiveness of the legal domain:

> Law functions as a mask for politics, precisely the role neofunctionalists originally forecast for economics. The need for a 'functional' domain to circumvent the direct clash of political interests is the central insight of neofunctionalist

> theory. This domain could never be completely separated from the political sphere but would at least provide a sufficient buffer to achieve results that could not be directly obtained in the political realm. (Burley & Mattli, 1993, p. 44)

Burley and Mattli linked their argument already explicitly to (de)politicisation: 'The strength of the functional domain as an incubator of integration depends on the relative resistance of that domain to politicisation' (Burley & Mattli, 1993, p. 44). Court judgments appear as 'technical', they deny the 'existence of policy discretion' and provide 'nonpolitical justification(s)' for 'purportedly neutral' decisions, which derive from their 'distinctive methodology and logic', in short: they follow the 'inexorable logic of law' (Burley & Mattli, 1993, p. 69–73). Due to these characteristics, case law 'functions both as a mask and shield' (Burley & Mattli, 1993, p. 74). The political implications of judgments are hidden behind their technical-legal language. And as long as no-one wants to call the Court's general authority into question, individual rulings are protected from outright political contestation, i.e., politically unwelcome case law can only be challenged on its own legal terms.

While Burley's and Mattli's argument deals with the depoliticising effect of law and courts in general, it applies, particularly, to the EU context. Appointments to the CJEU are much less prone to politicisation than, for example, to the US Supreme Court (Ferejohn, 2002, p. 65), and the selection process of CJEU judges has been largely professionalised on the basis of the Lisbon Treaty (Dumbrovsky, Petkova, & Van der Sluis, 2014). Moreover, apart from efficiency considerations, internal decision-making at the CJEU remains largely shielded from public scrutiny. While greater openness and transparent reasoning might arguably improve the legal quality of the Court's jurisprudence (Weiler, 2013), European judges have always cared greatly about maintaining the non-political appearance of their case law, e.g., through the short and apodictic style of many judgments, the confidentiality of their internal decision-making and the absence of dissenting opinions.

### *Two qualifications*

25 years after its original publication, the 'law as a mask and shield' argument is still one of the most prominent accounts of CJEU-driven integration through law; arguably holding a similar status as standard reference among political scientists as Joseph Weiler's 'Transformation of Europe' (1991) in the legal field. Yet, the neofunctionalist argument is not uncontested. Empirically, it has been noted that Burley and Mattli offered little evidence for their argument beyond the evolution of CJEU legal doctrine itself (Stone Sweet, 2010, p. 16). Subsequent research delivered strong support for some of their claims, e.g., regarding the enabling role of subnational actors such as domestic courts, lawyers and private litigants (Alter, 1998a; Cichowski, 2004; Kelemen, 2011; but see also Conant, Hofmann, Soennecken, & Vanhala,

2018 for many open questions regarding EU legal mobilisation). Theoretically, historical institutionalists explained the acceptance of expansive CJEU jurisprudence alternatively by emphasizing the short time horizons of politicians rather than the inherent qualities of law (Alter, 1998b; Pierson, 1996). Moreover, it has been criticised that neofunctionalists were largely ignorant of the limitations of integration through law (Alter, 1998b, p. 121). And indeed, Burley's and Mattli's original account shows only little concern for potential qualifications of the 'mask and shield' argument: in order to be accepted as law, CJEU jurisprudence just needs to exhibit 'a minimal degree of fidelity to both substantive law and the methodological constraints imposed by legal reasoning' (Burley & Mattli, 1993, p. 44) and in order not to lose its overall legitimacy, the Court must not 'outrun its constituency' (Mattli & Slaughter, 1998, p. 181).

In the following, we do not seek to present an alternative account, but we introduce two qualifications concerning both the shield and the mask aspects of CJEU jurisprudence, which are inspired by recent research on (i) judicial impact and on (ii) politicisation.

First, the shield of EU law is not impenetrable. When confronted with unwelcome case law, EU member state governments typically do not challenge the Court's overall authority politically, but they may seek to limit the Court's impact by legal means. Burley and Mattli captured judicial impact only partially. Although they defined their dependent variable in terms of a 'gradual penetration of EC law into the domestic law of its member states' (Burley & Mattli, 1993, p. 43), their empirical analysis focused on the development and acceptance of CJEU legal doctrine rather than on broader policy impact. Probably the most radical way to limit the Court without questioning its existing authority is the exclusion from new areas of integration (Burley & Mattli, 1993, p. 74). Apart from exclusion, a growing body of research on CJEU judicial impact has analyzed member states' more subtle ways to control and limit the effects of expansive jurisprudence. At the European level, member states may adopt secondary legislation to modify the implications of existing and to preempt future case law. Whereas outright legislative override of CJEU jurisprudence is rare, member states have been found to draft secondary legislation carefully in order to circumscribe the Court's policy impact (Martinsen, 2015). At the domestic level, the impact of unwelcome Court jurisprudence may be effectively limited in the process of implementation. As with legislative override at the EU level, member states rarely opt for open non-compliance at the domestic level. Rather, they resort to creative forms of compliance, e.g., by limiting the Court's impact to the individual conflict at issue (Conant, 2002) or by carefully designing domestic reforms 'with Luxemburg in mind', which are likely to survive future lawsuits while minimizing substantive policy change (Blauberger, 2012).

Secondly, the political substance of the Court's case law has become harder to mask. Burley and Mattli wrote their original piece still under the impression of the 'permissive consensus' (Hooghe & Marks, 2009). Since then, politicisation of European governance has increased in terms of visibility, polarisation and engagement beyond elite actors (Bresanelli, Koop, & Reh, 2020; de Wilde, Leupold, & Schmidtke, 2016). And, closely linked to this overall trend, CJEU jurisdiction has come to involve ever more politically sensitive issues such as citizenship or welfare rights, which forces the Court to engage in delicate value judgments and interest evaluations (Kelemen, 2016, p. 126f.). As a consequence, even when adhering perfectly to legal methodology and existing doctrine, CJEU judges may be confronted with politicisation. Particularly, the visibility or salience dimension of politicisation is important for our discussion of bottom-up pressures on the Court. Arguably, actor expansion might rather reinforce EU legal mobilisation (cf. Kelemen, 2011) and polarisation might increase CJEU independence as it reduces the risk of politically agreed counter-action (Larsson & Naurin, 2019, p. 12). By contrast, if politicisation involves salient public opposition against further integration in an area of CJEU jurisdiction, it can have a constraining effect on the Court. Studies on domestic high courts have shown that public opinion places a constraint on judicial decision-making and that judges respond to changes in the broader political context (McGuire & Stimson, 2004). Recent research on international courts also emphasises the importance of contextual factors for judicial authority (Alter, Helfer, & Madsen, 2018), including diffuse public support or opposition. Even if the vast majority of CJEU judgments do not reach broad visibility, newly collected data on newspaper coverage of CJEU jurisprudence shows that a considerable share of case law is in fact reported by main European newspapers (Dederke, 2018, p. 18). Moreover, there is empirical evidence that CJEU actually do 'read the morning papers' (Blauberger *et al.*, 2018).

### *Four constellations of CJEU contestation*

Following from the preceding discussion, we distinguish two kinds of bottom-up pressures for the Court. On the one hand, a large part of the political science literature on the CJEU takes a state-centric approach and addresses the Court's relationship to member state governments. Essentially, the question is how far CJEU judges can go in promoting integration through law and making it effective even against opposition from member state governments. While we cannot define a precise cut-off point of how many member governments constitute a bottom-up pressure on the Court, governmental contestation is typically regarded to be greater, the more member governments oppose an expansive EU legal interpretation in their written observations to the Court (Carrubba & Gabel, 2015, p. 84; Larsson & Naurin, 2016, p. 396). On the other hand, we add public politicisation as a separate kind of bottom-up pressure potentially affecting the Court's independence and impact.

Combining these two kinds of bottom-up pressures, four constellations of Court contestation are possible (see Table 1) and each constellation has different implications for the Court's strategic responses and their effectiveness in promoting integration through law. In constellation I, the Court is largely unconstrained by governmental contestation and public politicisation: integration through law is effective even without particular depoliticising efforts. In constellations II and III, the Court is faced with bottom-up pressures from *either* public politicisation *or* governmental contestation: both, 'law as a mask' and 'law as a shield' are responses of 'assertive depoliticisation' (Bressanelli *et al.*, 2019), i.e., they enable the Court to rule expansively despite bottom-up pressure. Finally, in constellation IV, public politicisation *and* governmental contestation constitute a 'constraining consensus' for the Court: a strategy of judicial self-restraint is necessary to protect the Court's recognition as a non-political institution and to avoid political backlash more generally.

(I) Unsurprisingly, the Court is least constrained in its role as an engine of integration in the absence of both, governmental contestation and public politicisation. Arguably, this constellation has predominated for the long period of the 'permissive consensus' and in particular in the core area of EU single market integration. The public exhibited a permissive attitude to elite-driven integration in general and largely ignored the 'quiet revolution' (Weiler, 1994) with the Court as the 'unsung hero' of integration (Burley & Mattli, 1993, p. 43) in particular. Member state governments disliked some rulings, but generally welcomed the Court's role in overcoming political obstacles to European market integration. Even if individual judgments were met with opposition from one or two governments, this hardly constrained the Court. As disagreement over the direction and contents of law are defining features of law-making (Madsen *et al.*, 2018, p. 202), contestation by individual member states hardly constrains the court or challenges its authority – but merely constitutes business as usual (Hofmann, 2018; Larsson & Naurin, 2016, p. 392).

(II) Burley's and Mattli's original argument about law as a mask mainly referred to the Court itself 'masking' the political implications of its jurisprudence. We amend this argument in light of our two qualifications above. Given that member state governments have become more alert to Court-

**Table 1.** Four constellations of CJEU contestation.

| | | Public politicisation | |
|---|---|---|---|
| | | No | Yes |
| Governmental contestation | No | (I) Permissive consensus | (II) Law as a mask |
| | Yes | (III) Law as a shield | (IV) Constraining consensus |

driven integration over time, they can unmask unwelcome integration through law more readily. However, they may prefer and protect the mask of law in light of public politicisation, i.e., whenever they share the Court's interest in promoting integration, but shy away from taking the political responsibility for unpopular decisions. As a consequence, the function of law as a mask is most powerful when the Court and member state governments collude. Under these circumstances, governments may prefer to shift decision-making to the seemingly neutral area of the judiciary, while tacitly agreeing with the political substance of Court-driven integration through law. By arguing 'We are sorry, but it's the law', member state governments can at least partly shift the blame to the Court. At the same time, the Court's authority remains unquestioned and member state governments do not undermine the impact of its jurisprudence.

(III) The Court can use law as a shield most forcefully, when governments are opposed to a specific ruling, but their opposition is not paralleled by strong public politicisation of that issue. In this constellation, the Court has a particular interest in delivering high quality judgments, which are difficult to challenge on legal grounds. References to established precedent serve to emphasise overall legal coherence and certainty (Schmidt, 2012, p. 10) and to justify further expansionary jurisprudence: 'where the "mask of law" has already fallen ... the Court argues more carefully, by means of reference to precedent' (Larsson, Naurin, Derlén, & Lindholm, 2016, p. 881). Under these circumstances, any attempt to deliberately politicise and to openly resist the Court's jurisprudence is likely to backfire for member state governments. Throughout the union, citizens tend to have greater trust in the CJEU than in their own government (or, actually, any other EU institution, see Kelemen, 2012, p. 48f.). Moreover, even if governments are very unhappy with an individual judgment, questioning the general authority of an otherwise functional court would be a high price to pay. Consequently, they seek ways to limit the impact of CJEU jurisprudence by legal means, e.g., through legislative modification at the EU level or creative compliance domestically (Hofmann, 2018). Such measures may contain the impact of individual rulings considerably, but by countering the case law on its own legal terms, they do not call into question the Court's overall authority.

(IV) Finally, CJEU judges may become confronted with the fourth constellation: a 'constraining consensus' where governmental contestation occurs together with public politicisation. While 'law as a mask' crucially depends on the collusion of governments and while law 'shields' the Court from political attacks without public resonance, both protective mechanisms fail in face of joint opposition from member state governments and the general public. This constellation occurs rarely since CJEU judgements usually do not reach broad visibility while at the same time being collectively opposed by several governments. Such bottom-up pressure is most likely to arise when the Court develops innovative rulings against the expressed intent of the EU legislature which affect matters of high political significance (Hofmann, 2018, p. 260; Madsen *et al.*, 2018, p. 205). If, however, the Court continues to drive integration against such a 'constraining consensus', it risks being perceived as a political actor who can also be challenged in political terms. Contestation, then, will not just aim at reducing the impact of individual rulings, but target the Court's general authority to rule expansively. Under these circumstances, the technical complexity of case law may even have the inverse effect of what neofunctionalists described, i.e., populists may (ab)use the opaque and complex character of individual cases and paint 'law as a caricature' to make vastly exaggerated anti-EU claims. As a consequence, we would expect CJEU judges to back down in the face of a 'constraining consensus' and to limit or even reverse expansive jurisprudence. Even if this scenario occurs only rarely, its relevance may be broader, namely if CJEU judges exert self-restraint in anticipation of possible backlash.

In sum, our typology refines the original mask and shield argument by specifying the constellations under which each of these functions of law plays a particular role and by adding public politicisation as an important contextual factor for European judges. It implies one basic hypothesis: effective integration through case law becomes less likely as we move from constellations (I) to (IV). Apart from the law itself, the Court is least constrained (I) under a permissive consensus and (II) when law serves as a mask. The Court may (III) continue to rule expansively even against member state opposition and use law as a shield against outright political attacks, but the impact of expansive jurisprudence is limited. Finally, (IV) under the rare constellation of a constraining consensus, the Court is limited not only with respect to its impact, but in its ability to rule expansively in the first place.

## Empirical illustration

In the following, we illustrate these four ideal-typical constellations with empirical evidence from a joint project on the free movement and equal treatment of EU citizens, complemented with well-researched examples from other policy areas. We, thereby, focus on a rather extreme set of cases, which are not meant to 'test' causal hypotheses or 'represent' CJEU case law in general. Instead, these cases are particularly useful for illustrative purposes as they come close to the ideal types conceptualised above and they cover the full spectrum of our typology. First, while case law on the free movement of workers reaches back to the earliest phases of integration and of the permissive consensus, it is arguably the area in which the Court ruled most strongly against member state opposition (Larsson & Naurin, 2016, p. 396). Secondly, while many CJEU judgments do not reach any public attention (Dederke, 2018, p. 18), the free movement of EU citizens and especially their cross-border access to social welfare has become increasingly politicised in recent years. We have thus chosen a set of cases where legal integration has occurred for long and considerably, while at the same time politics is a play (Martinsen, 2015, p. 10).

### *(I) Permissive consensus*

In terms of producing cases, the CJEU has been remarkably effective. Between 1961 and 2014, the Court decided in more than 7000 preliminary rulings and infringement proceedings (Martinsen, 2015, p. 11). Most cases have concerned agriculture and fisheries, second comes internal market interpretations concerning free movement of goods and thirdly judicial decisions within the social realm. Arguably, the largest pile of these cases were never politically controversial, but merely rather technical legal disputes, relevant for the parties involved but without broader implications. However, famous cases such as Van Gend en Loos and Costa v. E.N.E.L. from 1963 to 1964 certainly fall in this category of integration through law and were enabled by a permissive consensus. New historical research has shown that these landmark cases did indeed cause some political concern, but the majority of governments did not mobilise against the new legal order constructed (Rasmussen, 2017).

Expansive CJEU jurisprudence has largely shaped the free movement and equal treatment of workers for decades, enabled by the permissive consensus. Originally, the right to cross-border welfare in the European Union was restricted to workers by means of Regulation 1612/68 (now 492/2011) and Regulation 1408/71 (now 883/2004), entitling Community migrant workers to equal treatment with national citizens on social rights and tax advantages next to exporting social-security rights across member-states borders. This original regulatory framework of the 1960s has gradually extended its personal and material scope by means of CJEU case law and legislative revisions. The Court's early jurisprudence laid down that the purpose of the Treaty was to establish as 'complete a freedom of movement for workers as possible' (Case 75/63 *Hoekstra*). It later extended the personal scope to also include the self-employed (Case 17/76 *Brack*) and clarified the rights of the family members (Case 7/75 *Fracas*; C-308/93 *Cabanis-Issarte*). In addition, a permissive consensus allowed the Court to develop an inclusive concept of who is a worker according to EU law. In the case of *Kempf* (C-139/85), the CJEU established that working 12 h per week would suffice, and in the case of *Megner* and *Scheffel* (C-444/93), it ruled that 10 h of work per week did not exclude a person from being regarded as a worker.

EU gender equality has been another often cited cluster of case law, used to illustrate the power of integration through law (Cichowski, 2004). The *Defrenne* cases from 1971 and 1976 were crucial in defining the meaning and effect of the Treaty's declaration on equal pay and initiated an important process of judicial and political integration, which proved that litigation can be an important tool to push for change. In the Defrenne II case from 1976, a Belgian Court asked if the Treaty's article 119 had direct effect, creating enforceable rights for individuals in national courts without EU secondary legislation or national legislation transposing it. The Court disregarded objections by the UK and Ireland and confirmed the direct effect of article 119. Other important cases followed as for example *Danfoss* (C-109/88) on equal pay and *Dekker* (C-177/88) concerning the rights of pregnant workers among many others. The Court's jurisprudence was later codified into important pieces of secondary legislation (see for example the burden of proof directive 97/80 adopted in 1997). A large part of gender equality case law occurred without any significant governmental contestation despite their political and also financial implications. Although some member states disliked the rulings, there was no broader collective mobilisation or public politicisation for or against them.

### *(II) Law as a mask*

While law may hide political conflict in various ways, e.g., when the broader and long-term consequences of individual rulings go unnoticed by member state governments, the aspect of law as a mask is essential when governments tacitly endorse integration through law, but do not want to overtly take political responsibility. Theoretically, such a scenario in which governments shift decision-making (and blame) for unpopular decisions is highly plausible, but empirically, these cases are inherently difficult to document. The Court's role in these cases lies precisely in serving as a forum in which governments can hide politically conflictual issues behind a mask of technical, legal reasoning. And governments are assumed to remain silent or even to delude the public about their actual preferences.

Nevertheless, we can draw on some well-researched examples from the posting of workers to illustrate this constellation. The question of which labor standards apply to workers, who are posted from one EU member state to another, was at the heart of the 'Laval quartet' (Blauberger, 2012). In three of these four landmark judgments, the Court interpreted the Posting of Workers Directive extensively and ruled against national restrictions of the free movement of services (Martinsen, 2015). The cases were mainly perceived as pitting old against new EU member states, with the CJEU favoring further liberalisation and, thus, siding with new EU member states (Lindstrom, 2010). And yet, there is considerable evidence that the Court rulings were also received with the tacit approval of some conservative-liberal governments in the old member states. The *Rüffert* judgment (C-346/06) had the greatest impact in those German regions governed by conservative-liberal coalitions, where it was used to abolish the contested domestic rules without replacement (Sack, 2012). The *Laval* judgment (C-341/05) triggered various domestic reform processes, which went furthest in Sweden, where a conservative-liberal government was under strong influence from major business interests (Seikel, 2015). Arguably, in these cases, the mask of EU law worked better for the governments involved than for the CJEU itself. Since these cases were already politicised when they reached the Court, European judges were hardly able to mask the underlying political conflicts and had to take inevitably unpopular rulings. By contrast, the Court's rulings enabled liberal-conservative governments to enact domestic reforms, which could be portrayed as EU legal necessities.

Another policy area in which EU law typically serves to mask political conflict is the control of state aid. Over time, the Commission has been able to incrementally tighten the control of state aid in the EU, largely supported by the CJEU, but also with the tacit agreement of member state governments (Blauberger, 2009). Governments share a collective interest in avoiding subsidy races and reaping the benefits of undistorted competition, but they are vulnerable to political pressures from potential beneficiaries among their constituents. For example, governments are regularly called upon to save domestic enterprises (and their jobs) from bankruptcy by granting state aid. Under these circumstances, governments often readily refer to the constraints imposed by EU rules to deny state aid, while shifting the ultimate responsibility and blame to the European level.

### *(III) Law as a shield*

The case law on the free movement of workers post-Maastricht offers plenty of evidence on how the Court's jurisprudence is shielded from outright political attacks despite challenges by member state governments. Since Maastricht, the Court has significantly extended the rights to move freely and to be treated equally from workers to EU citizens more generally (Wollenschläger, 2011). The actual impact of the Court's citizenship jurisprudence, however, has been more limited. Already before the Court has shifted its own course (see next section), member state governments have effectively limited its impact through legislative modification at the EU level and contained compliance at the domestic level. Modification means compromises between legislative actors where specific articles or annexes insert more national control, more national discretion, exemptions or special rules (Martinsen, 2015, pp. 35–36). Such mitigating articles confines the implications of the case law nationally and in its practical application. For example, the expansive *Grzelczyk* ruling (C-184/99) from 2001 laid down that Union citizenship entitles students from other member states to the social assistance of a hosting member state if a certain link with the society of their host state has been established. Soon after, however, the member governments constructed a delicate compromise with the European parliament in the Citizenship directive 2004/38 (Wasserfallen, 2010), where article 24.2 aimed to modify the implications of the Court ruling by stating that member states are not obliged to confer entitlement to study grants or student loans before permanent residence has been acquired. Modification thus expresses governmental contestation to Court rulings, but is still a milder form of political pushback than upright rebellion against the authority of the Court. Moreover, there is increasing evidence that the impact of the Court's citizenship jurisprudence was limited from the beginning due to restrictive implementation at the domestic level (Heindlmaier & Blauberger, 2017; Martinsen, Rotger, & Thierry, 2019).

Moving beyond the area of EU citizenship, we also find examples of more severe measures to limit the Court's impact by legal means. Most often, the threshold to agree on legislative override is too high for member state governments, which is why they resort to modification as a second best option. And yet, there are some examples of legislative override. Again gender equality is illustrative, where the political receptiveness of legal innovations ended abruptly with the adoption of the Maastricht treaty in 1993. The Court's *Barber* case (C-262/88) from 1990 had laid down that the principle of equal treatment also applied to age of retirement. This time, member states and employers argued strongly against the Barber case's conclusions and the member states unanimously adopted the Barber protocol in the Maastricht Treaty to limit the implication of the judgement. Governments may also try to weaken the relative importance of the Court for the integration process more generally. For example, they restricted the power of the Court when they excluded its jurisdiction from two of the three Maastricht Treaty pillars (Burley & Mattli, 1993).

### *(IV) Constraining consensus*

Finally, the Court faces a 'constraining consensus' under very particular circumstances – namely, if the Court is continuously supplied with new cases in an area, in which further integration is opposed simultaneously by more member governments and public opinion. In this situation, the Court has to make decisions without, however, law serving as a mask or shield insulating the Court from governmental and public opposition. By extending integration through law regardless of political and public opposition, the Court would even exacerbate politicisation. As a consequence, the Court is likely to be responsive and to exert self-restaint in face of strongly voiced political and public objections.

In the area of free movement and cross border welfare, legal integration for many years advanced not only the social rights of workers but also of non-economically active EU citizens. Based on European citizenship enshrined in the Treaty, the Court was heralded for adding real rights and substance to an otherwise empty political concept. In core cases, such as *Martínez Sala* (C-85/96), *Grzelczyk* (C-184/99), *Baumbast* (C-413/99) and *Trojani* (C-456/02), the Court extended the principle of equal treatment to lawfully residing Union citizens, not on the basis of their economic activities but 'purely' as citizens of the Union. It thus declared that Union citizenship as 'destined to become the fundamental status of nationals of the Member States' (*Grzelczyk*, para. 31). However, during the last five years political and public critique against free movement and cross border welfare rights has sounded louder. Member state governments, not the least from the UK, had already called for greater national discretion regarding the regulation of EU migrants' welfare access for several years. In addition, between 2013 and 2015, the public debate around the theme of 'welfare migration' increasingly politicised EU citizens entitlements to welfare in a hosting member state in several member states (Blauberger *et al.*, 2018). 'Welfare tourism' came to feature as a negatively framed concept in the public debate. At the same time, the recent citizenship jurisprudence shows that the CJEU is not immune to the public temper. The previously expansive Union citizenship jurisprudence has turned into a remarkably restrictive course of legal integration with the cases of *Dano* (C-333/13) in November 2014, *Alimanovic* (C-67/14) in September 2015, Garcia-Nieto *Garcia-Nieto* (C-299/14) in April 2016 and in June 2016 with the *Commission v. UK* (C-308/14) infringement case. The Union citizenship of the treaty is no longer the reference point in the Court cases; instead the later restrictive interpretations are based on the conditions of secondary legislation as stated in the Citizenship directive. In its restrictive case law on free movement and cross border welfare, the Court not only proves attentive to the EU legislature, but sensitive to the broader political context and has turned away from expanding right of non-economically active EU citizens (Blauberger *et al.*, 2018).

The 'Laval quartet' was already discussed above as it provided interested governments with a short-term opportunity to mask their own preference and to shift the blame for unpopular decisions to the CJEU. In the longer run, however, the Court could not sustain its expansive jurisprudence as it became confronted with a constraining consensus. The Court's judgments triggered unprecedented public criticism (Scharpf, 2008) as well as resistance by a significant number of member states. In 2012, the Commission's attempt to codify the Court's case law in the so-called 'Monti II Regulation' led to the first activation ever of the Early Warning Mechanism by twelve national parliaments. When asked to further clarify its interpretation of the Posted Workers Directive in subsequent cases, the Court 'readjusted its position to the benefit of national social regulatory autonomy' (Garben, 2017, p. 38). In the case *Elektrobudowa* (C-396/13), the Court sided with the claims of a Finnish trade union and adopted an unexpectedly generous interpretation of what could be subsumed under the crucial term of 'minimum rates of pay'. In response to the

*Rüffert* judgment (C-346/06), most German regions revised their public procurement legislation in order to protect as much as possible of its original substance in an EU-compatible way (Blauberger, 2012, p. 118). When this legislation was challenged again in the *Regiopost* case (C-115-/14), the Court disagreed with the Commission and shifted its previous position: 'To avoid an explicit and principled reversal of its case law, the Court confines the ruling to the specific facts (...) But even if the extent to which Laval, Rüffert, Luxembourg and Bundesdruckerei have been overturned is open to discussion, the permissive signal to Member States and their courts is a strong one' (Garben, 2017, p. 39).

Finally, another politically sensitive area, in which the Court appears to exert self-restraint in anticipation of (rather than in response to) a constraining consensus, is the area of fundamental rights. Member state governments have been cautious not to facilitate unwarranted CJEU intervention into domestic affairs and limited the scope of application of the Charter of Fundamental Rights of the EU 'to the Member States only when they are implementing Union law' (Article 51 of the Charter). Obviously, any attempt to extend the Charter's scope of application through case law hinges on the interpretation of when member states 'are implementing Union law' and the Court has raised some expectations that might adopt an expansive interpretation (e.g., in the *Åkerberg Fransson* case, C-617/10). Yet, in contrast to these expectations and despite numerous 'invitations' to do so, the Court has so far refrained from an extensive interpretation of Article 51 of the Charter. Apart from the (lack of) legal basis, the current CJEU judge von Danwiz justifies the Court's restraint with a more or less explicit reference to the potential politicisation which could be caused by greater judicial activism (von Danwitz, 2014).

## Conclusion

25 years have passed since Burley and Mattli first presented legal integration to function as a mask and a shield (Burley & Mattli, 1993). Since then, political awareness of the outcomes of integration through law has grown significantly and EU legislative actions as well as national counter-actions limit the political power of the Court. Member states have become more skillful in penetrating the shield of law and as EU integration has moved into core areas of national sovereignty, the political implications of jurisprudence have become harder to mask. Public opinion increasingly forms for or against EU policies in general and partly even for or against specific judicial interpretations. As a consequence, growing politicisation has become an additional scope condition for the CJEU to acknowledge and, under peculiar circumstance, a 'constraining consensus' may restrict the possible outcomes of integration through law, when public politicisation is paralleled by member state opposition to expansive CJEU jurisprudence.

The judges in Luxembourg are not immune to this 'constraining consensus'. The CJEU appears to be sensitive to changes in the broader political context. This is not to say that the European Court has become or is likely to become politicised itself in the sense of taking a more ideological political side, but rather that public politicisation constrains the CJEU's ability to promote integration through law. Ultimately, the Court's legitimacy depends on its jurisprudence being accepted and complied with and there is only that much opposition a judicial authority can take. Moreover, once an issue has already become broadly politicised, we should not overestimate the Court's ability to simply depoliticise it again by the mere force of law. Hence, despite the function of law as a mask and shield, growing politicisation as a scope condition is largely exogenously given for the Court.

## Acknowledgements

We would like to thank Christine Reh, R. Daniel Kelemen and three anonymous reviewers for their very helpful comments.

## Disclosure statement

No potential conflict of interest was reported by the authors.

## Funding

The research for this article was part of a Norface Welfare State Futures (WSF)-funded project, TransJudFare [grant number 462-13-009].

## ORCID

*Michael Blauberger* http://orcid.org/0000-0002-3581-400X
*Dorte Sindbjerg Martinsen* http://orcid.org/0000-0002-2113-0950

## References

Alter, K. J. (1998a). Explaining national Court acceptance of European Court jurisprudence: A critical evaluation of theories of legal integration. In A.-M. Slaughter, A. Stone Sweet, & J. H. H. Weiler (Eds.), *The European Court and National Courts:*

*Doctrine and jurisprudence. Legal change in its social context* (pp. 227–252). Oxford: Hart Publishing.

Alter, K. J. (1998b). 'Who Are the 'masters of the Treaty'? European governments and the European Court of Justice'. *International Organization*, *52*(1), 121–147.

Alter, K. J., Helfer, L., & Madsen, M. R. (2018). *International court authority*. Oxford: Oxford University Press.

Blauberger, M. (2009). Of 'good' and 'bad' Subsidies: European state aid control through Soft and Hard Law. *West European Politics*, *32*(4), 719–737.

Blauberger, M. (2012). With Luxembourg in mind ... The Remaking of national policies in the face of ECJ jurisprudence. *Journal of European Public Policy*, *19*(1), 109–126.

Blauberger, M., Heindlmaier, A., Kramer, D., Martinsen, D. S., Sampson Thierry, J., Schenk, A., & Werner, B. (2018). ECJ judges read the morning papers. Explaining the turnaround of European citizenship jurisprudence. *Journal of European Public Policy*, *25*(10), 1422–1441.

Bresanelli, E., Koop, C. & Reh, C. (2020) 'EU actors under pressure: Politicisation and Depolicitisation as strategic responses', *Journal of European Public Policy*, *27*(3), 329–341.

Burley, A.-M., & Mattli, W. (1993). Europe before the Court: A political theory of legal integration. *International Organization*, *47*(1), 41–76.

Carrubba, C. J., & Gabel, M. J. (2015). *International Courts and the Performance of International Agreements. A General Theory with evidence from the European Union*. New York: Cambridge University Press.

Cichowski, R. A. (2004). Women's rights, the European Court, and Supranational Constitutionalism. *Law & Society Review*, *38*(3), 489–512.

Conant, L. (2002). *Justice contained: Law and politics in the European Union*. Ithaca, NY: Cornell University Press.

Conant, L., Hofmann, A., Soennecken, D., & Vanhala, L. (2018). Mobilizing European Law. *Journal of European Public Policy*, *25*(9), 1376–1389.

Dederke, J. (2018, June). *Media attention against all odds, or politicization as usual? Introducing Case Salience Data for CJEU Cases*. Paper presented at the ECPR-SGEU conference, Paris.

de Wilde, P., Leupold, A., & Schmidtke, H. (2016). Introduction: The differentiated politicisation of European governance. *West European Politics*, *39*(1), 3–22.

Dumbrovsky, T., Petkova, B., & Van der Sluis, M. (2014). Judicial appointments: The article 255 TFEU Advisory Panel and selection Procedures in the member states. *Common Market Law Review*, *51*(2), 455–482.

Ferejohn, J. (2002). Judicializing politics, politicizing Law. *Law and Contemporary Problems*, *65*(3), 41–68.

Garben, S. (2017). The constitutional (Im)balance between 'the market' and 'the social' in the European Union. *European Constitutional Law Review*, *13*(1), 23–61.

Heindlmaier, A., & Blauberger, M. (2017). Enter at your own risk: Free movement of EU citizens in practice. *West European Politics*, *40*(6), 1198–1217.

Hofmann, A. (2018). Resistance against the Court of Justice of the European Union. *International Journal of Law in Context*, *14*(2), 258–274.

Hooghe, L., & Marks, G. (2009). A postfunctionalist theory of European integration: From permissive consensus to constraining Dissensus. *British Journal of Political Science*, *39*(1), 1–23.

Kelemen, R. D. (2011). *Eurolegalism. The transformation of law and regulation in the European Union*. Cambridge: Harvard University Press.

Kelemen, R. D. (2012). The political foundations of judicial independence in the European Union. *Journal of European Public Policy, 19*(1), 43–58.
Kelemen, R. D. (2016). The Court of Justice of the European Union in the twenty-first century. *Law and Contemporary Problems, 79*(1), 117–140.
Larsson, O., & Naurin, D. (2016). Judicial independence and political uncertainty: How the risk of override Impacts on the Court of Justice of the EU. *International Organization, 70*(1), 377–408.
Larsson, O. & Naurin, D. (2019) "Split Vision: Multidimensionality in the European Union's legal policy Space", *International Studies Quarterly* 63(3): 492–506.
Larsson, O., Naurin, D., Derlén, M., & Lindholm, J. (2016). Speaking law to power: The strategic use of precedent of the Court of Justice of the European Union. *Comparative Political Studies, 50*(7), 879–907.
Lindstrom, N. (2010). Service liberalization in the Enlarged EU: A race to the bottom or the Emergence of Transnational political conflict? *Journal of Common Market Studies, 48*(5), 1307–1327.
Madsen, M. R., Cebulak, P., & Wiebusch, M. (2018). Backlash against international courts: Explaining the forms and Patterns of resistance to international courts. *International Journal of Law in Context, 14*(2), 197–220.
Martinsen, D. S. (2015). *An ever more powerful court? The political constraints of legal integration in the European Union*. Oxford: Oxford University Press.
Martinsen, D. S., Rotger, G. P. & Thierry, J. S. (2019) 'Free movement of people and cross-border welfare in the European Union: Dynamic rules, limited outcomes', *Journal of European Social Policy* 29(1): 84–99.
Mattli, W., & Slaughter, A.-M. (1998). Revisiting the European Court of Justice. *International Organization, 52*(1), 177–209.
McGuire, K. T., & Stimson, J. A. (2004). The least dangerous branch revisited: New evidence on Supreme Court responsiveness to public preferences. *Journal of Politics, 66*(4), 1018–1035.
Pierson, P. (1996). The path to European integration: A historical institutionalist perspective. *Comparative Political Studies, 29*(2), 123–163.
Rasmussen, M. (2017). How to enforce European law? A new history of the battle over the direct effect of Directives, 1958–1987. *European Law Journal, 23*(3-4), 290–308.
Sack, D. (2012). 'Europeanization through Law, compliance, and Party Differences. The ECJ's 'rüffert' judgment (C-346/06) and Amendments to public procurement Laws in German Federal states'. *Journal of European Integration, 34*(3), 241–260.
Scharpf, F. W. (2008). 'Der einzige Weg ist, dem EuGH nicht zu folgen'. *Mitbestimmung, 54*(7 + 8), 18–23.
Schmidt, S. K. (2012). Who cares about nationality? The path-dependent case law of the ECJ from goods to citizens. *Journal of European Public Policy, 19*(1), 8–24.
Seikel, D. (2015). 'Class struggle in the shadow of Luxembourg. The domestic impact of the European Court of Justice's case law on the regulation of working conditions'. *Journal of European Public Policy, 22*(8), 1166–1185.
Stein, E. (1981). Lawyers, judges, and the making of a transnational constitution. *American Journal of International Law, 75*(1), 1–27.
Stone Sweet, A. (2010). The European Court of Justice and the judicialization of EU governance. *Living Reviews in European Governance, 5*(2), 1–54.
von Danwitz, T. (2014). The rule of law in the recent jurisprudence of the ECJ. *Fordham International Law Journal, 37*(5), 1311–1346.

Wasserfallen, F. (2010). The judiciary as Legislator? How the European Court of Justice Shapes policy-making in the European Union. *Journal of European Public Policy, 17* (8), 1128–1146.

Weiler, J. H. H. (1991). The Transformation of Europe. *The Yale Law Journal, 100*(1), 2402–2483.

Weiler, J. H. H. (1994). A quiet revolution: The European Court of Justice and Its Interlocutors. *Comparative Political Studies, 26*(4), 510–534.

Weiler, J. H. H. (2013). Epilogue: Judging the judges – Apology and critique. In M. Adams, H. de Waele, & J. Meeusen (Eds.), *Judging Europe's Judges: The Legitimacy of the Case Law of the European Court of Justice* (pp. 235–254). Oxford: Hart Publishing.

Wollenschläger, F. (2011). A new fundamental freedom beyond market integration: Union citizenship and its Dynamics for shifting the economic Paradigm of European integration. *European Law Journal, 17*(1), 1–34.

# Let's speak more? How the ECB responds to public contestation

Manuela Moschella, Luca Pinto and Nicola Martocchia Diodati

**ABSTRACT**

Although the post-crisis politicisation of the ECB is widely acknowledged, little empirical evidence exists about how this important non-majoritarian institution has responded to public contestation. This article starts filling this gap by investigating whether and how public opinion affects ECB communication. Based on automated text analysis of the speeches delivered by Executive Board members (2001–2017), the article shows that negative public opinion is associated with an expansion of the scope of ECB communication and a reduction in the salience attributed to monetary policy issues. These results challenge the view according to which the ECB conceives of its sources of legitimation based almost exclusive on the achievement of its mandate. In particular, our findings suggest that increased politicisation leads the ECB to reassess the sources of its legitimation strategy from a strategy based on output achievement towards one based on participation to broader policy debates.

## Introduction

On the heels of the sovereign debt crisis, the European Central Bank (ECB) has been widely credited for its pivotal role in helping the Eurozone navigate the worst crisis since its creation. Through the adoption of unconventional policies, the ECB has contributed to disperse risks in the Economic and Monetary Union (EMU) (Schelkle, 2017), limit the potential for mass unrest in the member states (Genovese, Schneider, & Wassmann, 2016) and display the leadership (Verdun, 2017) and independence (Lombardi & Moschella, 2016) that ultimately preserved the same existence of the single currency. However, the crisis has also spurred a large public contestation of the ECB and its role: public

Supplemental data for this article can be accessed doi:10.1080/13501763.2020.1712457.

trust towards the ECB has sagged (Roth, Gros, & Nowak-Lehmann, 2014) and an unusual string of mass protests has brought to the surface widespread dissent towards the ECB and its policies.[1]

While several studies have investigated the causes of public discontent towards the ECB (Braun, 2016; Jones, 2009; Högenauer & Howarth, 2016), the purpose of this paper is to systematically investigate whether the ECB has responded to the politicisation of its role and to help illuminate on the legitimation strategies of this important non-majoritarian institution. Indeed, there is abundant evidence indicating that the ECB has not been impermeable to the criticisms, especially in the area of communication. For instance, in a notable shift for an institution that has been traditionally wary of disclosing too much information to the public (see Issing, 1999), the ECB moved in this direction by starting publishing accounts of its internal deliberations in January 2015. The ECB also started the practice of appearing before a number of national parliaments (Tesche, 2018), increased the frequency of communication with the European Parliament (Fraccaroli, Giovannini, & Jamet, 2018), engaged with debates on fiscal policy and structural adjustment (Ban & Patenaude, 2018; Diessner & Lisi, 2019); and even toured Europe in order 'to engage, explain and listen' to European public[2]

A straightforward explanation for the changes to the ECB traditionally guarded communication strategy lies in the (*de facto* and *de jure*) transformations in the ECB role throughout the crisis. As the ECB took on an increased political leadership by adopting unconventional policies and taking on new legal responsibilities in the realm of financial stability, its rhetoric expanded accordingly (Diessner & Lisi, 2019; Ferrara, 2019; Tortola & Pansardi, 2019). Although the changes in the policy context are certainly important to explain the ECB behavior, we argue that the ECB strategically responds to negative public opinion by using an expanded communication as a way to increase its perceived legitimacy. Expanding communication is instrumental to achieve this goal for two reasons. First, an expanded communication allows recasting the ECB public image so as to reject the accusation of being an institution obsessed with the achievement of price stability only. Second, an expanded communication allows the ECB to enhance its legitimation by addressing the policy concerns of several national publics simultaneously rather than focussing on a limited number of concerns that might be salient in some countries only.

Empirically, we investigate the impact of public opinion on the ECB communicative strategies by analysing the speeches delivered by the members of the Executive Board from 2001 to 2017. Specifically, we apply quantitative text analysis to identify how ECB policymakers share their attention among monetary and non-monetary policy issues in their communication with the public. The advantage of measuring the impact of public opinion on the salience attributed to issues that do not directly fall in the remit of the ECB price stability mandate is that it allows assessing what the ECB prioritises in its policy message and thus to appreciate whether the ECB deviates from past practice of focussing its rhetoric on its mandate as the way to achieve (output) legitimacy.

Our findings suggest that the ECB reacts to negative public opinion by allocating its attention to a wider set of issues rather than concentrating on those associated to its core mandate. This result challenges the view according to which the ECB conceives of its sources of legitimation based almost exclusive on the achievement of its mandate. In particular, our findings suggest that increased politicisation leads the ECB to reassess the sources of its legitimation strategy from a strategy based on output achievement towards one based on participation to broader policy debates.

The paper is organised as follows. Section 2 develops the theoretical arguments that informs our analysis. Section 3 details the research design used to gauge the impact of public opinion on ECB communication. Section 4 presents the results. Section 5 discusses the findings, their limitations and implications for future research.

## Speaking (more) to the public: why and how

Central banks' communication is usually analyzed to gauge the effectiveness of monetary policy to achieve its goals of price stability and output stabilisation. Given the central role that financial markets play in the transmission of the monetary policy impulse, scholarship has overwhelmingly focused on central banks' communication with financial markets (Blinder, Ehrmann, Fratzscher, De Haan, & Jansen, 2008). Recently, however, increasing attention has been devoted to exploring how central banks' communication affects public expectations, including households and societal groups' expectations (Haldane & McMahon, 2018). This attention stems from the recognition that communication with the general public is 'at least as important' as communication with financial markets (Blinder *et al.*, 2008, p. 941) also because, ultimately, the evolution of inflation is shaped by public's inflation expectations, through wage claims and savings, investment and consumption decisions.

In spite of the increased attention to communication with the public, existing literature has mainly focused on how central banks' messages impact on the behavior of societal actors. In contrast, studies that investigate the impact of public attitudes on central banks' communicative behavior are still sparse.

Yet, the relationship with the public is crucial not only for the effectiveness of monetary policy but also for the independence of central banks That is to say, like other non-majoritarian institutions, central banks care not only about effective policy solutions but also bureaucratic survival (Reh, Bressanelli, & Koop, 2020; Moschella & Pinto, 2019). Indeed, central banks' statutes are subject to legislators' interventions – unless the latter face a political cost for doing so. Indeed, several studies show that central bank independence is endogenous to the political system (Keefer & Stasavage, 2003) and that independence is more likely to be preserved if policymakers face high audience costs for interfering with the central bank's structure and legal status (Lohmann, 2003).

Although the prospect of legislators' interventions is higher for most central banks than it is for the ECB, whose independence is enshrined in an international treaty and not in domestic legislation, '[t]he ECB cannot ignore the possibility of an unfavourable political reaction' too (Jones, 2009, p. 1093). Negative public opinion can indeed weaken elected policymakers' support for central bank independence thus jeopardising the key feature of non-majoritarian institutions (also Blauberger and Martinsen 2020). This risk is all the more concrete because, by design, the ECB insulation from politics 'make[s] it difficult for the ECB to attract political stakeholders who have the ability and incentives to protect the integrity of the institution when it comes under political attack' (Lohmann, 1999, p. 17). Furthermore, the ECB cannot simply shrug off negative public opinion because it is formally accountable to the European Parliament as the representation of all EU citizens (Article 284 (3) TFEU).

The challenges that the ECB confronts should public support falters thereby suggest that the ECB is likely to strategically respond to negative public opinion. In particular, we argue that the ECB attempts to increase the degree of perceived legitimation and win back public support by expanding the scope of its communication beyond issues related to its core mandate.[3]

To understand why an expanded communication can be regarded as a legitimation strategy, it is important to take into consideration the characteristics of the ECB 'traditional' communication and the public audiences the ECB speaks to.

To start with the characteristics of the ECB traditional communication output, since its creation, the ECB has taken great care in molding a very guarded communication strategy aimed at limiting the amount of information disclosed on internal policy views and decision-making process.[4] Such cautiousness was a reflection of the view according to which ECB accountability lies primarily on the achievement of its mandate rather than on the amount of information provided to the public (Issing, 1999). The ECB has consistently justified its approach based on two arguments, both of which can be traced back to a conception of legitimacy as output legitimacy (Jabko, 2003; Schmidt, 2016). The first is that too much communication may confuse the European public about the central bank's policy intentions and decisions, thus undermining the central banks' ability to shape public expectations and achieve its mandated goal. The second argument against an expanded communication is that this practice could expose ECB policymakers to undue political pressures. The reasoning here is that the policy views expressed by ECB officials could be misread in national capitals leading domestic policymakers to exercise pressures on ECB policy choices. Because of the alleged risks deriving from an expanded communication output, ECB communication has thus been tailored in a way to limit the amount of information disclosed to the public, including by reducing information on the differences in the policy views among ECB policymakers (Blinder *et al.*, 2008, p. 923). These features in EU communication have also contributed fueling the accusation that the ECB eschews democratic accountability (Buiter, 1999) and that, often, the ECB has been reluctant to engage in public dialogue on broader issues that affect the general public (Transparency International, 2017).

By ditching its guarded communication approach in favor of an expanded communication, the ECB can thereby respond to the critics by signaling to the public that it is an institution not only interested in price stability but also attentive to a large set of policy debates. For instance, increasing the amount of information and communication capacity with the public is one of the strategies that international organisations (IOs) systematically pursue to respond to the politicisation of their role and thus (re)legitimize their activity especially after major scandals and public protests (Ecker-Ehrhardt, 2018; Gronau & Schmidtke, 2016). Similarly to what has been found in the realm of IOs, the ECB can rely on an expanded communication to legitimize its role and decisions before external audiences by recasting the central bank's public image away from the criticisms of the past. Furthermore, an expanded communication helps the ECB to manage its public image by allowing it to set out its views on multiple policy issues and, possibly, shape policy debates around them.

The expansion in communication can also be conceived as a legitimation strategy in light of the characteristics of the public audiences the ECB speaks to. As a supranational central bank of 19 countries, the ECB finds itself in the unique position of having to communicate its decisions to audiences based in different countries with potentially different conceptions of legitimacy. Indeed, studies on public opinion show that, in spite of growing Europeanisation, the concerns of EU public are fragmented along national lines: what is salient issue in one country is not necessarily the most salient issue in another (Serricchio, Tstakatika, & Quaglia, 2013). By expanding its communication, the ECB can thereby enhance its perceived legitimacy by showing to be attentive to the multiple concerns that run throughout Europe rather than to some of them, as it would be the case if the ECB sticks to a rhetoric on monetary policy only. This strategy is similar to the one that international courts have been found to follow in the use case law citations in their rulings: as international courts tend to maximise their legitimacy by avoiding fragmentation in their case law along lines of legal culture or country-specific factors (Lupu & Voeten, 2012, p. 413), so the ECB can maximise its legitimacy by avoiding fragmentation in the attention allocated to policy issues along country lines.

In short, variation in the scope of communication is indicative of how the ECB reacts to public signals. An expanded communication provides the ECB with more opportunities to increase its perceived legitimacy across different national audiences because the central bank can so address multiple concerns on a wider range of issues. It also helps the central bank to improve its public image, allowing it to participate and possibly orient multiple policy and societal debates. Hence, we expect the ECB to respond to negative public opinion by expanding its communication because this strategy helps the central bank legitimize its role and decisions to public audiences.

## Data and methods

### *Dependent variable*

To determine whether the ECB responds to the politicisation of its role by expanding its communication, we develop two interrelated dependent variables using communication output of the six members of the Executive Board. The first – *issue diversity* – captures the distribution of ECB policymakers' attention across the issues covered in their speeches. The second – *core salience* – tracks the salience attributed to monetary policy issues as compared to the other issues that appear in central bankers' speeches: the more the ECB communication is concentrated on the core mandate, the lower is issue diversity and vice-versa.

Specifically, we collected all the speeches delivered between 2001 and 2017 by the president of the ECB, the vice president, and the other four members of the Executive Board.[5] Our database consists of 1,427 speeches issued by 17 different speakers (see Appendix B).[6] Although the speeches do not exhaust the list of channels through which the ECB provides information on its activities,[7] these documents present a number of empirical advantages for the purposes of the analysis. To start with, the speeches here collected are directed at multiple audiences, allowing us to control for the impact they exert on communication outputs. Furthermore, speeches are strategically delivered, meaning that monetary policymakers generally choose what audiences to address and what to say.[8]

In order to develop our dependent variables, we first applied unsupervised topic modeling techniques to identify the topics in ECB policymakers' communication; second, we computed an index gauging issue diversity and core salience.

*Topic modeling*: We used structural topic models (STM) to identify topics. STM allows estimating general semantic themes within a corpus of documents and to simultaneously analysing the prevalence of each topic conditional on a number of factors.[9] Using STM we can, therefore, estimate the main topics that characterise our corpus of texts as well as the variation of their prevalence over time or as a consequence of the impact of major political and economic events.

Figure 1 reports the 20 topics extrapolated by the STM following standard tests aimed at assessing the validity of the topic model (see Appendix C). Figure 1 also reports the words that are both frequent in and exclusive to a topic. Frequent words, such as 'European', 'euro', 'central', 'bank', are common across many topics; however, they are characterised by lower levels of exclusivity – the opposite applies to infrequent words. The most informative words are therefore those that balance exclusivity and frequency (Roberts *et al.*, 2014): these words appear with a bigger font in Figure 1.

Based on the results of the topic model, we interpreted the content of each topic in order to identify the substantive issues policymakers attend to in their communication. We grouped the 20 topics according to whether they pertain to one of the following broad issues: EU integration process, financial stability, fiscal policy, global economic issues, monetary policy, statistics, and structural reforms.[10] These issues capture the main areas of operation of the ECB as well as its role in the functioning of the EMU. In order to validate topic interpretation, we examined the most frequent and exclusive words that characterise each topic as well as the most exemplar documents, e.g., the speeches that

**Figure 1.** Topics in executive board members' speeches, 2001–2017. Notes: Frequency indicates the probability of observing each word in the vocabulary of a given topic. Exclusivity identifies words associated with a topic that are unlikely to appear among the top words of another topic. Words' labels are weighted by joint frequency and exclusivity. Words are presented in their stemmed form.

have the highest proportion of words associated with each topic. To further validate our interpretation, we plotted the variation in topic prevalence over time, together with the average value of the expected topic proportion for each topic in the entire corpus (Figure 2).

Figure 2 thus shows the variety of issues that appear on ECB policy-makers communication based on our interpretation and validation techniques. Since our analysis is meant to distinguish ECB communication at large from communication focussed on monetary policy issues, here we provide more information on the topics that we classified as monetary policy topics, namely Topic 2, 6, 13, 17 and 18 (detailed information on the other topics is provided in Appendix C). The most discussed monetary issue in our corpus is topic 13, which is also the most discussed topic in the entire corpus. This topic captures talk on the ECB mandate. Indeed, the most frequent and exclusive words includes terms such as 'area', 'euro', 'price', 'rate', 'medium' and 'HICP' (i.e., Harmonised Index of Consumer Prices). These terms clearly reflect the ECB formal responsibility to achieve price stability over the medium term and set an interest rate for the euro area as a whole. Topic 13 is also associated to Topic 6. Indeed, Topic 6 identifies the monetary policy strategy that the ECB follows to achieve its price stability objective, as attested by words such as 'strategi*,' 'stabil*,' 'price', 'mediumterm', and 'pillar' – the latter is an explicit

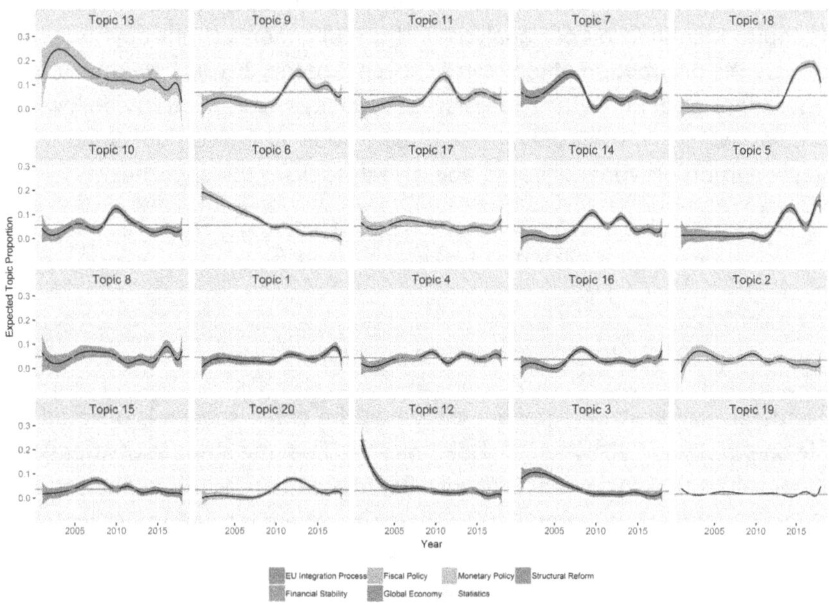


**Figure 2.** Topic prevalence over time in executive board members' speeches, 2001–2017. Notes: Topics are ordered based on their average prevalence. Red horizontal lines refer to the average topic prevalence over the period of analysis (2001–2017). 95 percent confidence intervals are reported.

reference to the two-pillar strategy that informs ECB monetary activity. Topic 2 identifies the working of the ECB monetary committee being characterised by words such as 'Eurosystem', 'bank', 'central', 'European', 'work' and 'Frankfurt', where the ECB policymakers collectively take decisions. Finally, Topic 17 and 18 identifies the ECB monetary policy tools. Topic 17 refers to conventional, interest rates tools, including terms such as 'polici*', 'monetary', 'price', 'inflat*', 'bank' and 'rate'. Topic 18 instead refers to unconventional tools being characterised by words such as 'measur*', 'purchas*', 'guidanc*', 'recoveri*', 'unconvent*', 'accommod*', 'negat*', 'zero'. All these words refer to the set of unconventional policies adopted by the ECB as interets rates approaches the zero lower bound, including asset purchases, forward guidance and even negative interest rates. The validity of interpretation of topic 18 as capturing talk on unconventional monetary policies is also supported by the prevalence pattern of this topic over time: the prevalence of this topic in the speech corpus intensifies following the sovereign debt crisis and the anaemic recovery in the Eurozone.

*Issues diversity and Core salience*: To compute our two dependent variables, we build on the STM's assumption according to which each speech can be represented as a mixture of a series of topics that always add up to one. This assumption implies that more attention on one topic in a speech necessarily reduces the attention on other topics (Roberts *et al.*, 2014).

To develop the measure of issue diversity, we retrieve the proportions of all the topics identified by our analysis and use Shannon's *H* entropy index to estimate the distribution of topics in a speech (Greene, 2016).[11] We then transform Shannon's *H* into a measure of issue diversity according to the following formulas, where $\theta_i$ is the prevalence of each topic in a given document (i.e., the proportion of words devoted about each topic in the speeches):

$$\text{Shannon's } H = -\sum_{i=1}^{20} \theta_i \ln \theta_i$$

$$\text{Issue Diversity} = \exp(\text{Shannon's } H)$$

Issue diversity can vary between 1, when the entire speech is devoted to only one topic, and 20, when all topics receive the same amount of attention. Higher values thus mean that Executive Board members distribute their attention across a greater number of different issues, whereas lower values indicate that they focus on a smaller set of topics. Among our speeches, issue diversity varies between 1.07 and 12.11, with a mean of 4.83 (see Appendix D for a plot of issue diversity as a function of time).

In order to measure core salience, we estimate the proportion of text belonging to the topics classified under the *Monetary policy* category for each document. The assumption here is that the higher the proportion of text dedicated to the monetary policy issues, the higher the salience attributed to these issues. On average, about 33 per cent of our corpus is devoted to the discussion of topics associated with the *Monetary policy* category, which is therefore the most prevalent one in ECB members' speeches (followed by the one related to *Financial stability*). The variable varies from 0.1, meaning that only very few words are devoted to a *Monetary policy* topic in a given speech, to 0.99, indicating that almost the entire speech covers issues related to ECB core mandate.

### Independent variable

Our argument suggests that the ECB responds to negative public opinion by strategically expanding the issues it deals in its external communication. Our main independent variable is thus a measure of public support. Specifically, we measure EU citizens' trust towards the ECB by coding the responses to the Eurobarometer question on this issue for each semester between 2001 and 2017.[12] In line with previous studies, we operationalise citizens' net trust as the difference between the percentage of respondents who tend to trust and those who tend do not trust the ECB (Roth *et al.*, 2014). In our data, net trust ranges from −17.64 to 27.57, with an average value of 2.01. Negative values indicate that a majority of respondents mistrust the ECB, vice-versa for positive values. Trust significantly declined with the onset of the sovereign debt crisis and its aftermath (see Appendix D).

### Controls

As discussed in the Introduction, an alternative explanation for the changes in ECB communication lies in the changes in the economic policy context in which the ECB operates. To control for the influence of this argument, our analysis control for the influence of economic growth, inflation and unemployment. Data were taken from the Eurostat database on a monthly base for unemployment and inflation (change of HICP) and on a quarterly base for GDP volume growth. To avoid multicollinearity problems, we also run a separate regression excluding unemployment because of its degree of collinearity with public trust variables (see Armingeon & Guthmann, 2014; Foster & Frieden, 2017; Roth *et al.*, 2014). As a further control for the economic situation, we employ a newspaper-based measure of economic policy uncertainty (EPU) that foreshadow declines in investment, output, and employment (Baker, Bloom, & Davis, 2016).

Since a more diverse communication could reflect the transformations in the ECB policies and legal role including in the area of financial stability and economic adjustment, we use a number of controls to investigate this counter-claim. In particular, we use the ECB balance-sheet liabilities as a proxy of the expansion of ECB (unconventional) policy interventions that could justify a broadening of its communication.[13] We also include a dummy variable that takes the value of one after July 2012, that is after the decision by European heads of government to create the Banking Union that has expanded the ECB mandate.

We also control for the characteristics of the audiences that central bankers address in their communication. Specifically, we classified each speech in three categories according to their target audience: political speeches, including hearings and testimonies before the European Parliament and national parliaments; press speeches, including press conferences and interviews to newspapers and magazines; and general speeches, including all the remaining speeches delivered, among the others, before societal actors and business associations.

Finally, we control for some characteristics related to the individual ECB policymakers, as their institutional duties and terms of office may be expected to influence communication. In particular, we distinguish between speakers' role by including a dummy variable coded one if the speaker is the President of the ECB and zero otherwise. We also control for the influence of the terms of office of each ECB policymakers by counting the number of days that are left to the end of the mandate when each speech is delivered. Lastly, to control for the longitudinal structure of the data, a year-counter variable is added to the model.

## Results

We perform our analysis using a multilevel model to account for the hierarchical nature of the data (i.e., speeches are clustered across different speakers).[14] Table 1 presents the regression results of our analysis. The dependent variable in Model 1 and 2 is issue diversity; while the dependent variable in Model 3 is core salience. Models 1 and 2 differ in the inclusion of the unemployment variable to address the multicollinearity problems discussed above, even if the results are consonant in both models.[15] In our discussion below, however, we prioritise results from Model 2 because it shows the best goodness of fits with the data (as confirmed by both the Akaike and Bayesian information criteria [AIC and BIC]).

Our analysis reveals that public opinion attitudes are a statistically significant predictor of the diversity of issues covered in Executive Board members' communication. Specifically, an increase in public trust significantly decreases the level of issue diversity in ECB speeches. The salience assigned to issues related to the ECB core mandate is also influenced by public opinion attitudes: the results indicate that an increase in public trust significantly increases core salience. That is to say, ECB policymakers tend narrowing their attention to a few issues when public contestation is low and,

**Table 1.** Determinants of issue diversity and core salience in ECB speeches.

| | Model 1 | Model 2 | Model 3 |
|---|---|---|---|
| Dependent variable | Issue diversity | | Core salience |
| Trust | −0.031* | −0.029** | 0.003** |
| | (0.015) | (0.010) | (0.001) |
| Type of Audience | | | |
| General | | Baseline | |
| Political Audience | 0.461* | 0.462* | −0.002 |
| | (0.182) | (0.183) | (0.031) |
| Press Audience | 0.054 | 0.054 | −0.005 |
| | (0.151) | (0.151) | (0.020) |
| Speaker | | | |
| EB member | | Baseline | |
| President | −0.377* | −0.377* | 0.211*** |
| | (0.153) | (0.153) | (0.051) |
| Time to end mandate | −0.010$^{+}$ | −0.010* | −0.001 |
| | (0.005) | (0.005) | (0.001) |
| Economic Growth (GDP) | −0.061$^{+}$ | −0.059 | 0.013*** |
| | (0.036) | (0.037) | (0.003) |
| Inflation | 0.065 | 0.067 | −0.034*** |
| | (0.081) | (0.079) | (0.09) |
| Unemployment | −0.019 | – | – |
| | (0.068) | | |
| Uncertainty | −0.002** | −0.002** | −0.0000 |
| | (0.001) | (0.001) | (0.0000) |
| Time | −0.023 | −0.021 | 0.005 |
| | (0.050) | (0.046) | (0.008) |
| Liabilities | 0.043 | 0.050 | 0.010 |
| | (0.156) | 0.165 | 0.025 |
| ECB Mandate | −0.073 | −0.074 | −0.058 |
| | (0.185) | (0.187) | (0.038) |
| Constant | 5.856*** | 5.617*** | 0.347*** |
| | (1.059) | (0.403) | (0.085) |
| SD (speaker) | 0.372*** | 0.372*** | 0.094*** |
| | (0.081) | (0.081) | (0.019) |
| SD (residual) | 2.003*** | 2.003*** | 0.284*** |
| | (0.090) | (0.090) | (0.023) |
| N | 1427 | 1427 | 1427 |
| N speaker | 17 | 17 | 17 |
| AIC | 6082.1 | 6080.2 | 525.8 |
| BIC | 6161.1 | 6153.8 | 599.5 |

Notes: Robust standard errors are reported in parentheses. Significance: $^{+}p < 0.1$, $*p < 0.05$, $**p < 0.01$, $***p < 0.001$.

consequently, expanding issue diversity when the ECB confronts higher levels of public contestation.

Substantively, moving from one standard deviation below the mean (roughly the average value of trust registered after 2010) to one standard deviation above the mean (the average value registered before 2010) results in a reduction of about one unit in the number of topics in ECB communication. The same shift in public trust increases the salience of core mandate-related topics by about ten percentage points. This is equivalent to say that, on average, issue diversity has increased by about 30 percent in relative terms before and after 2010, while core salience has decreased by the same figure.

To further assess the substantive magnitude of the findings, we use again STM to plot the relationship between net trust in the ECB and topic prevalence of the seven macro-areas of ECB communication identified above (Figure 3). STM allows testing the correlation patterns of public trust with topic prevalence in a regression-like framework.

Figure 3 shows an overall positive and strong correlation between public trust and the prevalence of most of the topics that pertain to *Monetary policy*. This result provides further support to the evidence reported above by showing that, in line with our theoretical expectations, ECB members tend to focus their public stance on price stability-related issues when net public trust is high – but not vice versa.

It is important to note, however, there is one relevant exception to this trend: Topic 18 shows a positive trend when public trust in the ECB decreases. As discussed above, this topic captures talk about unconventional monetary policy. While it is not straightforward to interpret this result, the positive relationship between public distrust and talk on unconventional policy may indicate that ECB policymakers felt the need to provide information on their unconventional actions given the lack of policy precedent and the widespread criticisms leveled by experts and elected policymakers levels. In general, however, the results reported in Figure 3 show that ECB policymakers

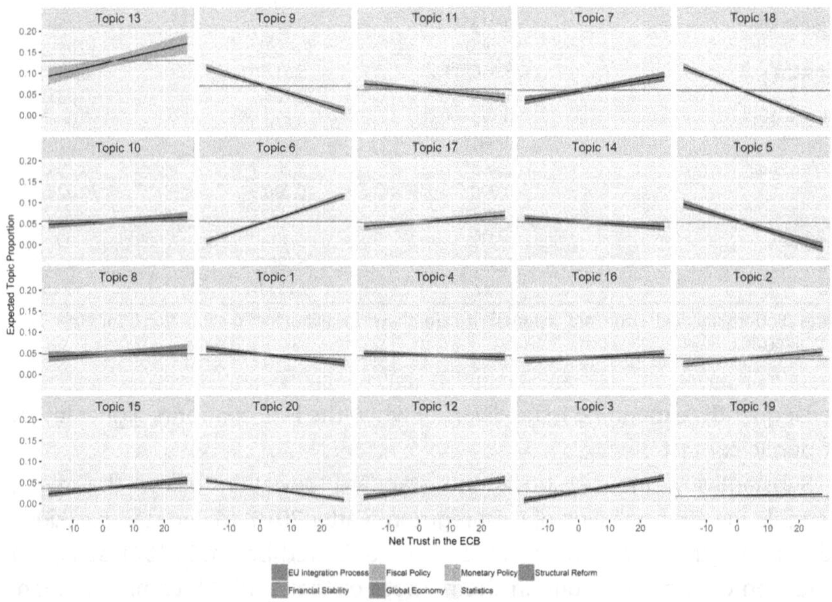


**Figure 3.** Topic prevalence in ECB communication and public trust in the ECB. Notes: Topics are ordered based on their average prevalence. Red horizontal lines refer to the average topic prevalence over the period of analysis (2001–2017). 95 percent confidence intervals are reported.

select the issues to include in their communication with great care when confronting a negative public opinion – including which issues within the monetary policy category.

In addition to the public opinion effect, Table 1 shows that speaking before political audiences predicts the level of issue diversity but not the salience attributed to monetary policy-related issues. This result is broadly in line with the observation that the format of the exchanges between the ECB and political audiences favor the expansion of the scope of attention. For instance, for the speeches delivered in context of the Monetary Dialogue, which constitute about 75 per cent in the political audience category, it is common practice that the ECB President incorporates into her introductory statement the topics selected by MEPs in advance to the meeting as deserving particular attention. The lack of a significant effect in the speeches before the press might be read in light of the fact that these categories of speeches include the press conferences that the ECB President regularly delivers following the meetings of the Governing Council where monetary decisions are taken. Since press conferences are primarily directed at providing information on the monetary policy decision just adopted, it may be the case that the ECB President tries to minimise the 'noise' in the policy message by narrowing it on a limited number of issues.

Some of the individual characteristics of ECB policymakers also have an impact on the ECB communicative strategies. In particular, we find that ECB Presidents are less likely to expand the scope of their communication while devoting more salience to price stability issues as compared to other Executive Board members. This finding suggests that, as the highest official in the institution, ECB Presidents tends to project the ECB organisational image and thus tend focussing on the core mandate of the institution. The results on the effect of the term of office is mild on issue coverage and non-significant for the salience attributed to monetary policy. It should also be noted that neither the dummy on the ECB mandate nor the control variable for ECB policies significantly impact our dependent variables.

In contrast, both economic growth and inflation significantly affect the salience on monetary policy, although in different directions. Indeed, a positive variation of the GDP leads to a significant expansion of the relevance of the issues related to the ECB core mandate, while higher levels of inflation reduces it (Model 3). While it is not straightforward to interpret this effect, one way to think about this result is that the emphasis attributed to monetary policy issues when the macroeconomic outlook is positive reveals the ECB 'anti-inflationary bias' – that is to say, the ECB tends to be more reactive to the inflationary risks that may stem from a growing economy than to deflationary risks in light of its German-inspired hawkish approach to monetary policy (Howarth & Loedel, 2003, p. 52). It should also be noted that economic uncertainty exerts a negative effect on the diversity of issues covered in ECB communication. This finding connects with the conclusion reached in monetary policy circles that 'a central bank should perhaps be wary of communicating about issues on which it receives noisy signals itself – such as the evolution of the economy' (Blinder *et al.*, 2008).

## Conclusions

In recent years, a growing number of EU citizens have lost trust in EU institutions and EU integration process at large. Although important differences exist among member countries, the emergence of what Hooghe and Marks (2009, p. 7) have called the 'constraining dissensus' in the European public sphere has posed new challenges for EU institutions. Nowhere are these challenges as evident as it is the case for the ECB. Indeed, the ECB is one of the EU institutions that has suffered the most from the growing dissatisfaction of EU citizens. Furthermore, this dissatisfaction is not entirely new for the ECB. Since its creation, the ECB has faced accusations of eschewing democratic legitimacy behind the veil of its independence.

The contribution of this article has been to examine how the ECB responds to public dissatisfaction and what this response tells us about the sources of ECB legitimacy. In particular, we examined the impact of public opinion on how the ECB crafts its policy message in order to shed light on whether the selected communicative strategy is geared at giving pride of place to the achievement of its mandate. After controlling for economic conditions and changes to the ECB mandate following the sovereign debt crisis, our findings show that negative public opinion pushes the ECB to expand the scope of its policy message rather than narrowing it on issues related to its core mandate.

Our findings provide some nuances to the debate on the ECB accountability framework by showing that the ECB listens to the public. More precisely, the ECB adapts the way in which it delivers its message when it confronts public contestation. While ECB response falls short of the full-fledged democratic control mechanisms that several ECB critics have called for (Transparency International, 2017), it nonetheless helps recast the debate on the ECB legitimacy framework by bringing back into the picture the ECB relationship with the public in addition to the one with the European Parliament. Our findings also to point to an unusual strategy to respond to public contestation for an institution that has traditionally signaled to rely on policy output as a justification for its independence and accountability.

In spite of these contributions, however, our analysis faces a number of limitations. For instance, a more detailed assessment of the extent to which the ECB seeks legitimacy by expanding communication would require a more refined analysis of the match between societal concerns and the topics covered in ECB policymakers' communication. This analysis would also allow assessing to what policy issues and national audiences the ECB is more attentive to. Still, a more fine-grained content analysis of ECB communication would allow assessing whether the ECB legitimation strategy is also informed by a blame-shifting logic. That is to say, by expanding its communication beyond monetary issues, the logic behind the ECB legitimation strategy might have been that of signaling to the public that the solutions to economic and societal problems lie not in central banks' hands. While future research will shed light on these important issues, our analysis provides the building blocks for this research agenda by shedding light on the importance of public trust for the ECB and showing the potential of applying automated content methods to further explore this relationship.

## Notes

1. Financial Times, *Anti-capitalist protesters target ECB in Frankfurt*, March 18, 2015; Financial Times, *ECB adjusts to life amid the protests*, April 23, 2015.
2. Benoit Coeuré, ECB Executive Board Member, as reported in The Financial Times, *ECB hits the road to pitch its policies*, 8 October 2018.
3. We also investigated whether reverse causality exists between public support and communication expansion. Our empirical tests (Clausen, Kraay, & Nyiri, 2011) suggest that the presence of reverse causation does not undermine our conclusions (see Appendix A).
4. For instance, as compared to other major central banks in the advanced economies, the ECB has not published account of monetary policy meetings until 2015 and these accounts do not provide information on the individual preferences of ECB policymakers.
5. Our analysis starts in 2001 in order to discount potential problems related to data availability and public awareness of ECB activity that might have been limited in the first years of its operations.
6. All speeches were automatically retrieved from the Bank for International Settlements website. The speeches of Sirkka Hämäläinen (1998–2003) and Eugenio Solans (1998–2004) were not available.
7. Information is regularly provided also through research publications and, since 2015, through the publication of the accounts of monetary policy meetings.
8. More than 80 per cent of the speeches in our corpus are not part of the ECB legal and operational obligations such hearings and press conferences.
9. We estimate topic models using the *stm* package in R (Roberts, Stewart, & Tingley, 2018).
10. We aggregated topics to help the reader to better visualise the results of the topic model analysis. The only relevant macro-category for the purpose of the statistical analysis is the one on monetary policy, which we discuss in what follows.
11. Measures of issue or attention diversity have been extensively used in several studies related to public policy, agenda formation and party competition (see Greene, 2016).
12. Respondents were asked to choose among three categories: "Tend to trust it", "Tend not to trust it" and "Do not know". For each year, data were taken from the Eurobarometer of May and October. Data on net trust in the ECB were

matched to the speeches according to the date of the document. Population-weighted trust values are employed. We also compute a measure of net trust limited to Eurozone countries. The results show that there is no significant difference between the impact of the former compared to net trust at the European level (see Appendix E). Given the role played by the ECB also in non-eurozone countries, we thus used data on EU trust. We also included two variables measuring the difference between net trust toward the ECB and net trust toward the EU Parliament and the EU Commission. We found that only trust in the ECB is significant for ECB communication (data are available upon request).

13. Data are taken from the annual consolidated balance sheet of the Eurosystem at the end of each month.
14. We run the analysis using different model specifications: a speaker-level fixed effects; random intercepts for speaker and time; a random slope for time-counter between speakers; a model including all the ECB representatives who delivered at least ten speeches; and, finally, a model including only observations starting from 2002 (the year of Euro introduction). The results are similar to those reported. Data are available upon request.
15. Both unemployment and public trust show a very high variance inflation factor, indicating that knowing the former is possible to predict the latter quite well.

## Disclosure statement

No potential conflict of interest was reported by the authors.

## Funding

This work was supported by Italian Ministry of Education, SIR Grant 2014 'Unconventional Central Banks: Making Monetary Policy in Hard Times' [RBSI14KCWY].

## ORCID

*Manuela Moschella* http://orcid.org/0000-0002-3159-9533
*Luca Pinto* http://orcid.org/0000-0003-1165-4475
*Nicola Martocchia Diodati* http://orcid.org/0000-0003-4743-8918

## References

Armingeon, K., & Guthmann, K. (2014). Democracy in crisis? The declining support for national democracy in European countries, 2007–2011. *European Journal of Political Research*, *53*(3), 423–442.

Baker, S. R., Bloom, N., & Davis, S. J. (2016). Measuring economic policy uncertainty. *The Quarterly Journal of Economics, 131*(4), 1593–1636.

Ban, C., & Patenaude, B. (2018). The Professional politics of the austerity debate: Comparing the European central bank and the international monetary Fund. *Public Administration*, doi:10.1111/padm.12561

Blauberger, M., & Martinsen, D. (2020). The court of justice in times of politicisation: 'Law as a mask and shield' revisited. Journal of European Public Policy, *27*(3), 382–399.

Blinder, A. S., Ehrmann, M., Fratzscher, M., De Haan, J., & Jansen, D.-J. (2008). Central bank communication and monetary policy: A survey of theory and evidence. *Journal of Economic Literature, 46*(4), 910–945.

Braun, B. (2016). Speaking to the people? Money, trust, and central bank legitimacy in the age of quantitative easing. *Review of International Political Economy, 23*(6), 1064–1092.

Buiter, W. H. (1999). Alice in Euroland. *Journal of Common Market Studies, 37*(2), 181–209.

Clausen, B., Kraay, A., & Nyiri, Z. (2011). Corruption and confidence in public institutions: Evidence from a global survey. *World Bank Economic Review, 25*(2), 212–249.

Diessner, S., & Lisi, G. (2019). Masters of the 'masters of the universe'? Monetary, fiscal and financial dominance in the Eurozone. *Socio-Economic Review*. doi:10.1093/ser/mwz017

Ecker-Ehrhardt, M. (2018). International organizations "going public"? An event history analysis of public communication reforms 1950–2015. *International Studies Quarterly, 62*(4), 723–736.

Ferrara, F. (2019). The battle of ideas on the euro crisis: Evidence from ECB inter-meeting speeches. *Journal of European Public Policy*, 1–24. doi:10.1080/13501763.2019.1670231

Foster, C., & Frieden, J. (2017). 'Crisis of trust: Socio-economic determinants of Europeans' confidence in government'. *European Union Politics, 18*(4), 511–535.

Fraccaroli, N., Giovannini, A., & Jamet, J.-F. (2018). The evolution of the ECB's accountability practices during the crisis. In European Central Bank (Eds.), *Economic bulletin* (pp. 47–71). Frankfurt: European Central Bank.

Genovese, F., Schneider, G., & Wassmann, P. (2016). 'The Eurotower strikes back: Crises, adjustments, and Europe's austerity protests'. *Comparative Political Studies, 49*(7), 939–967.

Greene, Z. (2016). Competing on the issues: How experience in government and economic conditions influence the scope of parties' policy messages. *Party Politics, 22*(6), 809–822.

Gronau, J., & Schmidtke, H. (2016). 'The quest for legitimacy in world politics – international institutions' legitimation strategies'. *Review of International Studies, 42*(3), 535–557.

Haldane, A., & McMahon, M. (2018). Central bank communications and the general public. *AEA Papers and Proceedings, 108*, 578–583.

Högenauer, A. L., & Howarth, D. (2016). 'Unconventional monetary policies and the European central bank's problematic democratic legitimacy'. *Journal of Public Law, 17*(2), 1–24.

Hooghe, L., & Marks, G. (2009). A postfunctionalist theory of European integration: From permissive consensus to constraining dissensus. *British Journal of Political Science, 39* (1), 1–23.

Howarth, D., & Loedel, P. (2003). *The European Central Bank: The New European Leviathan?* Basingstoke: Palgrave.

Issing, O. (1999). The Eurosystem: Transparent and accountable or 'willem in Euroland'. *Journal of Common Market Studies, 37*(3), 503–519.

Jabko, N. (2003). Democracy in the age of the euro. *Journal of European Public Policy, 10* (5), 710–739.

Jones, E. (2009). Output legitimacy and the global financial crisis: Perceptions matter. *JCMS: Journal of Common Market Studies, 47*(5), 1085–1105.

Keefer, P., & Stasavage, D. (2003). The limits of delegation: Veto players, central bank independence, and the credibility of monetary policy. *American Political Science Review, 97*(3), 407–423.

Lohmann, S. (1999). The dark side of European monetary union. In E. E. Meade (Ed.), *The European Central Bank. How accountable? How decentralized?* (pp. 15–38). Washington: American Institute for Contemporary German Studies.

Lohmann, S. (2003). Why do institutions matter? An audience–cost theory of institutional commitment. *Governance, 16*(1), 95–110.

Lombardi, D., & Moschella, M. (2016). The government bond buying programmes of the European central bank: An analysis of their policy settings. *Journal of European Public Policy, 23*(6), 851–870.

Lupu, Y., & Voeten, E. (2012). Precedent in international courts: A network analysis of case citations by the European Court of human rights. *British Journal of Political Science, 42*(2), 413–439.

Moschella, M., & Pinto, L. (2019). 'Central banks' communication as reputation management: How the Fed talks under uncertainty'. *Public Administration, 97*(3), 513–529.

Reh, C., Bressanelli, E., & Koop, C. (2020). Responsive withdrawal? The politics of EU agenda-setting. Journal of European Public Policy, *27*(3), 419–438.

Roberts, M. E., Stewart, B. M., & Tingley, D. (2018). STM: R package for structural topic models. *Journal of Statistical Software, 91*(2), 1–40.

Roberts, M. E., Stewart, B. M., Tingley, D., Lucas, C., Shana, J. L.-L., Gadarian, K., … Rand, D. G. (2014). Structural topic models for open-ended survey responses. *American Journal of Political Science, 58*(4), 1064–1082.

Roth, F., Gros, D., & Nowak-Lehmann, D. F. (2014). 'Crisis and citizens' trust in the European central bank - Panel data evidence for the euro area, 1999–2012'. *Journal of European Integration, 36*(3), 303–320.

Schelkle, W. (2017). *The political economy of monetary solidarity: Understanding the Euro experiment*. Oxford: Oxford University Press.

Schmidt, V. A. (2016). Reinterpreting the rules 'by stealth' in times of crisis: A discursive institutionalist analysis of the European central bank and the European Commission. *West European Politics, 39*(5), 1032–1052.

Serricchio, F., Tstakatika, M., & Quaglia, L. (2013). Euroscepticism and the global financial crisis. *JCMS: Journal of Common Market Studies, 51*(1), 51–64.

Tesche, T. (2018). 'Instrumentalizing EMU's democratic deficit: The ECB's unconventional accountability measures during the eurozone crisis'. *Journal of European Integration, 41*(4), 447–463.

Tortola, P. D., & Pansardi, P. (2019). The charismatic leadership of the ECB presidency: A language-based analysis. *European Journal of Political Research, 58*(1), 96–116.

Transparency International EU. (2017). Two sides of the same coin? Independence and accountability of the European Central Bank, Berlin.

Verdun, A. (2017). Political leadership of the European central bank. *Journal of European Integration, 39*(2), 207–221.

# Responsive withdrawal? The politics of EU agenda-setting

Christine Reh*, Edoardo Bressanelli* and Christel Koop *

**ABSTRACT**

This contribution asks whether and why the newly political environment of EU law-making impacts on the European Commission's choice (not) to announce the withdrawal of legislative proposals. We argue that the Commission uses 'responsive withdrawal' in response to bottom-up pressure, so as to signal self-restraint or policy-determination to different audiences. Bottom-up pressures are driven by (1) the national contestation of 'Europe'; (2) visible controversy about optimal (crisis) governance; and (3) the domestic salience of EU legislation. Our hypotheses are tested on a new dataset of all codecision files concluded, withdrawn, rejected or ongoing between 2006 and 2018. We show that the Commission reacts to bottom-up pressure by either politicising or depoliticising the EU's legislative agenda: 'withdrawal announcements' are more likely when Euroscepticism is high and when legislation touches core state powers, but less likely when legislation is domestically salient. We also demonstrate the continued importance of cyclical and technical reasons. Our analysis complements extant explanations of withdrawal as the upshot of functional factors or of uncertainty, and contributes to the nascent debate about whether, why and how supranational actors respond when the systems in which they operate – and the policies they produce – come under attack.

## Introduction

Over the past decades, the European Union (EU) and its policies have become more visible, contested and relevant across its member states. The European Commission is at the forefront of such contestation. Frequently framed as the 'epitome of Brussels', it is seen and criticised as symbolic of the system under attack. The Commission is also increasingly salient: its presidency has been

*The authors would like to acknowledge their equal contribution to the article.

Supplemental data for this article can be accessed at https://doi.org/10.1080/13501763.2020.1712453

deliberately politicised, and the Commission itself claims to have become a more 'political' supranational actor.

We ask whether this 'new environment' impacts on the Commission's key role in the EU's legislative process: agenda-setting. More specifically, we explore the Commission's choice to announce the withdrawal of its legislative proposals. We argue that the Commission, motivated by both survival and policy, uses withdrawals as a tool to respond to political pressure. 'Responsive withdrawal' can have different effects on EU law-making: by taking legislation off the table, the Commission signals self-restraint, reduces supranational visibility and, thus, depoliticises the agenda; by keeping legislation on the table under adversity, the Commission signals political determination and policy clout. Our analysis contributes to the wider debate about whether, why and how supranational actors respond when the systems in which they operate – and the policies they produce – come under attack.

Indeed, it is well-established in both public debate and scholarship that 'Europe' is becoming more politicised. At the national level, contestation is on the rise, shown by Eurosceptic public opinion, the popularity of challenger parties, European integration as an issue in national elections, and highly polarised referendum campaigns. At the supranational level, more visible conflict emerged with the 2014 and 2019 *Spitzenkandidaten* process, European Central Bank (ECB) decisions during the Eurozone crisis, more openly confrontational relations between member states, and the composition of the Eighth and Ninth European Parliaments (EPs). In short, visibly debated, fundamentally contested and increasingly relevant, European integration (in)famously has gone from 'permissive consensus' to 'constraining dissensus' (Hooghe & Marks, 2009).

We explore whether this new environment matters for agenda-setting by the European Commission. Does the oft-repeated diagnosis of a 'more political Commission' actually bear out empirically? Does the Commission respond to political pressure, in particular when choosing what to withdraw from the legislative agenda? What consequences do these decisions have for the (de)politicisation of EU law-making?

To answer these questions, we analyse the Commission's announcements to withdraw proposals, made in its annual work programmes (WPs) between 2006 and 2018. Under political pressure, we assume, the Commission uses these announcements as signals. Drawing from scholarship on responsiveness and non-majoritarian institutions, we argue that the Commission's response to pressure is driven by two motivations: bureaucratic survival and policy solutions that matter for Europe's citizens; drawing from the literature on politicisation, we suggest that pressure increases with (1) national contestation over 'Europe'; (2) visible controversy about (crisis) governance; and (3) the domestic salience of EU legislation.

In testing these arguments, we aim to make two contributions. Empirically, we know a lot about the EU's politicisation at the domestic level (e.g., De

Wilde, Leupold, & Schmidtke, 2016; Grande & Kriesi, 2014). There is also a vivid debate about the 'newly political' Commission and the tension between its non-majoritarian mandate and its increasing visibility, including in Europe's electoral politics (e.g., Nugent & Rhinard, 2019; Peterson, 2017). Finally, scholars have analysed the Commission's influence, success and failure in EU agenda-setting (e.g., Boranbay-Akan, König, & Osnabrügge, 2017; Kreppel & Oztas, 2017). Yet, we know a lot less about whether and how political pressure affects the Commission's everyday role in EU law-making. Legislative programming more specifically – including priorities and withdrawals – and its communication in the Commission's WPs has remained surprisingly unexplored, and surprisingly untapped as a data source (but see Kreppel & Oztas, 2017; Lupo, 2018; Osnabrügge, 2015; Tholoniat, 2009). Our analysis contributes to filling this gap.

Theoretically, we develop an explicitly political argument to explain the Commission's choice to withdraw legislative proposals. In doing so, we complement two extant explanations of withdrawal: first, the position that withdrawals are, essentially, functional and technical (Ponzano, Hermanin, & Corona, 2012); second, the view of withdrawal as 'failure', resulting from the Commission's incomplete information about the co-legislators' future positions when proposing laws (Boranbay-Akan *et al.*, 2017). Individual instances of politicised withdrawal are well-known – the circular economy is a prominent case (Bouts, 2014). Yet, a systematic analysis of whether and why 'politics matters' for the Commission is still lacking. In developing and testing our argument, we build on – and contribute to – a nascent literature that shows the impact of domestic (electoral) politics on EU-level actors and behaviour (e.g., Hagemann, Hobolt, & Wratil, 2017; Koop, Reh, & Bressanelli, 2018; Rauh, 2019; Schneider, 2018; Wratil, 2018).

The paper proceeds as follows. The next section introduces the process and politics of withdrawal. We then develop our theoretical argument; introduce our dataset and operationalisation; and test our hypotheses. We show that 'withdrawal announcements' are more likely when Euroscepticism increases and when legislation touches on core state powers, but less likely when legislation is domestically salient. Cyclical and technical reasons also drive announcements to withdraw. The final section concludes on 'responsive withdrawals', suggests that responsiveness can politicise *and* depoliticise the EU's agenda, and discusses our contribution to the debate about supranational responsiveness.

## The process and politics of withdrawal

This article explores the Commission's response to domestic political pressure when carrying out its core task in EU law-making: agenda-setting. Empirically, we zoom in on one specific signal the Commission can send into this process, namely the announcement to withdraw its proposals. Since 2006, such announcements have been annexed to the annual WP so as to 'pre-alert the other institutions' (Lupo, 2018, p. 320). Usually published in October, WPs serve as the roadmap for the legislative year ahead. We explain the Commission's *intention* to withdraw, not *actual* withdrawal. Actual withdrawal can – but need not – follow the announcement.

Legislative programming is a key executive tool across political systems; in the EU, programming is driven by the Commission. After a European election, the new Commission, in a process called '(dis)continuation', reviews the pipeline of legislation left by the previous EP and Commission, and decides which files to withdraw and keep (Corbett, Jacobs, & Neville, 2016, pp. 313–315). Since the late 1990s, an incoming Commission has also published 'Political Guidelines' – previously known as 'Multi-Annual Strategic Objectives' (Tholoniat, 2009) – to set overall parameters and political structure for policy activity over its term. Fine-tuned annual programming, involving the President's 'State of the Union' address, intra-institutional coordination between General Secretariat and Directorates-General (Hartlapp, Metz, & Rauh, 2014, pp. 247–252), and inter-institutional coordination between Commission and co-legislators (Lupo, 2018, pp. 319–322) eventually results in the annual WP, with annexed lists of files to be prioritised and withdrawn in the 12 months to follow.

To capture when the Commission marks a proposal as 'to be withdrawn', we generated a dataset of all legislative files concluded, withdrawn, rejected or ongoing under the Ordinary Legislative Procedure (OLP) by the end of June 2018.[1] The 2007 WP – published in October 2006 – was the first to include an appendix with announced withdrawals; therefore, our data starts with all proposals on the agenda by October 2006. A file remains 'at risk' of being withdrawn from the moment it is tabled until the Council of the EU has acted (Lupo, 2018, p. 313). Therefore, the observations in our dataset are 'file-years': each proposal is included in every year in which its withdrawal could have been announced. The dataset has 3,681 file-year observations for a total of 1,288 OLP files. Withdrawal announcements are relatively rare; they account for 151 observations. Eight legislative files were announced to be withdrawn, but not actually taken off the agenda. Figure 1 shows announced withdrawals, as a number and percentage of all legislative files on the Commission's agenda in a given year.

Contrary to the Commission's monopoly of legislative initiative (Art. 17(2) TEU) and right to amend a proposal '[a]s long as the Council has not acted' (Art. 293(2) TFEU), withdrawal is not regulated in the EU's Treaties. Yet, withdrawal has been seen as the logical flipside of initiative and amendment. The Court of Justice of the European Union (CJEU) confirmed this view in 2015, but tied the Commission's right to a set of conditions: withdrawal should not amount to a veto right, be justified, and comply with 'the principles of conferral of powers, institutional balance and sincere cooperation' (Lupo, 2018,

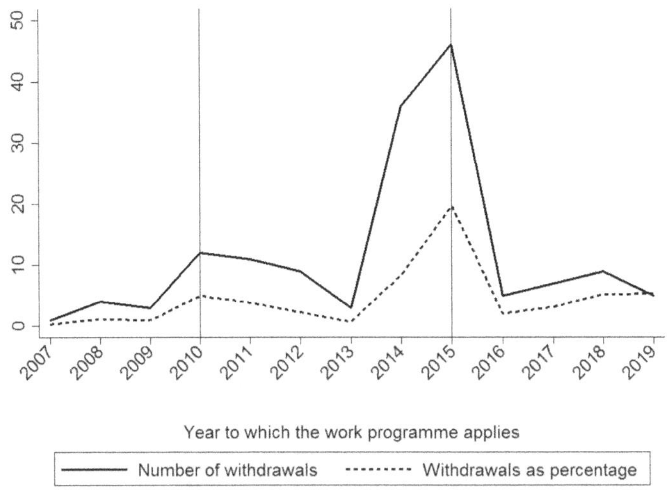


**Figure 1.** Number and percentage of announced withdrawals, by WP year.

p. 313). In 2016, and as part of more general 'proceduralisation and parliamentarisation' (Lupo, 2018, p. 319), the Commission and the co-legislators enshrined the Court's principles in the *Interinstitutional Agreement on Better Law-Making* and in a new Rule 37(4) in the EP's *Rules of Procedure*. The CJEU and the inter-institutional agreement (temporarily) settled the conflict over when and how the Commission is allowed to take its own proposals off the table (Corbett *et al.*, 2016, pp. 313–315).

Announcing the intention to table, prioritise and withdraw EU legislation is the Commission's prerogative. In this process, WPs translate political guidelines into concrete annual agendas; hence, they are at the core of the Commission's political narrative, strategic communication and signalling of legislative intentions to the co-legislators and the public. Traditionally framed as 'technical', withdrawals may therefore matter for a Commission that has described itself as 'political'. Indeed, the Juncker Commission's first two WPs demonstrate a marked shift in framing and listing withdrawals: the main text links withdrawals explicitly to political priorities and legislative ambition (European Commission, 2014, pp. 2–4; 2015, p. 3); the annexes distinguish between withdrawals due to 'obsolescence' and other reasons. Yet, so far, evidence of the Commission announcing withdrawals for more 'political reasons' has remained anecdotal.

In sum, the annual WPs offer us the most explicit data available on what (no longer) matters to the Commission in EU law-making, and the most comprehensive insights into how the Commission intends to use its agenda-setting power in the legislative year to come. We draw on this data to systematically explore whether and when the Commission uses withdrawal announcements as a tool in response to bottom-up political pressure.

## 'Responsive withdrawal': the argument

The Commission sets the EU's legislative agenda in a new environment: the Union and its policies are increasingly important across the member states, and this importance generates political pressure across the multi-level system. We develop a three-step argument about why and how the Commission uses withdrawals in response. First, bottom-up pressure on the Commission varies with national contestation over 'Europe', visible controversy about the EU's (crisis) governance, and the domestic salience of European legislation. Second, under pressure the Commission uses withdrawal announcements to signal either self-restraint or policy-determination. Third, when doing so, the Commission is driven by two motivations: survival and policy. Hence, the Commission's choice of signals is shaped by the interplay between political pressure and actor motivation, with visible contestation triggering agenda-restraint, and the salience of (crisis) legislation triggering agenda-responsiveness.

This argument complements two extant explanations of withdrawal. First, recent inter-institutional conflict over the Commission's right to withdraw notwithstanding (Lupo, 2018, p. 311), actual withdrawal has been explained with functional and temporal factors, as well as obsolescence and non-adoptability (Lupo, 2018, pp. 325–327; Ponzano *et al.*, 2012). We explore whether legislative programming has, instead, become a political tool. Second, scholars have demonstrated, for an earlier time period, that withdrawal, effectively, equals legislative failure; withdrawal happens because the Commission, when proposing legislation, has incomplete information about the co-legislators' future positions (Boranbay-Akan *et al.*, 2017). We agree that conflict can increase, and legislative positions change, during a file's 'lifetime'; yet, we argue that withdrawal announcements can also be deliberate political signals.

To identify bottom-up pressure, we draw on De Wilde *et al.*'s three dimensions of EU politicisation in national politics (2016), namely (1) the EU has become *more visible*; (2) it has become *more contested*; (3) there is *broader engagement* with the EU. Our analysis translates these dimensions into pressure-generating conditions: contestation is expressed in mass-level Euroscepticism; controversy over the optimal scope and level of (crisis) governance increases visibility; stakes and engagement show in the salience of EU legislation. Pressure subsequently travels bottom-up, requiring EU-level actors to respond (see Bressanelli, Koop, & Reh, 2020).

Indeed, recent studies show, *inter alia*, that Euroscepticism impacts Council decision-making (Hagemann *et al.*, 2017; Wratil, 2018), and that national election proximity affects voting behaviour in the EP (Koop *et al.*, 2018). Likewise, the role of the Commission in this context – in particular, the politicisation of its top-level appointments and policy choices, and the greater relevance of ideological cleavages and coalitions within and across the EU's institutions – has been subject to vivid commentary and debate (e.g., Nugent & Rhinard, 2019; Peterson, 2017; Rauh, 2019). By analysing the Commission's use of its agenda-role in response to bottom-up pressure we aim to connect these literatures.

Albeit originally designed as a non-majoritarian institution, insulated from ideological and electoral conflict (Majone, 2002), the Commission should respond to political pressure for two reasons. First, the Commission's monopoly of legislative initiative, in particular, was to protect the agenda from constituency-level politics, short-term bias and the 'cycling' of proposals (Pollack, 2003). Yet, the new environment visibly contests delegation to 'technocrats' at the supranational level, with the Commission – the 'public face' of technocracy in Europe – at the centre of attacks. Hence, sheer survival is on the line: of the Commission and the political system it serves. Under such conditions, the Commission – like a survival-oriented bureaucracy – needs to avoid the loss of competences, defend its 'turf', and protect its reputation (cf. Carpenter, 2001). In response to bottom-up pressure, the Commission should therefore aim for depoliticisation through self-restraint, shrinking the agenda and taking visible conflict out of EU law-making. Withdrawal announcements are well-suited to do so.

Yet, the view of the Commission as an 'insulated bureaucracy', designed to provide expertise, lower transaction costs, and facilitate credible commitment has always been contested (e.g., Sandholtz & Zysman, 1989). Motivated, first and foremost, by policy-problems that matter for Europe's citizens, the Commission, instead, aims to shape the agenda politically (e.g., Becker, Bauer, Connolly, & Kassim, 2016; Nugent & Rhinard, 2019; Peterson, 2017). This view gained particular traction with the Juncker Commission. Entering office in 2014, after an EP election aiming for a more direct electoral connection between the Commission's President and Europe's voters, President Juncker, indeed, used his first State of the Union address to pledge a more political Commission. Yet, Juncker's pledge was policy-seeking, not party-political, emphasising a Commission committed to its priorities, and to addressing the challenges faced by Europe's citizens (Juncker, 2014).[2] In response to pressure, a policy-seeker will politicise the EU's agenda through determination – even if clout is perceived as activism. Not withdrawing legislation under visibility and adversity is a well-suited signal to do so.

In sum, both survival and policy should drive the Commission to use the announcement (not) to take legislation off the table strategically, with the concrete signalling choice shaped by how bottom-up pressure interplays with the actor's motivations. Bottom-up pressure on the Commission increases under three conditions: contestation, visibility and salience.

First, political pressure increases with mass-level contestation over 'Europe'. Euroscepticism puts the Commission at the centre of its critique, and the louder the critique, the more incentivised the Commission will be to respond (cf. Rauh, 2019). Perceptive of domestic dissent and of being its prime target, the Commission is acutely aware of the need to be seen to 'listen' – as shown in former President Barroso's statement on 'the challenge of winning citizens' trust' in the midst of the Eurozone crisis (European Commission, 2012). Euroscepticism, ultimately, questions the EU as a political system, its institutions, and the Commission's competences and reputation. Hence, we expect mass-level contestation to trigger agenda-restraint; as a survival-oriented bureaucracy, the Commission will fight to protect its turf and reputation by signalling its willingness to listen and by countering perceived 'over-bureaucratisation'. Displaying behaviour similar to Europe's Court (Blauberger & Schmidt, 2017), the Commission should use withdrawal announcements as part of this 'fight'. 'Less action but better action' (Santer, 1995) is a much-quoted slogan, summing up the Santer (and subsequent) Commissions' attempts to take legislation off the table to signal restraint under public pressure 'against' Brussels. We therefore submit:

> H1 The European Commission is more likely to announce the withdrawal of a legislative proposal under higher levels of Euroscepticism.

Second, conflict over legislation is more visible – with pressure increasing accordingly – when a policy-problem is pressing and when the competence to address the problem is contested; we also know that responsiveness increases on visibly important files (Page & Shapiro, 1983, pp. 181–182l, 183l). Legislation on core state powers (Genschel & Jachtenfuchs, 2018) falls into this category. On the one hand, legislation on finance and migration is at the core of national sovereignty and, more recently, of national electoral politics; hence, supranational involvement is controversial. On the other hand, legislation on finance and migration is integral to Europe's multiple crises; hence, pressure has been put on the EU to act in precisely these areas. In short, legislation on core state powers is both visible and visibly contested. In response, the Commission should use withdrawal announcements strategically, but the signalling choices of a survival-oriented bureaucracy and a policy-seeker will differ. A survival-oriented bureaucracy should announce withdrawal to signal restraint to governments that feel challenged to the core of their sovereignty; a policy-seeker, by contrast, would want to act precisely on crisis-files, to signal responsiveness on issues that matter to Europe's citizens. We therefore submit two alternative hypotheses:

> H2a The European Commission is more likely to announce the withdrawal of a legislative proposal if the file touches on a core state power.

> H2b The European Commission is less likely to announce the withdrawal of a legislative proposal if the file touches on a core state power.

Finally, bottom-up pressure on the Commission increases with issue-specific salience. Indeed, both the comparative and the EU-specific literature tell us that salience drives the responsiveness of national and supranational actors (e.g., Hagemann *et al.*, 2017; Rauh, 2019; Soroka & Wlezien, 2010). In line with this argument, a policy-seeking Commission should prioritise issues of direct concern to Europe's citizens, and show commitment to solve policy problems that attract public attention across member states (cf. Klüver & Spoon, 2015; Sternberg, 2016). Hence, the Commission is likely to keep salient legislation on the agenda, as announcing its withdrawal would signal lacking political determination and policy clout in the face of adversity. We therefore submit:

> H3 The European Commission is less likely to announce the withdrawal of a legislative proposal if the file is domestically salient.

## Data and operationalisation

To analyse the conditions under which the Commission marks a file as 'to be withdrawn' in its annual WP, we generated a dataset of all OLP files 'at risk' of withdrawal between October 2006 and June 2018. As noted, a file is 'at risk' from its tabling until the Council has formally expressed a position. The data starts in 2006, as no withdrawals annex was published before. WPs are normally published in October; therefore, 1 October is the start of the year to which the WP applies, and the following 30 September is the end point. To recall, our dataset includes 3,681 file-year observations for 1,288 OLP files; hence, on average, 2.9 observations per file.

Our dependent variable *withdrawal* is dichotomous and coded 1 when a file is mentioned in the withdrawals annex of a WP in a given year. Withdrawal announcements are rare: only 151 of the 3,681 observations in our dataset (4.1 per cent). In theory, the same procedure could be 'at risk' in multiple years. Yet, this is the case for only two procedures in our dataset.[3] The Online Appendix includes the descriptive statistics (Table A) and correlation matrix (Table B).

To test our first hypothesis (H1), *Euroscepticism* captures the percentage of citizens who answer 'a bad thing' to the question: 'Generally speaking, do you think that [our country]'s membership of the EU is ... ? (a good thing/a bad thing/neither good nor bad)'. We use data from the Eurobarometer's autumn waves. The variable is lagged by one year, because the Commission will need some time to perceive, process and react to national-level pressure.

*Core state powers* (H2) is a dummy variable capturing contestation in policy areas close to national sovereignty: economic governance, budgetary policy, asylum and migration (cf. Genschel & Jachtenfuchs, 2018). These policies were also at the core of Europe's recent crises and are, therefore, integral to the new environment of EU decision-making.

*Issue salience* (H3) captures a file's media attention. The variable is measured as the average number of references in English-, German-, French- and Italian-language print media, made between the Commission proposal and the date of the file's conclusion, withdrawal or rejection, or, for ongoing procedures, the end of June 2018 (following Bressanelli, Koop, & Reh, 2016; Reh, Héritier, Bressanelli, & Koop, 2013). Given the positive skewness of the variable, we use its natural log.

Our analysis includes two sets of control variables. These capture the two extant explanations of withdrawal – uncertainty due to incomplete information, and functional factors – which have not been tested on the data used and the time period covered in our analysis.

The first two variables capture the uncertainty of agenda-setting, and control for factors shown to drive actual withdrawals between 1993 and 2009 (Boranbay-Akan *et al.*, 2017). The variables are adapted to fit our data structure. *Gridlock* measures the interval between the left-most and right-most pivotal actors needed to pass legislation under an extant procedural rule.[4] A larger gridlock interval makes approval of legislation more difficult (Crombez & Hix, 2015) and may not have been anticipated by the Commission when tabling its proposal (Boranbay-Akan *et al.*, 2017). Hence, the likelihood of announced withdrawal should increase with the size of the gridlock interval. Due to the increased importance of ideological alignment and conflict within and between EU institutions, we assume a one-dimensional, left-right policy space, (Crombez & Hix, 2015; Klüver & Sagarzazu, 2013). In addition, we focus on 'ordinary' legislation rather than 'constitutional' choices, where the 'pro-anti integration' dimension would be more dominant.

We calculated the gridlock interval by estimating the positions of the OLP's three pivotal actors under the relevant majority rules: the left and right pivots in the Council, and the median Europarliamentarian (MEP; see Crombez & Hix, 2015). The two most 'extreme' positions make up the gridlock interval. We draw on Broniecki, Obholzer, and Reh (2018) for October 2006 to September 2014, and update the data until June 2018. Positions are obtained from the Chapel Hill Expert Survey (Bakker *et al.*, 2015; Polk *et al.*, 2017). The Council pivot positions are the average positions of the governing parties, weighted by their seats in national parliaments. The EP position for the entire period is the national party position of the median MEP, who is needed for an (absolute) majority. A single point-estimate was calculated on 1 October of each year and matched to our annual periods. Like *Euroscepticism*, *gridlock* is lagged by one year.

Following Boranbay-Akan *et al.* (2017), we include the variable *national elections*. This control accounts for the uncertainty about future positions which the Commission faces when tabling a proposal, and when deciding whether or not to withdraw. We calculated the population-weighted number of parliamentary and (directly-elected) presidential elections held during the year of the respective WP. By including elections in all member states, our measure differs from Boranbay-Akan *et al.*'s (2017, p. 179): although the largest member states 'matter' more in our variable, the Commission is unlikely to be insensitive to elections held in other member states, particularly when elections are clustered.

The second set of controls captures functional explanations. Starting with file-characteristics, our variable *substantive* distinguishes between procedural changes (adaptation, recast, and codification are coded 0), and substantive amendments as well as new legislation (coded 1). The EU has changed the implementation of broader procedural changes over time, and withdrawn procedurally-obsolete proposals (particularly under Barroso II; see below). Hence, *substantive* should have a negative sign. We also control for *complexity*. Our continuous variable counts the number of recitals in the proposal, updating data in Reh *et al.* (2013) for 2009–2018. Given greater up-front investment by the Commission, complex proposals should be less likely to be withdrawn. As the variable is positively skewed, we used its natural log. Similarly, given the Commission's investment and institutional interest, withdrawal announcements should be less likely when files expand the Union's competences. Our variable *EU expansion* is coded 1 if the file increases (i) the level, (ii) the scope, or (iii) the inclusiveness of EU action (cf. Franchino 2007, Ch. 3; for details see Online Appendix).

We also control for temporal factors. *Time on agenda* captures the years passed since a proposal's introduction. The longer this time, the more likely a withdrawal announcement. The variable takes the value 1 in the first year of a file's existence, and then counts every subsequent agenda year. *Cycle: first-last year* is a dummy controlling for regular 'activity peaks'; the variable separates the first and last years of a legislative cycle from the 'in between' years.

Finally, we control for the different *Commissions* (Barroso I, Barroso II, Juncker). Given specific contextual factors and dynamics, Commissions may use WPs differently (cf. Kreppel & Oztas, 2017). For instance, Juncker applied 'political discontinuity' liberally when taking office, while Barroso-II is known for 'cleaning up', by removing procedurally-obsolete proposals that are pending, because there is no 'time-out' for legislative proposals.

## Analysis

As our dependent variable is dichotomous, we used logistic regression to estimate the likelihood of withdrawal announcements. Such announcements are uncommon, but their number in our data (151 'events') allows us to use regular logistic regression rather than logistic regression for rare events. We clustered our observations by legislative file as our observations are pending proposals in a specific annual period.

We estimated five models. Table 1 presents the models and includes both coefficients and odds ratios. Models 1–3 include the control variables to explore established explanations of withdrawal. Model 1 includes the functional-temporal controls, capturing the Commission's work cycle (*cycle: first-last year*), *time on agenda*, and the different Commissions. Model 2 adds file-characteristics (*substantive; complexity; EU expansion*). Model 3 includes the controls for uncertainty: *gridlock* and *national elections*. Models 4 introduces our 'political' variables: Euroscepticism, core state powers, and issue salience.[5] Finally, Model 5 is a reduced version of Model 4, excluding the controls that did not have a significant effect.

All controls in Models 1 and 2 have significant effects, except *EU expansion*. As expected, the Commission announces significantly more withdrawals in the *first and last year* of its time in office. Indeed, as Figure 1 suggested, both Barroso II and Juncker used their first WP to 'clean up' (there are no withdrawals annexes for the first years of Barroso I), while the last WP of the cycle mattered in particular for Barroso II. Compared to Barroso I, *Barroso II* and *Juncker* announced more withdrawals, suggesting 'normalisation'. Finally, *time on agenda* is positive and strongly significant. Proposals staying on the agenda for long are more likely to become obsolete, and, finally, removed. In line with extant explanations, Model 2 demonstrates that *substantive* and more *complex* proposals are less likely to be withdrawn. The link between *expansion* and withdrawal is negative, but not significant.

We also find some support for the extant explanation of withdrawal based on incomplete information and uncertainty. Model 3, which adds *gridlock* and *national elections*, shows a weak positive link between the gridlock interval and withdrawal. Hence, the larger the interval, the more likely a withdrawal announcement. Yet, this relationship is only just significant; in line with the extant literature (cf. Osnabrügge, 2015, pp. 248–9, 253), gridlock seems at best a weak predictor of Commission behaviour. We do not find a relationship between *national elections* and withdrawal announcements; depending on the model specification, the effect is either positive or negative, but never significant.

Importantly, our models show that politics matters. Model 4 adds *Euroscepticism, core state powers* and *issue salience*. In line with H1, the Commission is more likely to announce a withdrawal under higher levels of Euroscepticism. The model includes all controls; hence, the effect holds even when controlling for *Barroso II* – the Commission operating under peak Euroscepticism. The results are substantively the same in Model 5, which excludes those variables that were not significant in Model 4. This is a first indication of withdrawal announcements in response to what is perceived as bottom-up pressure; more specifically, the Commission seems to signal agenda-restraint when Europe's public becomes more sceptical.

Models 4 and 5 also include our measure of *core state powers*. In line with H2a, the effect of this variable is positive and significant. Hence, in the face of

**Table 1.** The likelihood of Commission withdrawal announcements (2006–2018).

| | Model 1 | | Model 2 | | Model 3 | | Model 4 | | Model 5 | |
|---|---|---|---|---|---|---|---|---|---|---|
| | Coef (SE) | $e^{\beta}$ | Coef (SE) | $e^{\beta}$ | Coef (SE) | $e^{\beta}$ | Coef (SE) | $e^{\beta}$ | Coef (SE) | $e^{\beta}$ |
| Euroscepticism | | | | | | | 0.30 (0.07)*** | 1.35 | 0.29 (0.07)*** | 1.33 |
| Core state powers | | | | | | | 0.86 (0.29)*** | 2.35 | 0.74 (0.30)** | 2.10 |
| Issue salience | | | | | | | −0.75 (0.35)** | 0.47 | −0.80 (0.33)** | 0.45 |
| Gridlock | | | | | 1.26 (0.69)* | 3.54 | 1.53 (0.87)* | 4.64 | 1.30 (0.70)* | 3.66 |
| National elections | | | | | 0.24 (0.72) | 1.27 | −0.73 (1.02) | 0.48 | | |
| Substantive | | | −0.78 (0.22)*** | 0.45 | −0.77 (0.22)*** | 0.46 | −0.79 (0.22)*** | 0.46 | −0.82 (0.22)*** | 0.44 |
| Complexity | | | −0.47 (0.14)*** | 0.63 | −0.44 (0.14)*** | 0.64 | −0.34 (0.14)** | 0.71 | −0.41 (0.12)*** | 0.67 |
| EU expansion | | | −0.48 (0.29) | 0.62 | −0.48 (0.29)* | 0.62 | −0.46 (0.29) | 0.63 | | |
| Cycle: first-last year | 1.25 (0.20)*** | 3.49 | 1.24 (0.21)*** | 3.46 | 1.27 (0.21)*** | 3.54 | 1.57 (0.26)*** | 4.80 | 1.62 (0.26)*** | 5.06 |
| Time on agenda | 0.57 (0.07)*** | 1.77 | 0.54 (0.07)*** | 1.71 | 0.56 (0.08)*** | 1.75 | 0.60 (0.07)*** | 1.82 | 0.60 (0.07)*** | 1.82 |
| Commission | | | | | | | | | | |
| Barroso II | 0.80 (0.39)** | 2.23 | 1.09 (0.42)*** | 2.98 | 1.59 (0.55)*** | 4.91 | 1.04 (0.72) | 2.83 | 0.85 (0.61) | 2.34 |
| Juncker | 1.00 (0.41)** | 2.71 | 1.55 (0.45)*** | 4.72 | 1.98 (0.54)*** | 7.27 | 1.48 (0.65)** | 4.38 | 1.31 (0.58)** | 3.72 |
| Constant | −6.47 (0.43)*** | | −4.74 (0.52)*** | | −6.67 (1.06)*** | | −11.56 (1.81)*** | | −11.11 (1.56)*** | |
| *N* | 3681 | | 3681 | | 3681 | | 3681 | | 3681 | |
| Log-pseudolikelihood | −471.07 | | −448.62 | | −446.08 | | −431.51 | | −433.86 | |
| McFadden-adj. $R^2$ | 0.24 | | 0.28 | | 0.28 | | 0.30 | | 0.29 | |
| Nagelkerke $R^2$ | 0.29 | | 0.32 | | 0.33 | | 0.35 | | 0.35 | |

Note: Robust standard errors, clustered by proposal. $^{***}p < 0.01$, $^{**}p < 0.05$, $^{*}p < 0.1$ (two-tailed).

member states' opposition and concerns over sovereignty, the Commission seems more likely to announce withdrawals and does not push 'its' legislation. Two examples are the '2014 Visa Policy Package' and the '2013 Smart Border Package'; in both cases, the Juncker Commission withdrew its original proposal following criticism from the co-legislators, particularly the Council. Initially, we submitted alternative hypotheses on core state powers. Our findings suggest a Commission driven by survival and ready to announce the withdrawal of contentious legislation in areas sensitive for the member states, such as economic governance, budgetary policy, asylum and migration.

Finally, the models show a negative and significant relationship between *issue salience* and withdrawal: legislation 'show-cased' in the national media is less likely to be withdrawn. As hypothesised (H3), this result demonstrates a Commission focused on policy outputs in areas of direct concern, relevance and visibility for Europe's citizens.

In a next step, we delved deeper into the question of variation across Commissions. In particular, does the allegedly 'more political' Juncker Commission focus on files with different characteristics than its predecessor? To address these questions, we ran our analyses on subsets of the data for Barroso II and Juncker, including those variables that significantly affected withdrawal announcements in the above models.[6] We excluded *Euroscepticism* from the analysis: the variable only varies over time, and including five of its values in the separate Commission analyses (for the five years in office), together with the *cycle* variable, would be problematic. The results – coefficients and confidence intervals – are plotted in Figure 2.

Figure 2 demonstrates that Barroso II and Juncker use withdrawal announcements somewhat differently. Both are more likely to announce the withdrawal of files that spent a long time on the agenda, and in the *first and last year* of their terms. In both cases, withdrawal announcements are more likely when the *gridlock* interval is large – although the large

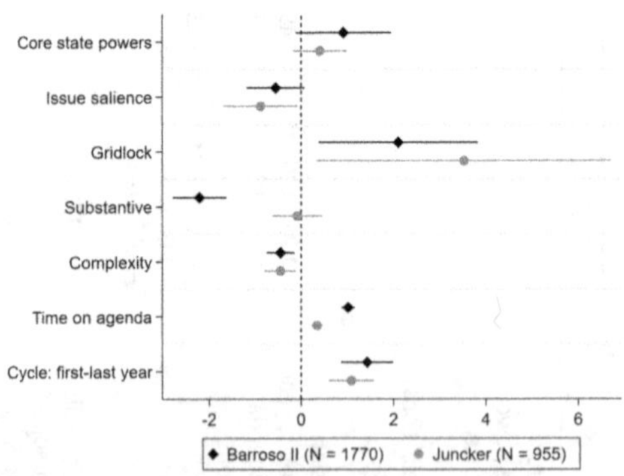


**Figure 2.** Withdrawals under Barroso II and Juncker.

Note: Robust standard errors, clustered by proposal.

**Table 2.** Marginal changes (based on Model 4).

| Variables | Change |
|---|---|
| Euroscepticism | 0.06*** |
| Core state powers | 0.03** |
| Issue salience | −0.04*** |
| Gridlock | 0.06 |
| National elections | −0.01 |
| Substantive | −0.03*** |
| Complexity | −0.06** |
| EU expansion | −0.01* |
| Cycle: first-last year | 0.05*** |
| Time on agenda | 0.83*** |
| Barroso II | 0.03 |
| Juncker | 0.06* |

Note: Change from minimum to maximum value. ***$p < 0.01$, **$p < 0.05$, *$p < 0.1$.

confidence intervals call for cautious interpretation – and less likely when *complexity* increases. Yet, under Barroso II, the likelihood of withdrawal announcements decreases considerably for *substantive* files, while this file characteristic does not seem to affect Juncker.[7] This is in line with the previous emphasis on a 'cleaning exercise' initiated by Barroso II. *Issue salience* also makes withdrawal announcement less likely, but only under Juncker. The variable *core state powers* remains (just) outside conventional significance levels in the subset analyses.

Finally, Table 2 shows the marginal effects based on Model 4, which included all 'political' variables. These effects need to be interpreted with care, but the values add insight into the relative importance of the variables. By far the largest change is 'caused' by *time on agenda*; very 'old' files face almost certain withdrawal announcement. A considerable – if smaller – difference is made by *Euroscepticism*, *complexity* and legislative *cycle*, followed by *issue salience*, *core state powers* and *substantive*. The marginal effects of *EU expansion* and *Juncker* are less significant; the effects of *gridlock*, *national elections* and *Barroso II* are not significant.

## Conclusion and discussion

This study theorised and analysed how the new environment of EU lawmaking impacts on the Commission as an agenda-setter, and on its choice to announce withdrawal of legislative proposals. We argued that bottom-up pressure on the Commission intensifies under domestic contestation, visibility and salience; that the Commission faces pressure as both a survival-oriented bureaucracy and a policy-seeker; and that withdrawal announcements serve as signals.

Our analysis suggests that established functional and temporal explanations continue to apply: withdrawal announcements are more likely at the beginning and end of the legislative term; for technical, obsolete or non-complex legislation; and for 'old' proposals. Yet, politics matters too. The Commission signals agenda restraint when Euroscepticism grows and when legislation is close to core state powers. By contrast, the Commission seeks policy on issues of importance for Europe's citizens; domestically salient files are less likely to be withdrawn. Importantly, the Commission is more responsive to pressure from the public and from the member states than to the co-legislators' conflict on the left-right dimension.

In a nutshell, withdrawals continue to be announced on functional and temporal grounds. Yet, the Commission also uses withdrawal announcements as signals in response to bottom-up pressure. It does so in a nuanced way: as a survival-oriented bureaucracy, the Commission aims to actively depoliticise the agenda, to protect its prerogatives and to de-escalate through restraint; as a policy-seeker, the Commission politicises the agenda by keeping strategically important legislation in play, even under visible adversity. In other words, the Commission uses strategies of assertive depoliticisation and politicisation (Bressanelli *et al.*, 2020).

Finally, our findings on 'responsive withdrawal' provide evidence for a 'more political' Juncker Commission. Indeed, the WPs indicate that Juncker announces withdrawals more strategically – using political discontinuity to focus on and promote legislative priorities, and making announcements to pressure the co-legislators (for instance, European Commission, 2014, pp. 2–4; 9). We also show that the Juncker Commission – different from Barroso I and II – selects non-substantive *and* substantive proposals for withdrawal, and – as befits a Commission with clear agenda-priorities – is particularly responsive to issue salience.

Our analysis contributes to the nascent debate about bottom-up politicisation, and signposts a number of future research avenues. First, we know that political pressure matters for those actors at the supranational level that have an electoral connection into domestic democratic arenas; our results show that even the Commission's announcements to withdraw legislation – arguably, the most technical dimension of agenda-setting by a non-majoritarian institution – are affected by contestation, visibility and salience. This finding encourages extended exploration of the Commission's agenda-setting and communication under pressure and speaks directly to the comparative literature on how agencies, bureaucracies and courts respond to public opinion and issue salience (see Koop & Lodge, 2019, pp. 10–15).

Second, by presenting an institution that seeks both survival and policy, we contribute to the debate about the Commission's different – arguably competing – roles in the EU's political system: non-majoritarian bureaucracy on the one hand, proto-executive on the other. In using withdrawal announcements under pressure, the Commission is clearly responsive, but not to party ideology or electoral politics. Instead, a 'political' Commission responds to Europe's public and governments by focusing on legislative priorities and outputs – even if these outputs have become more contested and visible – and by protecting its competences to continue agenda-setting in future. Fine-graining our understanding of how the Commission responds to public opinion across issues would be fruitful, and generate more extensive empirical evidence to assess the (political) nature of the Commission.

Finally, our analysis of annual WPs leads us to, tentatively, expect more 'responsive withdrawals' in future. The withdrawal process is subject to inter-institutional debate; there is anecdotal evidence of withdrawal announcements to pressure the co-legislators; and given both Barroso's and Juncker's 'clear-out' of obsolete proposals, the Von der Leyen Commission can announce withdrawals more strategically on the fewer files left on the table. Truly far-reaching, in the run-up to her appointment, Commission President von der Leyen supported a right of legislative initiative for the EP. Hence, agenda-setting, legislative programming and the Commission's strategic use – and defence – of its prerogative are likely to feature prominently in intra- and inter-institutional conflict to come.

## Notes

1. We only include ongoing legislation proposed before the end of 2016, because by June 2018, these files would have either been withdrawn or would still be ongoing.
2. This is also reflected in the Juncker Commission's WPs. For instance, the first programme stated that the Commission was 'voted into office with a commitment to make a difference: to do different things and to do things differently' (2014, p. 2).
3. Procedures 2005/0127(COD) and 2013/0059(COD).
4. Unlike Boranbay-Akan *et al.* (2017), we exclude 'procedural change' as a variable. Our 'codecision-only' dataset starts in 2006 and does not include proposals transferred to the OLP.
5. As robustness checks, we ran a model with an alternative operationalisation of ideological conflict; a model estimated on a subset of observations excluding Barroso I (where withdrawals were rare); and two models changing the sequence of including different categories of variables. The results do not differ substantively. All models are presented in Table C in the Online Appendix.
6. Our data also include the Barroso I period, but the number of announced withdrawals is so low (only eight) that we cannot run a separate analysis for that Commission. This is relevant in itself, suggesting that the power to withdraw has only recently been embraced as an agenda-setting tool.
7. The difference in approaches is confirmed when adding an interaction between *Juncker* and *substantive* files to Model 4 in Table 1 (see Table D and Figure A in the Online Appendix).

## Acknowledgements

We would like to thank Berthold Rittberger, two anonymous reviewers and participants at the Workshop 'Politicising and De-Politicising the European Union' (King's College

London, 15 and 16 December 2017) for their helpful feedback. Nicolò Conti, Simona Piattoni as well as audiences at the King's College Public Policy and Regulation Workshop (15 February 2019) and the European Governance Colloquium at the Hertie School (4 March 2019) also provided constructive comments on earlier versions of this article. We are grateful to Niccolò Massei, Francesca Minetto and Michele Scotto di Vettimo for their excellent research assistance.

## Disclosure statement

No potential conflict of interest was reported by the authors.

## Funding

Research for this article was supported by a British Academy/Leverhulme Small Research Grant (SG160582; 'Politicising Europe').

## ORCID

*Christel Koop* http://orcid.org/0000-0002-7125-6439

## References

Bakker, R., de Vries, C., Edwards, E., Hooghe, L., Jolly, S., Marks, G., … Vachudova, M. A. (2015). Measuring party positions in Europe: The Chapel Hill expert survey trend file, 1999–2010. *Party Politics*, *21*(1), 143–152.

Becker, S., Bauer, M. W., Connolly, S., & Kassim, H. (2016). The Commission: Boxed in and constrained, but still an engine of integration. *West European Politics*, *39*(5), 1011–1031.

Blauberger, M., & Schmidt, S. K. (2017). The European Court of Justice and its political impact. *West European Politics*, *40*(4), 907–918.

Boranbay-Akan, S., König, T., & Osnabrügge, M. (2017). The imperfect agenda-setter: Why do legislative proposals fail in the EU decision-making process? *European Union Politics*, *18*(2), 168–187.

Bouts, E. (2014, December 14). Withdrawal of the circular economy package: A missed opportunity for sustainable growth. *Euractiv*.

Bressanelli, E., Koop, C., & Reh, C. (2016). The impact of informalisation: Early agreements and voting cohesion in the European Parliament. *European Union Politics*, *17*(1), 91–113.

Bressanelli, E., Koop, C., & Reh, C. (2020). EU actors under pressure: Politicisation and depoliticisation as strategic response. *Journal of European Public Policy, 27*(3), 329–341.

Broniecki, P., Obholzer, L., & Reh, C. (2018). Against the odds: Overcoming gridlock in EU legislative decision-making. Paper presented at the ECPR-SGEU conference in Paris, June.

Carpenter, D. P. (2001). *The forging of bureaucratic autonomy: Reputations, networks, and policy innovation in executive agencies, 1862–1928*. Princeton, NJ: Princeton University Press.

Corbett, R., Jacobs, F., & Neville, D. (2016). *The European Parliament* (9th ed.). London: John Harper.

Crombez, C., & Hix, S. (2015). Legislative activity and gridlock in the European Union. *British Journal of Political Science, 45*(3), 477–499.

De Wilde, P., Leupold, A., & Schmidtke, H. (2016). Introduction: The differentiated politicisation of European governance. *West European Politics, 39*(1), 3–22.

European Commission. (2012, April 25). 'The challenge of winning citizens' trust', Remarks by President Barroso at the Seminar Organised by European Ombudsman. MEMO/12/276.

European Commission. (2014, December 12). 'Work programme 2015: A new start' (COM(2014) 910), Strasbourg.

European Commission. (2015, October 27). 'Work programme 2016: No time for business as usual' (COM(2015) 610), Strasbourg.

Franchino, F. (2007). *The powers of the Union: Delegation in the EU*. Cambridge: Cambridge University Press.

Genschel, P., & Jachtenfuchs, M. (2018). From market integration to core state powers: The Eurozone crisis, the refugee crisis and integration theory. *JCMS: Journal of Common Market Studies, 56*(1), 178–196.

Grande, E., & Kriesi, H. (2014). The restructuring of political conflict in Europe and the politicization of European integration. In T. Risse (Ed.), *European public spheres: Politics is back* (pp. 190–224). Cambridge: Cambridge University Press.

Hagemann, S., Hobolt, S. B., & Wratil, C. (2017). Government responsiveness in the European Union: Evidence from Council voting. *Comparative Political Studies, 50*(6), 850–876.

Hartlapp, M., Metz, J., & Rauh, C. (2014). *Which policy for Europe? Power and conflict inside the European Commission*. Oxford: Oxford University Press.

Hooghe, L., & Marks, G. (2009). A postfunctionalist theory of European integration: From permissive consensus to constraining dissensus. *British Journal of Political Science, 39*(1), 1–23.

Juncker, J.-C. (2014, July 15). 'A new start for Europe: My agenda for jobs, growth, fairness and democratic change', Political guidelines for the next European Commission, Opening statement in the European Parliament plenary session, Strasbourg.

Klüver, H., & Sagarzazu, I. (2013). Ideological congruency and decision-making speed: The effect of partisanship across European Union institutions. *European Union Politics, 14*(3), 388–407.

Klüver, H., & Spoon, J.-J. (2015). Bringing salience back in: Explaining voting defection in the European Parliament. *Party Politics, 21*(4), 553–564.

Koop, C., & Lodge, M. (2019). British economic regulators in an age of politicisation: From the responsible to the responsive regulatory state? Paper presented at the ECPR General Conference 2019.

Koop, C., Reh, C., & Bressanelli, E. (2018). When politics prevails: Parties, elections and loyalty in the European Parliament. *European Journal of Political Research*, *57*(3), 563–586.

Kreppel, A., & Oztas, B. (2017). Leading the band or just playing the tune? Reassessing the agenda-setting powers of the European Commission. *Comparative Political Studies*, *50*(8), 1118–1150.

Lupo, N. (2018). The Commission's power to withdraw legislative proposals and its "parliamentarisation", between technical and political grounds. *European Constitutional Law Review*, *14*(2), 311–331.

Majone, G. (2002). The European Commission: The limits of centralization and the perils of parliamentarization. *Governance*, *15*(3), 375–392.

Nugent, N., & Rhinard, M. (2019). The 'political' roles of the European Commission. *Journal of European Integration*, *41*(2), 203–220.

Osnabrügge, M. (2015). The European Commission and the implementation of its legislative programme. *European Union Politics*, *16*(2), 241–261.

Page, B. I., & Shapiro, R. Y. (1983). Effects of public opinion on policy. *American Political Science Review*, *77*(1), 175–190.

Peterson, J. (2017). Juncker's political European Commission and an EU in crisis. *JCMS: Journal of Common Market Studies*, *55*(2), 349–367.

Polk, J., Rovny, J., Bakker, R., Edwards, E., Hooghe, L., Jolly, S., & Koedam, J. (2017). Explaining the salience of anti-elitism and reducing political corruption for political parties in Europe with the 2014 Chapel Hill Expert Survey data. *Research & Politics*, *4* (1), 1–9.

Pollack, M. A. (2003). *The engines of European integration: Delegation, agency, and agenda-setting in the EU*. Oxford: Oxford University Press.

Ponzano, P., Hermanin, C., & Corona, D. (2012). The power of initiative of the European Commission: A progressive erosion? Notre Europe, Study No. 89.

Rauh, C. (2019). EU politicization and policy initiatives of the European Commission: The case of consumer policy. *Journal of European Public Policy*, *26*(3), 344–365.

Reh, C., Héritier, A., Bressanelli, E., & Koop, C. (2013). The informal politics of legislation: Explaining secluded decision making in the European Union. *Comparative Political Studies*, *46*(9), 1112–1142.

Sandholtz, W., & Zysman, J. (1989). 1992: Recasting the European bargain. *World Politics*, *42*(1), 95–128.

Santer, J. (1995, January 17). Speech to the European Parliament.

Schneider, C. J. (2018). *The responsive union: National elections and European governance*. Cambridge: Cambridge University Press.

Soroka, S. N., & Wlezien, C. (2010). *Degrees of democracy: Politics, public opinion, and policy*. Cambridge: Cambridge University Press.

Sternberg, C. (2016). Public opinion in the EU institutions' discourses on EU legitimacy from the beginnings of integration to today. *Politique Européenne*, *54*(4), 24–56.

Tholoniat, L. (2009). The temporal constitution of the European Commission: A timely investigation. *Journal of European Public Policy*, *16*(2), 221–238.

Wratil, C. (2018). Modes of government responsiveness in the European Union: Evidence from Council negotiation positions. *European Union Politics*, *19*(1), 52–74.

OPEN ACCESS

# Understanding the European Commission's use of politicisation in the negotiation of interinstitutional agreements: the role of consultations and issue framing

Adriana Bunea

**ABSTRACT**

The negotiations that precede the adoption of EU interinstitutional agreements present relevant opportunities for political entrepreneurs to politicise the interinstitutional dialogue. This study asks *when and how does the European Commission politicise the negotiations of EU interinstitutional agreements?* Building on a classic model explaining the politicisation of EU at domestic level, the study argues that the Commission has incentives to politicise negotiations when these revolve around substantive agreements that propose relevant change, when it anticipates autonomy or power losses and opposition on behalf of negotiations counterparts. Politicisation is used as a tool for re-legitimisation with a view to strengthening the power to shape negotiation outcomes. Stakeholder consultations and issue framing are instruments used to deploy classic politicisation strategies of expanding publicity, the universe of actors and controversy. The study shows how the Commission politicised the negotiations of two most recent agreements on a mandatory Transparency Register and Better Law-making.

## Introduction

Interinstitutional agreements (IIAs) are a well-established form of coordination and collaboration on procedural and substantive matters between the Commission (EC), the European Parliament (EP) and the Council. IIAs emerged as a practice in the 1960s and played a key role in building 'the fabric of EU governance', serving as a 'sub-constitutional driving force of European integration' (Riekmann, 2007, p. 4). An interesting theoretical puzzle regarding IIAs is the extent to which the negotiations preceding their adoption may be politicised. On the one hand,

IIAs are an instrument offering pragmatic, ad-hoc solutions to procedural issues or substantive institutional disagreements. They allow efficient solutions to key interinstitutional tensions by circumscribing procedural hurdles and 'avoiding the cumbersome procedures of treaty amendment' (Monar, 1994, pp. 695–696). IIAs offer a 'coordinating or even peace-building tool for interinstitutional conflicts' (Eiselt, Pollak, & Slominski, 2007, p. 77). This (functionalist) perspective suggests that interinstitutional negotiations are less susceptible to politicisation. On the other hand, IIAs are opportunities used by institutional actors to pursue specific policy and political goals (e.g., enhancing their role in legislative decision-making or their oversight powers, cf. Stacey, 2010). This (political) perspective suggests that IIAs are likely to increase conflict and their negotiations are more susceptible to politicisation (Kietz & Maurer, 2007). The implications of this perspective are important insofar they suggest that politicisation is also a top-down phenomenon characterizing the EU polity and a strategy employed by supranational institutional actors (see also Blauberger & Martinsen, 2020 and Reh, Bressanelli, & Koop, 2020).

This study taps into this second perspective and asks: *when and how does the European Commission politicise the negotiations of EU interinstitutional agreements?* Its analytical focus on the Commission is justified in two ways. First, the literature analyzing IIAs as a legal instrument of informal constitutionalisation, parliamentarisation and institutionalisation of EU governance focuses primarily on EP's role in negotiations and the Council-EP power dynamic (Eiselt *et al.*, 2007). IIAs rest in-between a legal document and a political declaration and tackle various substantive and procedural issues. They can result in important changes to the institutional status quo. However, the literature pays little attention to the Commission's role in these negotiations (exceptions are Stacey, 2012 and Cini, 2013). This neglect is surprising given that the Commission enjoyed agenda-setting (drafting) power in some negotiations and several agreements introduced additional constraints on its institutional autonomy and power. It is reasonable to assume that in some negotiations the EC has incentives to act as a political entrepreneur seizing political opportunities facilitating competence and status gains as part of interinstitutional negotiations (Wille, 2013). Second, research shows that politicisation is part of the Commission's institutional structure and exercise of executive power (Haverland, de Ruiter, & Van de Walle, 2018) and of its policy formulation strategies (Rauh, 2019). However, we lack a study of how the EC may politicise IIAs negotiations when it enjoys drafting and agenda-setting prerogatives. Considering the Commission's loss of power following treaty reforms (Kreppel & Oztas, 2017) and that IIAs became increasingly 'more integrative in the last 20 years' by 'reallocating political power among the Three' institutions (Stacey, 2012, p. 397), it is important to examine when and how the Commission chooses to politicise negotiations to ameliorate status and power losses and/or enhance its relevance and power. The EP set a successful example regarding the use of these negotiations to recalibrate (inter)institutional power dynamics: the 2005 Framework Agreement between the EC and EP gave 'the EP a veto power over the nomination of individual commissioners' (Stacey, 2010, p. 197). Therefore, it is important to understand to what extent the Commission learned from EP's success in negotiating IIAs, and is now able to use both agenda-setting and strategic 'politicisation management' (Schimmelfenning, 2020) to get what it wants in negotiations.

This study focuses on the politicisation of interinstitutional negotiations, which taps directly or indirectly into all three forms of politicisation of the EU: 'politicisation of EU institutions, [...] decision-making processes and [...] of issues related to European integration' (De Wilder, 2011, p. 560). In line with the research on the politicisation of EU integration (Grande & Hutter, 2016; Statham & Trenz, 2015), I define politicisation as a process through which: an issue becomes 'a subject of public regulation and/or a subject of public discussion' (De Wilde & Zürn, 2012, p. 139); the visibility/publicity of issues is significantly increased; the range of actors involved in debates is expanded; and a polarisation of actors' positions emerges. Key to this process is the presence of one (or more) political actors that publicly present themselves as representatives and contest other representatives (De Wilder, 2011, p. 560). They fuel and drive the process forward. These actors usually face the challenge of lacking direct democratic legitimacy and a traditional representative mandate. This makes them more prone to use politicisation as a tool of re-legitimatisation. This study adopts a more complex definition of politicisation and departs from more traditional conceptualisations that define it as simply the domination exerted by 'elected politicians' over 'assumed neutral bureaucratic actors' (Smismans, 2017).

I argue that in a hostile environment marked by increasing contestation of its democratic legitimacy, the Commission chooses to use its drafting prerogatives to strategically politicise interinstitutional negotiations. The goal is to increase its legitimacy, enhance its negotiation leverage and maximise chances to shape negotiation outcomes. The Commission decides to engage in political entrepreneurship and 'assertive politicisation' (Bressanelli, Koop, & Reh, 2020). Politicisation is chosen and employed as an instrument of re-legitimisation and empowerment for a bureaucracy facing democratic contestation. Politicisation allows the EC to build input legitimacy, to make a claim the draft agreement was informed by public debates, reflects policy controversies, and is thus embedded in a legitimate process and constitutes an attempt to ensure representation and responsiveness to the European public demands, broadly defined. This in turn legitimatises the Commission's negotiating position and enhances its bargaining power. When drafting the text of IIAs and setting the agenda for negotiations, the Commission can use three dimensions to politicise interinstitutional dialogue: increasing the *public visibility* (publicity) of issues subject to negotiations; increasing the *number of actors* involved in debates; increasing the level of *conflict* over discussed issues. Stakeholder consultations and issue framing are instruments used to implement these dimensions. Adopting a case-study research design, I show how the Commission deployed this politicisation strategy when negotiating two recent agreements: the IIA on a mandatory Transparency Register (still under negotiation since 2016) and the IIA on Better Law-making (2016).

The study builds on the extensive literature on EU agenda-setting (Kreppel & Oztas, 2017), that on the politicisation of supranational policymaking (Rauh, 2019; Van der Veer & Haverland, 2018) and that on politicisation of EU integration in domestic politics (De Wilde, Leupold, & Schmidtke, 2016). Its contribution is threefold. *Conceptually*, it proposes an innovative perspective over the politicisation of EU policymaking from within. It provides one of the few analytical accounts explaining how politicisation can be injected in the EU polity by supranational institutional actors (Schmidt, 2019). In line with the innovative analytical approach proposed by Bressanelli *et al.* in this issue, and different from the mainstream research on EU politicisation, I argue that politicisation is not confined to the realm of domestic politics. Instead, it transcends national arenas and constitutes a phenomenon that plays a key role in EU interinstitutional dialogue. *Theoretically*, the study contributes by illustrating how key dimensions used to politicise the EU in national and multi-level politics also work when deployed by a different kind of political entrepreneur (a supranational bureaucracy) in interinstitutional negotiations. *Empirically*, the study analyses politicisation strategies used in negotiating two IIAs addressing fundamental issues of EU democratic governance. This provides relevant insights illustrating the innovative re-conceptualisation of EU politicisation proposed in this special issue and presents interesting findings about an institutional actor less studied in the literatures on politicisation and IIAs.

## EU interinstitutional agreements

IIAs are informal (non-sanctioned by a third party) accords used by EU institutions to coordinate and further institutionalise their cooperation (Stacey, 2010). Alongside 'unwritten agreements, exchanges of letters, informal declarations, Rules of Procedures' (Stacey, 2010, p. 66), IIAs allow supranational institutions to find suitable solutions to legal, procedural or substantive issues unaddressed or only partially addressed by Treaties. They contribute towards institutionalizing the EU and furthering European integration through informal constitutionalisation of supranational governance. IIAs had distributive effects and 'enhanced the democratic quality of the EU by empowering the EP relative to both the Council and the Commission' (Riekmann, 2007, p. 5). Research unanimously acknowledges their contribution to the parliamentarisation of EU by facilitating a continuous reallocation of powers from Council and Commission to the EP. The Parliament benefited most from agreements on budgetary issues, legislative and oversight procedures, and Council's communication practices (Stacey, 2010). Interinstitutional negotiations helped the EP to shape interinstitutional dynamics. This raises the question of whether, how and to what extent these negotiations are also used by the Commission to address anticipated redistributive consequences of IIAs and eventual power struggles.

A classic interpretation of IIAs is that they are instruments of informal ad-hoc problem-solving and consensus-building that facilitate compromise solutions, and improve in time collaboration and the overall quality of interinstitutional relations (Riekmann, 2007). Traditionally, IIAs involved a limited number of actors: a combination of two of the three main EU institutions. They were concluded through informal negotiations conducted behind closed doors, enjoying little publicity and formal recording. This feature makes their empirical research notoriously difficult (Stacey, 2010, p. 76). Opaqueness facilitated compromise-building, scaling-down disagreement and avoiding actors' polarisation. This is why from a functionalist perspective IIA negotiations are a less probable venue for politicisation. This is particularly the case when negotiations revolve around technical specifications of primary law or establishing the working procedures of new institutions: i.e., the Ombudsman or comitology committees (Eiselt & Slominski, 2007, p. 214).

However, an alternative view indicates that 'IIAs are often used by institutional actors as a lever to pursue a given political goal, thus causing interinstitutional conflict' (Eiselt *et al.*, 2007, p. 77). When negotiating "higher level' issues such as general principles of democracy' (Eiselt & Slominski, 2007, p. 215), political entrepreneurs may seek to achieve specific goals and enhance their power. They use the drafting of IIA text proposed for negotiations as an opportunity to increase the publicity surrounding negotiations, the level of policy conflict and the number of actors involved in debates. Here, negotiations are susceptible to politicisation.

Stacey (2010:, pp. 100–103) proposed a threefold typology of IIAs, using as key criteria the amount and type of institutional change introduced. Category I are *procedural agreements* bringing little to no institutional change or power shifts but merely 'institutionalise the status quo' (the 1994 IIA on the codification of legal texts). Category II are *substantive agreements* that 'adjust interorganisational relations' and introduce small institutional changes that augment authority (the 2003 IIA on better law-making). Category III are *substantive agreements* introducing new rules which alter significantly the balance of power and result in 'power transfers' between institutions (the 2007 IIA on co-decision, the 2006 IIA on comitology, the 1993 IIA on budgetary discipline). Stacey's study shows a constant increase in the number of substantive agreements indicative of their role in furthering integration.

## The Commission and the politicisation of interinstitutional negotiations

This study examines the Commission's approach to interinstitutional negotiations. It builds on a classic model of politicisation proposed by De Wilde and Zürn (2012), filtered through the theoretical lenses of agenda-setting and bureaucratic politics. This model contends that an increase in levels of EU authority increases the likelihood that European integration issues (which are otherwise decided in elitist and secluded decision-making forums) enter the public sphere and become subject to increased levels of public scrutiny and controversy. This leads to their politicisation, evident in rising publicity and citizen awareness, increased mobilisation of actors and resources in policy controversies and a polarisation of key actors' demands and positions (De Wilde & Zürn, 2012, p. 141).

This theoretical approach is justified in two ways. First, IIAs contribute to furthering integration by consolidating and institutionalizing the supranational institutional order. Over time, they contribute towards increasing EU's authority by strengthening its institutional structures and 'governance fabric', which is fundamental in the politicisation of European integration (De Wilde & Zürn, 2012, p. 140). By strengthening the supranational order, IIAs allow EU institutions to address the pressures coming from both citizens and Member States, which demand increasing the legitimacy and efficiency of supranational institutions and decision-making. Second, IIAs are used to address key issues that remained unaddressed or were only partially addressed in Treaties. Their initiation, negotiation and adoption create a unique *'political opportunity structure'* (De Wilde & Zürn, 2012, p. 143) for political entrepreneurs interested in shifting decision-making from secluded bargaining to public debate (Statham & Trenz, 2013, p. 967).

### *Incentives to politicise negotiations*

Politicisation narratives feature actors that play an active role in driving politicisation by increasing 'issue salience, actor expansion and actor polarisation' (Grande & Hutter, 2016, p. 8). These entrepreneurs are usually parties or political elites when the EU is politicised in domestic politics (Statham & Trenz, 2013). Actors employ politicisation to serve their legitimacy needs. The link between politicisation and legitimacy is explicitly recognised: Zürn (2016, p. 244) describes politicisation as 'the process of confronting EU governance with the normative requirements of a legitimate political order'.

Building on theories of agenda-setting, I argue the role of political entrepreneur setting the agenda of interinstitutional negotiations is played by the institutional actor enjoying the prerogative of drafting the agreement text proposed for negotiations. EP employed this strategy when negotiating

IIAs on budget, legislative procedures and comitology (Stacey, 2010). When the Commission enjoys drafting prerogatives, it has incentives to act as a political entrepreneur and politicise negotiations. These incentives depend on several considerations: whether the agreement is procedural or substantive and whether it tries to institutionalise a practice, modify a procedure or 'overhaul interorganisational rules' (Stacey, 2010, p. 101); whether the agreement leads to a redistribution of power or resources amongst institutions; whether the Commission anticipates opposition to its draft text from counterparts; whether it needs to build a reputation for democratic legitimacy to shape negotiation outcomes.

I contend the Commission has strong incentives to politicise negotiations when the agreement is *substantive* and proposes *a non-negligible (relevant yet moderate) amount of change* to the interinstitutional power dynamics. The level of politicisation varies according to the amount of change proposed: the more significant the change of status quo, the higher the politicisation of negotiations in order to create the policy and political momentum required for a shift in the institutional status quo. The amount of change proposed constitutes the key background condition that takes precedence over all others.

Second in importance is a consideration of whether the proposed text and status quo change will result in power or autonomy losses on behalf of any of IIA signatories. High levels of politicisation are more likely when either the Commission or its negotiation counterparts expect to incur important power or autonomy losses. If the Commission incurs losses, it has incentives to politicise negotiations in order to increase its bargaining power and try to prevent or reduce the magnitude of these losses by moving negotiations outcomes closer to its ideal point. If the EP and/or the Council incur losses, the Commission anticipates high levels of opposition during negotiations on their behalf. The Commission has incentives to politicise negotiations to increase its bargaining power, fight effectively against this opposition and shape negotiation outcomes. In both scenarios, the Commission needs to enter negotiations with a draft IIA text for which it can claim input legitimacy and a solid democratic mandate that would enhance its negotiation leverage and allow it to overcome opposition to proposed measures (Van der Veer & Haverland, 2018). Table 1 summarises this. When all or some of these conditions emerge, the Commission deploys its politicisation strategy described next.

## ***Politicisation strategy: dimensions***

Building on bureaucratic politics research, I argue the Commission has incentives to act as a 'purposeful opportunist' and a political entrepreneur (Kreppel & Oztas, 2017) during negotiations. It strategically uses a *three-dimensional politicisation strategy,* congruent with de Wilde and Zürn's model. First, it

**Table 1.** Conditions informing the Commission's incentives to politicise negotiations.

| Background condition | Power or autonomy losses foresight | Legitimacy need | Incentives to politicise |
|---|---|---|---|
| Substantive IIA proposing significant change | Important autonomy or power losses for any of the IIA signatories<br>EC anticipates opposition from EP and/or Council if they incur power or autonomy losses | EC needs input legitimacy to boost its negotiation leverage/power | High |
| Substantive IIA proposing relevant but largely incremental change | Limited distributive consequences and autonomy or power losses for any of the IIA signatories<br>EC anticipates limited opposition on behalf of EP and/or Council | EC does not need input legitimacy to boost its negotiation leverage/ power | Low |

increases the visibility/publicity of agreement's substantive content and negotiations. Second, it expands the number and range of actors involved in debates. Third, it creates controversy and increases conflict over text and negotiations. The ultimate goal is strengthening the Commission's input legitimacy and eventually enhancing its power to shape negotiation outcomes. The extent to which the Commission employs all three or a combination of these dimensions provides an indication of how much politicisation it decides to inject in negotiations.

### *Politicisation strategy: instruments*

To implement this strategy, the Commission employs two key instruments available to bureaucratic agenda-setters: the prerogative to consult stakeholders during policy-formulation and the advantage of issue framing early in the policy cycle (Daviter, 2007). *Stakeholder consultations* contribute to politicisation by increasing publicity, facilitating the participation of the public and stakeholders in policymaking and increasing conflict and controversy (Smismans, 2017). The Commission enjoys high levels of discretion on when and how to consult (Bunea & Thomson, 2015, p. 520). Therefore, consultations may inject varying levels of politicisation, depending on their format: open vs. closed consultations. Consultation format affects levels of issue publicity, the number and types of actors involved in policy controversy and the polarisation of decision-makers' and stakeholders' positions. Consultations impact on all three politicisation dimensions. Open consultations are particularly well-suited to increase publicity, expand the universe of involved actors and facilitate polarisation. These consultations are likely to inject *high levels of politicisation* in negotiations. Conversely, closed consultations such as public hearings or advisory groups (in which participation is by invitation-only and access is restricted) decrease publicity, reduce the number of engaged actors and

**Table 2.** Dimensions and instruments for politicising negotiations.

| Incentives to politicise | Politicisation dimensions | Politicisation instruments | Levels of politicisation |
|---|---|---|---|
| High | Increase publicity<br>Expand universe of actors involved in debate<br>Increase controversy and conflict | Open consultations & Political frames | High |
| Low | Limit publicity<br>Limit the universe of actors involved in debate<br>Limit controversy and conflict | Closed consultations & Technical frames | Low |

facilitate compromise solutions, which in turn prevents polarisation. These consultations inject a significantly *lower level of politicisations* in negotiations.

*Issue framing* represents a key EC agenda-setting strategy to increase publicity and build credibility/authority over policy issues (Princen, 2011, p. 931). The literature distinguishes *generic* vs. *specific frames, policy vs. institutional frames* (Eising, Rasch, & Rozbicka, 2015) and *thematic frames* (i.e., public, economic) (Klüver, Mahoney, & Opper, 2015). The distinction between *political* and *technical frames* is particularly relevant here because they capture 'a classic choice made available to the Commission [on] whether to 'politicise' or 'depoliticise' a particular issue' (Rhinard 2010: 31). Political frames emphasise the political weight of an issue and its alignment with political priorities. Technical frames highlight policy implications and emphasise technical details to explain or justify a policy option. These two frames contribute differently towards politicising IIA negotiations. *Political frames* increase publicity, augment conflict, expand mobilisation of stakeholders and facilitate polarisation. They contribute to all three politicisation dimensions. Conversely, *technical frames* increase issue-publicity only among specific, specialised stakeholders. They address a restricted audience and mobilise fewer actors and employ evidence-based arguments in debates. They are less partisan in nature and less polarizing. They contribute towards decreasing levels of politicisation.

Table 2 summarises this argument and the theoretical expectations regarding the combination of politicisation dimensions and instruments leading to different levels of politicisation. It is worth noting that since procedural IIAs propose the institutionalisation of a procedural status quo, the Commission has no incentives to politicise their negotiations. Therefore, these agreements are not included in the analytical and theoretical focus of this analysis.

## Research Design

This study examines two recently negotiated IIAs for which the Commission was agenda-setter: the 2016 IIA on Better Law-making (2016/512 OJ

L 123) and the IIA on a mandatory Transparency Register (2016/2829, under negotiation). It employs a qualitative, comparative case-study approach suitable for its theory-testing focus. This design allows circumventing some important challenges in mapping and examining empirically IIAs: a high variety of their format and substantive content and, absolutely crucial, the informal character of negotiations preceding their adoption (Stacey, 2010). This makes a large-n, comparative study of IIAs negotiations virtually impossible and justifies the case-study approach and focus on recent agreements.

A complete list of IIAs is currently missing. A research team at the University of Innsbruck attempted once the task of their systematic identification. Their list includes 123 accords titles concluded between 1958–2005 and provides a brief content description. It provides no information about negotiations. This makes impossible the systematic reconstruction of the contextual variables and relevant information allowing a large-n, empirical assessment of whether, how and to what extent politicisation played a role in negotiations. Identifying the texts of agreements included in this list proved equally challenging and possible only for texts concluded after 1990.

## *Case selection*

This study adopts a theory-centric approach (Beach & Pedersen, 2013: 144). It aims to test empirically the theoretical conjectures developed to explain when and how the European executive has incentives to politicise interinstitutional negotiations. The case selection technique employs the *logic of diverse cases.* This strategy allows 'the achievement of maximum variance along relevant dimensions' (Seawright & Gerring, 2008, p. 300). The two cases illustrate the range of values relevant for the explanans: type of substantive agreement (introducing significant vs. incremental change) and contextual conditions.

They are *substantive agreements* aiming to introduce new procedures and rules relevant for policymaking and institutional dynamics. Both tackled relevant issues of democratic governance. They differ with respect to the amount of change proposed. The IIA on Better Law-making proposed relevant yet *incremental* changes to the institutional status quo, and did not involve major shifts in the institutional power balance (Stacey's category II agreement). The IIA on a mandatory TR proposed a significant change: it proposed a mandatory register, that the Council would join, despite it rejecting this for years, and that the EP makes all interactions between MEPs and interest groups (conducted both inside and outside EP premises) conditional upon groups' registration. This agreement imposed more constraints on the Council and EP and resulted in important (re)distributive effects (Stacey's category III agreement). Differences in substantive content correspond to differences in *contextual conditions* structuring the Commission's incentives to politicise negotiations to different extents. This enables the empirical test and illustrating the theoretical argument.

I used qualitative content analysis of primary data sources to identify relevant information about the IIAs. I used news reports, official statements and online press releases of institutional actors to document the contextual conditions of negotiations. To document the EC's politicisation strategies, I used official documents issued by the Commission (e.g., EC Communication on Better EU law-making, 2016 Political Guidelines, official reports on consultations, etc.) and the EP Legislative Observatory.

## Analysis

### *Negotiating the IIA on a mandatory TR: high politicisation*

This agreement proposed important status quo changes regarding the transparency of interactions between decision-makers and interest organisations. The draft agreement asked the EP and Council to increase the amount of publicly available information about their interactions with private actors. The autonomy losses incurred by the legislative actors were important, while the Commission entailed no further costs since it was already implementing similar measures and treating the Register as being *de facto* mandatory (Bunea, 2018). The IIA did not imply a transfer of powers between institutions but imposed significantly more formal constraints on EP and Council, which unsettled the institutional power balance. Moreover, the agreement offered the Commission the opportunity to become a champion of lobbying regulation and transparent politics and policymaking.

The Commission anticipated high levels of opposition from EP and Council to its draft text because of these constraints and because regulating the interactions between organisations and decision-makers was always a contentious issue in interinstitutional dialogue (Bunea, 2018). This is evident in the slow progress of negotiations that are still ongoing since October 2016. In a November 2018 press interview, Sylvie Guillaume, EP Vice-President and member of the Constitutional Affairs Committee negotiating the agreement, highlighted important disagreements between EC and EP regarding key issues such as definition of lobbying and what would be a suitable regulatory regime for MEPs. She openly admitted the presence of a 'stalemate' in negotiations (Euractiv, 2018).

Thus, the Commission had incentives and chose to politicise negotiations to a significant extent so as to increase its legitimacy and enhance its leverage to shape negotiation outcomes (scenario one in Table 1).

***Increasing publicity***

The Commission employed both consultations and framing to increase the publicity of its draft agreement and its negotiation. As part of its formulation process, the Commission organised a broad public stakeholder consultation, explicitly entitled *'Public Consultation on a proposal for a mandatory TR'* (March-June 2016). The draft agreement was sent to legislators following the consultation, in September 2016. The Commission intensely publicised the consultation which attracted a very high number of stakeholders. The important role played by this consultation in EC's politicisation strategy is evident in the explanatory memo accompanying the press release announcing the draft agreement: *'[t]oday's proposal follows intensive discussions carried out with all relevant stakeholders. A 12-week public consultation concluded on 1 June, receiving 1,758 replies, with 975 responses from individual citizens and 783 from organisations Respondents shared their views on the functioning of the current TR and put forward suggestions for the design of the future regime'* (EC, 2016b). This explanatory text described at length how the Commission prepared the proposal based on stakeholders' views expressed in the broad public consultation. This consultation helped the Commission to increase the publicity of its initiative amongst stakeholders and the European public, and to publicly signal its negotiation partners that its draft text was formulate together with and having the support of large parts of this public (Bunea, 2018). This constitutes an evident attempt to politicise negotiations and enhance EC's input legitimacy.

The memo also mentions a public debate hosted by the EP Vice-President Sylvie Guillaume and Commission First Vice-President Timmermans, bringing together *'stakeholders from Brussels as well as Member States, to debate key themes of the consultation'* (EC, 2016b). This closed (targeted) consultation complemented the open one and indicates their possible co-existence in the formulation of draft agreements and legislative initiatives. What is however absolutely crucial is the Commission purposely organised a broad public consultation attracting the participation of high numbers of citizens and organisations, and it could thus show its proposed measures were widely supported by the European public broadly defined.

Furthermore, the Commission framed the issue of transparency and lobbying regulation as a top political priority. President Juncker's tenth political priority ('A Union of Democratic Change') and commitment was: *'to enhanced transparency when it comes to contact with stakeholders and lobbyists. Our citizens have the right to know with whom Commissioners and Commission staff, Members of the EP or representatives of the Council meet in the context of the legislative process. I will therefore propose an Inter-Institutional Agreement to Parliament and Council to create a mandatory lobby register covering all three institutions. The Commission will lead by example in this process'* (Political

Guidelines , p. 12). This signals the strong political charge of interinstitutional dialogue around a long-lasting controversy: finding an optimal regulatory regime for supranational lobbying.

Second, the Commission framed the adoption of a mandatory Register as a basic yet fundamental democratic issue of institutional credibility and openness. The press release announcing the agreement quoted Timmermans stating that: *'EU institutions need to work together to win back the trust of our citizens. We must be more open in everything we do'* (EC, 2016a). To strengthen this political frame, the explanatory memo accompanying the press release highlights the initiative was announced in the 2014 Political Guidelines as a Commission priority and was included in its Work Programme. The agreement was *'delivering on this [political] commitment'* (EC, 2016b).

### *Expanding the universe of actors*

Consultations and (political) issue framing also helped expanding the universe of actors aware of the initiative and engaged in its formulation and negotiation. The public stakeholder consultation helped increasing the number and diversity of organisations involved in the *public debate*. The consultation attracted an unusually high number of citizens from across all EU Member States (Bunea, 2018, p. 365), and organisations representing various interests: business organisations, public interests, consultancies, professional, local and regional authorities. Some organisations had a representative mandate and participated in consultation as European, national or regional/local-level representative associations.

Issue framing helped expanding the universe of institutional actors involved in the *interinstitutional debate*. The EC press statement accompanying the release of the draft agreement explicitly mentioned that the agreement aims to make *'all three institutions – including the Council – [to] be subject to the same minimum standards for the first time'* (EC, 2016a). The Commission framed transparency as a collective institutional responsibility, which is a political frame. The memo accompanying the press statement detailed all institutional and political actors covered by the register: *'MEPs, the Secretary-General, Directors-General and Secretaries-General of political groups'*, and the Council's *'Secretary-General and Directors-General or the Ambassador of the current or forthcoming Presidency, as well as their deputies'* (EC, 2016b). It also indicated the draft agreement *'foresees a mechanism allowing Member States, on a voluntary basis, to make certain interactions with their Permanent Representations conditional upon prior registration'* (EC, 2016b). This explicit, detailed mention increased the universe of institutional actors involved in debate and emphasised the political stake of negotiations.

### *Increasing controversy*

To increase controversy and conflict around negotiations, the Commission employed both consultations and issue framing. First, since the Commission knew the Council's longstanding reluctance to join any lobbying regulation regime, it asked stakeholders participating in the public consultation to indicate whether they 'agree with the Commission's view that the Council of the EU should participate in the new Inter-institutional Agreement on a mandatory Register'. An overwhelming majority of respondents agreed. This increased the public legitimacy of the proposal to include the Council in a mandatory register but increased controversy and conflict around the issue of lobbying regulation in general and of lobbying the Council in particular.

Second, the Commission used issue framing to increase the controversy around the agreement. It discarded the EP's insistent requirement to regulate interactions between institutions and organisations with the help of a binding regulatory instrument, i.e., a regulation or directive. Instead, it proposed an interinstitutional agreement. This move indirectly yet explicitly framed transparency and lobbying regulation as a political matter pertaining to the EU constitutional order and not a matter of ordinary regulatory policymaking. This political frame elevated the matter from a low-order policy issue to a high-order political one, susceptible to more public scrutiny, controversy and conflict.

## *Negotiating the IIA on Better Law-making: low politicisation*

This agreement aimed to enhance the transparency, accountability and efficiency of supranational policymaking. It did not imply a reallocation of power between institutions nor autonomy losses on behalf of signatories. The changes proposed were relevant but substantively incremental. For example, the provisions required the Commission to implement a set of measures to increase transparency of its decision-making: the agreement stipulated the Commission had to set up a joint public register of delegated and implementing acts to increase the public oversight of their adoption. This tackled the Commission's prerogative to adopt non-legislative acts that change non-essential aspects of legislative decisions. Another example is the EC obligation to consult Member State experts when preparing delegated acts and allowing EP and Council experts to access all expert groups engaged in drafting these acts. These changes were relevant but incremental: the Commission was asked to essentially extend to a more diverse set of processes and acts the transparency and public information provision regime used for formulating legislative proposals.

The agreement imposed more constraints on the Commission, and significantly fewer on the EP and Council. The legislative actors were required to carry out impact assessments in relation to their substantial amendments of

Commission's proposals only 'when they consider this appropriate and necessary for the legislative process' (EC, 2015b). However, the constraints faced by EC also enhanced its institutional reputation and provided important benefits. The agreement increased the amount of public information about supranational governance and its provisions made the Commission a champion of transparent decision-making (EC, 2015a). The Commission secured important reputational gains from the agreement which compensated for the additional transparency and procedural constraints imposed by it. The overall distributive consequences of the agreement were limited, in line with scenario two in Table 1. Furthermore, the Commission anticipated limited opposition on behalf of EP and Council given that these actors were incurring significantly fewer constraints as part of the agreement. The Commission's need to build input legitimacy to strengthen its negotiation leverage was much lower than in the negotiations on a mandatory TR agreement. So were its incentives to politicise the negotiations. The expectation is the Commission decided to limit publicity and controversy around its draft agreement and to limit the universe of actors involved in debate with the help of closed consultations and technical frames.

However, the empirical evidence points otherwise: the observed politicisation dimensions and instruments diverged from the expected pattern. Instead of using closed consultations and technical frames to limit publicity, the universe of actors and levels of controversy and conflict, the Commission used political frames to increase the level of publicity, expand the universe of actors responsible for the implementation of the agreement, increase public controversy but limit institutional conflict (EC, 2015a and 2015b). Although two public consultations preceded the drafting of the agreement[1], the Commission decided not to use and reference them in support of its draft text. Closed consultations were also missing from the formulation process, contrary to the expectations outlined in Table 2 regarding a scenario in which the Commission has low incentives to politicise. Overall, this case presents lower levels of politicisation than the previous one (in line with the theoretical argument) but the politicisation instruments used differ significantly from the ones expected. Issue framing played a significantly more important role in this politicisation strategy than consultations.

### *Managing publicity*

Contrary to the theoretical expectations, the Commission used political frames to deal with the publicity of the draft agreement and its negotiation. This increased its publicity and visibility. This was evident when the new Juncker Commission defined better regulation as a key political issue at the heart of his political agenda. His political guidelines explicitly linked better regulation to *'restoring European citizens' confidence'* and *'strengthening democratic legitimacy on the basis of the Community method'* (2014 Political Guidelines: 1). Adopting a new IIA on better regulation was framed as a top political priority: Juncker committed *'to entrust the responsibility for better regulation to one of the Vice-Presidents in [his] Commission'* (Idem: 4). The Commission's First Vice-President would become responsible for better regulation and interinstitutional relations. This signalled EC's political commitment to the better regulation agenda and an explicit political framing of the initiative.

Later on, the EC press release announcing the proposal for an IIA on Better Law-making used a political frame by explicitly linking better regulation measures with the democratic performance of supranational policymaking: they *'will open up the EU decision-making process, allowing for more transparency and scrutiny, and providing more opportunities for people to give their views'* (EC, 2015a).

### *Identifying the responsible actors*

Issue framing was also used to explicitly identify and define the universe of institutional and private actors responsible for the successful implementation of the agreement. First, the EC press release introducing the draft agreement stated that: *'Better Regulation can only work if it is a shared commitment of the Commission, Council and EP'* (EC, 2015a). Second, the release described one of it key provisions (the Regulatory Fitness and Performance Programme REFIT) by comprehensively indicating all public and private actors that would be actively engaged in its design, implementation and performance: *'the REFIT Platform will bring together high-level experts from business, civil society, social partners, the Economic and Social Committee, the Committee of Regions and Member States'* (EC, 2015a). This 'collective responsibility' political frame expanded the number of relevant actors from across levels of government that were considered responsible for the design and performance of key parts of the agreement. This move aimed to increase the publicity of the agreement amongst these responsible actors.

### *Managing controversy and conflict*

To increase controversy but keep conflict low, the Commission used again the political frame of collective responsibility for the adoption of the agreement, projected over all three European institutions. The explanatory memo accompanying the press statement announcing the draft agreement publicly acknowledged that although better regulation *'concerns its own working methods'*, the Commission *'cannot deliver this agenda alone'* and therefore *'it relies on a commitment from the co-legislators to do their part'* (EC, 2015b). Therefore, *'the inter-institutional agreement proposed to the Parliament and Council calls on them to take up their responsibilities for [it]'* (EC, 2015b). To increase pressure on counterparts, a timeline for reaching an agreement was mentioned: *'the Commission's ambition is to finalise negotiations on this agreement before the end of 2015'* (EC, 2015b).

Political frames were also used to reduce conflict by systematically explaining why and how the draft agreement does not constitute a 'power grab' attempt on behalf of Commission (Euractiv, 2015). The EC invoked the power conferred by Treaties to the EP and Council and explicitly stated that no power transfers would ensue following the agreement: *'All of the measures set out today are in full respect for the imperative of the co-legislators in the EP and Council. These powers are clearly defined in the Treaties and the Commission is not seeking to change them'* (EC, 2015b). This was meant to reduce conflict by reassuring its negotiation counterparts that no direct or indirect transfer of power or authority would follow the agreement. Similarly, to tackle the potentially divisive provision demanding the EP and Council to conduct impact assessments for any major amendments of Commission proposals, the European executive publicly indicated that this measure was *'not seeking to reduce the political scope of the Parliament or Council, it is merely asking them to consider the impact of any major amendments they propose'*. This reduced conflict by subtly juxtaposing the political logic of legislative decision-making with the evidence-based fundamentals of bureaucratic policymaking (illustrated by impact assessments), while openly recognizing the primacy of the former over the latter in the context of EU decision-making.

## Conclusions

This study built on theories of EU politicisation and examined the role of politicisation in the negotiation of IIAs. It focused on the Commission and argued that politicisation strategies employed in domestic politics by political elites also serve supranational entrepreneurs facing the challenge of re-legitimisation in a hostile policy environment. The study outlined the conditions under which the Commission has incentives to act as a purposeful political entrepreneur and use stakeholder consultations and issue framing to implement its (otherwise classic) politicisation strategy. Empirically, it examined two recent agreements and showed why and how the negotiations of the agreement on a mandatory TR were significantly more politicised than the ones on better law-making. The extent of politicisation varied in line with theorised background conditions, indicative that politicisation is deployed when EC's re-legitimisation needs are high, the distributive effects of changes are significant and it anticipates hostile negotiation partners. The study refined, extended and tailored the application of concepts and arguments developed in the mainstream research on the politicisation of EU (De Wilde, Leupold, & Schmidtke, 2016; Grande & Hutter, 2016; Zürn, 2016) to a less examined yet fundamental for European integration decision-making venue: the negotiation of IIAs.

The study proposed stakeholder consultations and issue framing as relevant instruments of politicisation the Commission strategically uses as part of agenda-setting and formulation prerogatives. This contributes to the research describing the toolkit of politicisation strategies political entrepreneurs employ and deploy at supranational (and national) level (Rauh, 2019; Schmidt, 2019). The first case illustrated well the link between theorised contextual conditions and the corresponding dimensions and strategies. The evidence about the second case diverged significantly from the argument regarding politicisation instruments, suggestive that the relative and absolute importance of the two politicisation tools (consultations and framing) may vary significantly across contexts and events.

The study circumvented important challenges of empirically studying EU informal governance: the reconstruction of contextual variables describing agenda-setting and negotiation dynamics. Yet it is also marked by clear shortcomings: a limited power to generalise its findings to a broader set of IIAs. This represents a venue for further research and motivates a research agenda aiming to reconstruct in a systematic manner the complexity of negotiations for recent and future agreements by mapping the positions of institutional actors and stakeholders, actors' moves during negotiation stages, decision-making outcomes and characteristics of policy context.

## Note

1. The 2012 'Stakeholder Consultation on Smart Regulation in the EU' and the 2014 consultation on 'Draft Stakeholder Consultation Guidelines'.

## Acknowledgements

The author is grateful to Christine Reh, Christel Koop, Edoardo Bressanelli and Raimondas Ibenskas for their constant and helpful feedback on this manuscript. A special thank you goes to Christine Reh for her kind and wise advice on key conceptual and analytical aspects of the article.

## Disclosure statement

No potential conflict of interest was reported by the author.

## Funding

This article is part of a project that has received funding from the European Research Council (ERC ) under the European Union's Horizon 2020 research and innovation programme (ERC StG 2018 CONSULTATIONEFFECTS, grant agreement no. 804288).

## ORCID

*Adriana Bunea* http://orcid.org/0000-0002-2348-9676

## References

Beach, D., & Pedersen, R. B. (2013). *Process-tracing methods: Foundations and guidelines*. Oxford: Oxford University Press.

Blauberger, M., & Martinsen, D. (2020). The court of justice in times of politicisation: 'law as a mask and shield' revisited. *Journal of European Public Policy*, *27*(3), 382–399.

Bressanelli, E., Koop, C., & Reh, C. (2020). EU actors under pressure: Politicisation and depoliticisation as strategic responses. *Journal of European Public Policy*, *27*(3), 329–341.

Bunea, A. (2018). Legitimacy through targeted transparency? Regulatory effectiveness and sustainability of lobbying regulation in the European Union. *European Journal of Political Research*, *57*(2), 378–403.

Bunea, A., & Thomson, R. (2015). Consultations with interest groups and the empowerment of executives: evidence from the European Union. *Governance*, *28*(4), 517–531.

Cini, M. (2013). EU decision-making on inter-institutional agreements: Defining (common) rules of conduct for European lobbyists and public servants. *West European Politics*, *36*(6), 1143–1158.

Daviter, F. (2007). Policy framing in the European Union. *Journal of European Public Policy*, *14*(40), 654–666.

De Wilde, P., Leupold, A., & Schmidtke, H. (2016). Introduction: The differentiated politicisation of European governance. *West European Politics*, *39*(1), 3–22.

De Wilde, P., & Zürn, M. (2012). Can the politicisation of European integration be reversed? *Journal of Common Market Studies*, *50*(1), 137–153.

De Wilder, P. (2011). No polity for old politics? A framework for analysing the politicisation of European integration. *Journal of European Integration*, *33*(5), 559–575.

Eiselt, I., Pollak, J., & Slominski, P. (2007). Codifying temporary stability? The role of inter-institutional agreements in budgetary affairs. *European Law Journal*, *13*(1), 75–91.

Eiselt, I. and Slominski, P. (2007) 'Sub-constitutional engineering: Negotiation, content, and legal value of interinstitutional agreement in the EU', *European Law Journal* 12 (2): 209–225.

Eising, R., Rasch, D. and Rozbicka, P. (2015). Institutions, policies, and arguments: Context and strategy in EU policy framing. *Journal of European Public Policy*, 22(4): 516–533.

Euractiv. (2015). *Commission denies power grab claims over 'Better Regulation'*. May 19th, 2015. Retrieved from https://www.euractiv.com/section/science-policymaking/news/commission-denies-power-grab-claims-over-better-regulation/.

Euractiv. (2018). *Parliament VP: We cannot 'copy and paste' Commission transparency rules*. November 17th, 2018. Retrieved from https://www.euractiv.com/section/politics/interview/parliament-vp-we-cannot-copy-and-paste-commission-transparency-rules/.

European Commission. (2015a). *Better Regulation Agenda: Enhancing transparency and scrutiny for better EU law-making*. Press release. (Strasbourg, 19.05.2015).

European Commission. (2015b). Fact Sheet. *Better Regulation Agenda: Questions and Answers*. (Strasbourg, 19.05.2015).

European Commission. (2016a). *Delivering on transparency: Commission proposes mandatory Transparency Register for all EU institutions*. Press release. (Brussels, 28.09.2016).

European Commission. (2016b). Fact Sheet. *Questions and Answers: Proposal for an Interinstitutional Agreement on a mandatory Transparency Register*. (Brussels, 28 September).

Grande, E., & Hutter, S. (2016). Introduction: Europe integration and the challenge of politicisation. In S. Hutter, E. Grande, & H. Kriesi (Eds.), *Politicising Europe: Integration and mass politics* (pp. 3–31). Cambridge: Cambridge University Press.

Haverland, M., de Ruiter, M., & Van de Walle, S. (2018). Agenda-setting by the European Commission. Seeking the public? *Journal of European Public Policy*, *25*(3), 327–345.

Kietz, D., & Maurer, A. (2007). The European Parliament in treaty reform: Predefining ICGs through interinstitutional agreements. *European Law Journal*, *13*(1), 20–46.

Klüver, H., Mahoney, C. and Opper, M. (2015). Framing in context: How interest groups employs framing to lobby the European Commission. *Journal of European Public Policy*, 22(4): 481–498.

Kreppel, A., & Oztas, B. (2017). Leading the band or just playing the tune? Reassessing the agenda-setting powers of the European Commission. *Comparative Political Studies*, *50*(8), 1118–1150.

Monar, J. (1994). Inter-institutional agreements: The phenomenon and its new dynamics after Maastricht. *Common Market Law Review*, *31*, 693–719.

President Juncker's Political Guidelines for the Next European Commission. Opening statement in the European Parliament Session. (Strasbourg, 15.07.2014). Retrieved from https://ec.europa.eu/commission/publications/president-junckers-political-guidelines_en.

Princen, S. (2011). Agenda-setting strategies in EU policy processes. *Journal of European Public Policy*, *18*(7), 927–943.

Rauh, C. (2019). EU politicisation and policy initiatives of the European Commission: The case of consumer policy. *Journal of European Public Policy*, *26*(3), 344–365.

Reh, C., Bressanelli, E., & Koop, C. (2020). Responsive withdrawal? The politics of EU agenda-setting. *Journal of European Public Policy*, *27*(3), 419–438.

Rhinard, M. (2010). *Framing Europe: The policy shaping strategies of the European Commission*. Dordrecht: Mrtinhus Nijhoff Publishers.

Riekmann, S. P. (2007). The cocoon of power: Democratic implications of interinstitutional agreements. *European Law Journal*, *13*(1), 4–19.

Schimmelfenning, F. (2020). Politicisation management in the European Union. *Journal of European Public Policy*, *27*(3), 342–361.

Schmidt, A. V. (2019) Politicisation in the EU: Between national politics and EU political dynamics. *Journal of European Public Policy*, 26(7): 1018–1036.

Seawright, J., & Gerring, J. (2008). Case selection techniques in case study research: A menu of qualitative and quantitative options. *Political Research Quarterly*, *61*(2), 294–308.

Smismans, S. (2017). The politicisation of ex post policy evaluation in the EU. *European Journal of Law Reform*, *19*(1), 74–96.

Stacey, J. (2010) *Integrating Europe. Informal politics and institutional change*. Oxford: Oxford University Press.

Stacey, J. (2012) Informal governance in the EU: The European Commission versus the European Parliament. In T. Christiansen and C. Neuhold (Eds.), *International handbook of informal governance* (pp. 395–411) Cheltenham: Edward Elgar.

Statham, P., & Trenz, H. J. (2013). How European Union politicisation can emerge through contestation: The constitution case. *Journal of Commons Market Studies, 51*(5), 965–980.

Statham, P., & Trenz, H. J. (2015). Understanding the mechanisms of EU politicisation: Lessons from the Eurozone crisis. *Comparative European Politics, 13*(3), 287–306.

Van der Veer, R. A., & Haverland, M. (2018). Bread and butter or bread and circuses? Politicisation and the European Commission in the European Semester. *European Union Politics, 19*(3), 524–545.

Wille, A. (2013) *The normalization of the European Commission politics and bureaucracy in the EU Executive*. Oxford: Oxford University Press.

Zürn, M. (2016). Opening up Europe: Next steps in politicisation research. *West European Politics, 39*(1), 164–118.

# Politicisation and economic governance design

Fabio Franchino and Camilla Mariotto

**ABSTRACT**
The functional pressures shaping policy design may be disrupted in salient policies and politicised contexts, according to recent postfunctionalist/new intergovernmentalist theories. We contrast these expectations with those derived from liberal intergovernmentalism and neofunctionalism by analysing the reforms of the European Union economic governance. Its Council-centred enforcement, which has been a dominant feature until the euro crisis, despite noncompliance, does not sit comfortably with traditional theories but can be explained by policy salience and implementation uncertainties. Instead, the emphasis that traditional approaches assign to noncompliance, commitment problems, threats of exclusion and veto, issue linkages, path dependencies and supranational decision-making, allows to adequately account for the overall direction of reforms toward more tightening and delegation, notwithstanding the pooled enforcement in recent ancillary measures. Postfunctionalist theories overall fall short in highly politicised contexts, exactly where they should do most of the explaining. We conclude discussing politicisation as a strategic elite response.

## Introduction

The rules governing economic and fiscal policies in the European Union (EU) are a centrepiece of the economic and monetary union. Over the years, they have become subject to heated public debates. Reforms that originally attracted only the interest of the specialised press generate now broad and polarised public discussions (Kriesi & Grande, 2016, p. 253). How has such politicisation been managed and what are the consequences for the design of these rules? When legislators adopt any EU policy, they take three key design decisions. First, they establish common rules. Second, they determine the modality and extent to which they are involved in policy-making. Third, they determine the prerogatives and constraints of the authorities in charge of implementation. In this article, we compare and contrast expectations of

Supplemental data for this article can be accessed at https://doi.org/10.1080/13501763.2020.1712456.

policy design derived from liberal intergovernmentalism and neofunctionalism with those arising from a new wave of theorising, which originates from postfunctionalism and falls under the general rubric of new intergovernmentalism. These new theories argue that politicisation has consequences for policy design that are unaccounted for by traditional approaches. We subject these claims to test by focusing on a policy that is prone to politicisation and by taking advantage of the fact that its most recent reform was significantly more politicised than previous ones.

Studies of economic governance take mainly one theoretical perspective, such as liberal intergovernmentalism (Biermann, Guérin, Jagdhuber, Rittberger, & Weiss, 2019; Schimmelfennig, 2015), neofunctionalism and its variants (Niemann & Ioannou, 2015; Verdun, 2015) or postfunctionalist-based approaches (e.g., Börzel & Risse, 2018; Fabbrini, 2016; Genschel & Jachtenfuchs, 2018; Puetter, 2012). We follow Heipertz and Verdun (2005, 2010) and Schimmelfennig (2014) and consider all the most relevant theories of policy design. Additionally, most works concentrate solely on the most recent reform. We instead analyse economic governance since its inception, building on the extant analyses of the 1997 and 2005 reforms (Heipertz & Verdun, 2005, 2010; Schure & Verdun, 2008; Segers & van Esch, 2007).

But unlike these studies, we subject expectations to empirical corroboration through a systematic analysis of the bargaining dynamics and the provision-specific patterns of governance design adopted between 1993 and 2013. We conceive the *design* of a policy as characterised by a set of provisions with specific and, occasionally, multiple properties. *Tightening* provisions impose requirements and obligations on national authorities, whereas *loosening* ones relax such demands or offer them leeway. For instance, the deficit and debt reference values in the treaty protocol on excessive deficit procedure tightened control over national fiscal policies, while the adoption in 2005 of country-specific (rather than common) medium-term budgetary objectives (MTOs), which can diverge from a balance position, loosened control. *Pooling* provisions are those where the Council takes decisions by voting procedures other than unanimity and *delegating* ones are those where policy prerogatives are conferred upon the European Commission. Both pooling and delegation can be subject to *constraints*. For instance, the decision to establish the existence of an excessive deficit is pooled within the Council, but until 2005 exceptional circumstances could be granted only in case of an annual fall of real gross domestic product (GDP) of at least 2 per cent. Since 2005, the Commission can amend poor quality data on public finances, subject to prompt communication to the relevant member state and the Economic and Financial Committee.

Do established theories help explain the patterns we observe? Or do they need to be qualified, given the salience and politicisation of the policy? In the conclusion we will engage with the concept of politicisation as strategic response but, for the most part the article, *politicisation* is conceptualised as an expansion of the scope of conflict within national political systems which translates into bottom-up pressures on EU-level actors (Bressanelli, Koop, & Reh, 2020; Schimmelfennig, 2020). We leverage the documented observation that the recent reform was characterised by significantly more extensive and polarised involvement of public actors – two key politicisation dimensions – than earlier ones (Kriesi & Grande, 2016), making such reform a most-likely case for politicisation to shape policy design. How have EU-level actors reacted in response to such pressures? We begin our investigation by introducing the theoretical predictions.

## Integration theories, politicisation and policy design

We limit our attention to integration theories, or variants therein, that offer clear expectations about policy design. Length constraints prevent us from discussing the full richness of these approaches. These expectations focus on tightening, loosening, pooling and delegation.

For liberal intergovernmentalism, pooling and delegation are driven by the need to bolster the *credibility of policy commitments*, when incomplete contracting and incentives to renege on agreements create problems of time consistency (Moravcsik, 1998, pp. 73–77). Pooling and delegation occur when future decisions are *uncertain*, joint gains are high and distributional conflicts are moderate. Pooling entails less loss of governmental control than delegation. It is preferred when policies require additional measures because it undermines unilateral vetoes to secondary legislation. In addition to reducing legislative workload, delegation addresses concerns about domestic compliance and it is more likely in enforcement since a supranational bureaucracy pursues this activity more credibly than a Council of elected ministers. *A higher risk of noncompliance should therefore tilt policy design toward delegation* (i.e., Commission empowerment) *and* plausibly *tightening*.

Opposition is likely to be voiced by governments that expect being either in a minority position or noncompliant. The preferences of governments with superior bargaining power, resulting from asymmetric interdependence, eventually shape outcomes. Most influential are those that (a) place relatively higher value to the best alternative to an agreement and (b) can form viable alternative coalitions that are costly to the excluded countries. The first situation underlies credible *threats to veto*, the second credible *threats to exclude*. *Issue linkages* may play a role as well, but within issue areas, if interests are asymmetrically distributed, benefits concentrated and costs diffused (Moravcsik, 1998, pp. 60–67).

Neofunctionalism encompasses more variegated contributions but a common thread is the emphasis on *endogeneity*, as well as uncertainty, in policy design (e.g., Heipertz & Verdun, 2010, pp. 64–67; Schimmelfennig,

2014, pp. 326–327). According to its institutionalist variant, past decisions have profound consequences for current bargaining because of endogenous interdependencies, spillovers and path dependencies (Garrett & Tsebelis, 1996; Pierson, 1996). Consider an obvious example: a flexible exchange rate is costlier now for Eurozone countries compared to when they were members of the European monetary system. The uncertainty and *exit cost* associated with leaving a monetary union are significant, effectively precluding this option.

Except for the need of centralised expertise which may justify delegation, neofunctionalism does not suggest new logics of policy design (Schimmelfennig, 2014, p. 334). One of its key insights is that a more supranational policy process may lead to different outcomes (i.e., a 'cultivated' spillover effect). The agent/agenda setter's position, institutional hurdles (lower voting thresholds), inter-institutional conflicts may all shape the final design. For instance, demands for tightening and delegation are more likely to be met under qualified majority voting since recalcitrant governments, preferring ample national discretion and narrowly defined Commission's competences, can be overruled. The outcome may tilt further in this direction under the ordinary legislative procedure if the position of European Parliament is closer to that of the supranational executive than to that of the Council (Franchino, 2007, pp. 64–65, 285–286).

There is however reason to believe that these traditional rationales may not be at play. According to Genschel and Jachtenfuchs (2018, pp. 181–182), fiscal policy is a core state power where bargaining is zero-sum. Compliance falls predominantly on governmental rather than societal actors; it faces tighter capacity constraints and may require the building up of capacity at the EU level. Negotiations are therefore highly politicised. Moreover, the bargaining context has changed. In a study of six European countries, Kriesi and Grande (2016, p. 253) report that the latest economic governance reform has been 'the integration debate with the highest public visibility' in the mass media since the early 1970s. Its politicisation, including the involvement and polarisation of actors, was on a par with the debate on the ratification of the Maastricht Treaty. In sum, economic governance is more politicised than other policies and its politicisation has increased over time.

Accordingly, Schimmelfennig (2014, p. 322) argues that the recent euro crisis contains the conditions for Hooghe and Marks' (2009) postfunctionalism to offer better guidance. For these scholars, in an age of politicisation and public dissensus on European integration, outcomes may not reflect functional pressures any longer and identity-based contestation may make all the difference. If European issues are politicised on identity lines, we should see a 'downward pressure on the level and scope of integration' and a narrowing of the 'substantive ground of possible agreement' (Hooghe & Marks, 2009, pp. 21–22). For our purposes, this could be interpreted as *loosening, less pooling and delegation*, but Hooghe and Marks (2009, p. 21, 22) are more ambivalent. They tentatively conclude that politicisation may lead to both less integration (*loosening*) *and* more delegation – the latter presumably seen as a means to depoliticise an issue.

This indeterminacy is resolved in the recent wave of new intergovernmentalist theorising that shares postfunctionalist premises such as the relevance assigned to the post-Maastricht rise in public dissensus and politicisation (Bickerton, Hodson, & Puetter, 2015, pp. 709–711; Fabbrini & Puetter, 2016, p. 486). According to this variant, the post-Maastricht period is marked by 'integration without supranationalism' (Bickerton *et al.*, 2015, p. 703). Initiatives are characterised by *greater reliance on the European Council and the Council for policy execution and implementation* (Fabbrini & Puetter, 2016, p. 481). Delegation of powers 'to traditional supranational institutions such as the Commission [is] increasingly discredited among member state governments' (Puetter, 2016, p. 604), *de novo* institutions are preferred, and unanimous decision-making within intergovernmental institutions acquires greater prominence (Fabbrini, 2016, p. 593; Fabbrini & Puetter, 2016, p. 488). This reluctance to pool and delegate is particularly relevant in highly salient or core state powers such as fiscal policy. These scholars do not seem to associate 'integration' with tighter national obligations, but rather with loose coordination measures that marginally encroach upon national policy autonomy. This is plausible in light of how politicisation operates. Once an issue becomes politicised, public dissensus restricts governments' room to manoeuvre, making them less inclined to relinquish sovereignty and even temped to reining in lost control (Hooghe & Marks, 2009, pp. 18–22; Puetter, 2012, p. 168). Postfunctionalist scholars do not differentiate the impact of politicisation by country or government, but it could be argued for instance that politicisation may have led Germany to demand more delegation and tightening in the last reform and Greece to push for the opposite. But this proposition is undistinguishable from liberal intergovernmentalist predictions as it is based on a government's expectation of being compliant, thus making politicisation epiphenomenal.

In conclusion, if the euro crisis has been an highly politicised identity conflict (Börzel & Risse, 2018) or represents the 'apex of the [new] intergovernmental moment' (Fabbrini, 2013, p. 1010), the functional pressures in policy design identified by liberal intergovernmentalism and neofunctionalism are disrupted and concerns about losing control are heightened. Therefore, *economic governance should rely less on pooling and delegation and* plausibly *more on loosening, especially in politicised contexts.* Table 1 summarises the key expectations. Next, we explain our coding of policy design.

## Measuring the design of economic governance measures

The EU economic governance regime is based on the chapter on economic policy and the protocol on the excessive deficit procedure (EDP) of the

**Table 1.** Expectations and driving mechanisms of policy design.

| Integration theories | Expectations | Driving mechanisms |
|---|---|---|
| Liberal intergovernmentalism | Pooling for additional measures, delegation for enforcement and implementation. Noncompliance leads to more delegation and plausibly tightening | Veto threats, exclusion threats and issue linkages shape outcomes |
| Neofunctionalism (institutionalist variant) | Delegation also to benefit from centralised expertise | Exit costs, supranational institutions and decision-making also shape outcomes |
| Postfunctionalism / New intergovernmentalism | Less pooling and delegation, and plausibly loosening in salient policies and politicised contexts[a] | Governments object to pooling and delegation and try to loosen obligations |

[a]Loosening and *more* delegation for Hooghe and Marks (2009).

Treaty on European Union. Secondary measures include an EDP regulation, the stability and growth pact (SGP), made of a preventive, a corrective and a recent enforcement regulation. There are also ancillary acts harmonising and monitoring national budgetary procedures. Additional measures, which we can only briefly discuss here, are the macroeconomic imbalance procedure (MIB) and the fiscal compact treaty (the Online Appendix lists the provisions and the seventeen acts subject to our study).

We broadly follow the method of coding provisions developed in the American congressional literature and applied by Franchino (2007) to EU legislation. Each legal act, including treaty provisions and protocols, is subdivided into major provisions. Each major provision is coded if it imposes obligations on member states (*tightening*) or gives them leeway in implementing measures (*loosening*). Similarly, each major provision is coded if it pools policy authority within the Council (*pooling*), it delegates authority to the Commission (*delegation*) and it sets *constraints* upon these institutions. A provision can have multiple properties. For instance, it may delegate a policy prerogative, subject to constraints. We also determine whether pooled and delegated authority is related to an enforcement activity, such as establishing noncompliance or monitoring budgets. Provisions have been coded independently first, then disparities have been settled (coding rules are in the Online Appendix). Intercoder agreement is 89 per cent greater than what would be expected by chance.

This procedure is reliable, easily replicable and produces data that greatly facilitate comparison across measures, time, and even policies, but it is not devoid of drawbacks. It treats policy prerogatives equally. A provision that confers upon the Commission the power to determine noncompliance has the same weight as one that asks this institution to adopt data collection guidelines. Also, a small change to an existing constraint, such as the shortening of a time limit, has to be either disregarded or double counted (we opted for the former). These shortcomings are not serious enough to distort the broad patterns we observe and, where necessary, we will compensate for this coarseness by distinguishing among types of policy prerogatives. On the other hand, we took two coding decisions to make sure that some important changes are detected. First, we code as constraint on the Council if this institution has to co-operate or co-decide with the Parliament, while we disregard simple consultation. Second, delegation is the granting of substantive policy authority to shape outcomes (Franchino, 2007, p. 84). It excludes the sole examination of documents and the proposal prerogatives of the Commission, unless they are enhanced, that is, if less than a Council qualified majority is sufficient to adopt proposals. Here, the Commission has a significant chance of affecting outcomes.

Figure 1 displays the number of provisions in force after important reforms (see Online Appendix for detailed breakdowns). Major and tightening provisions have quintupled since the completion of the initial framework in 1997. Initially no provisions loosened control or conferred some policy leeway to member states, but since 2005 the number has moderately increased. Pooling provisions have remained constant until 2005, and then they almost tripled. The associated constraints tripled both with the initial SGP and with the latest reforms. Instead, apart from standard proposal prerogatives, no provisions delegated powers to the Commission until the 2005 reform of the EDP. The total tally is now almost ten times larger and the associated constraints have sextupled since.

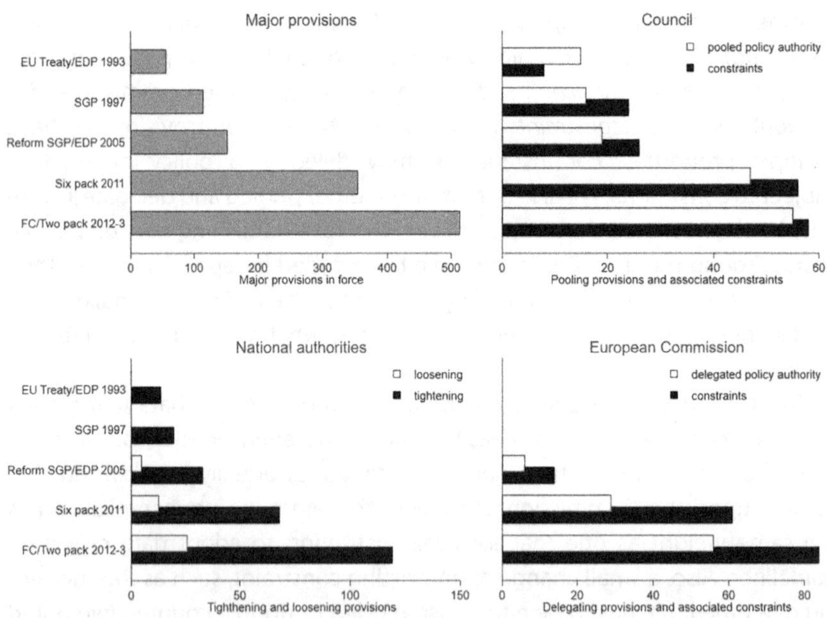


**Figure 1.** Major and design economic governance provisions in force. Note: Cumulative figures. EDP: Excessive Deficit Procedure, SGP: Stability and Growth Pact, FC: Fiscal Compact

The following analysis of negotiations is also based on information on contested issues and positions of institutional and governmental actors. The methodology for collecting these data, including a detailed account of the sources and strategies of identification and cross-validation, is available in the Online Appendix.

## The initial design: Why so much pooling?

### *Council-centred enforcement*

Figure 2 displays the regime after major reforms in terms of shares of design provisions, while Figure 3 displays the share of pooling and delegating provisions that are related to an enforcement activity. Only pooling occurred by the time the initial framework was completed in 1997. Apart from proposal competences, no provisions delegated powers to the Commission or granted some leeway to member states. Council constraining provisions and tightening provisions were similarly employed.

The Maastricht treaty (and the proximate EDP regulation) set some general demands on member states on coordination and reporting of economic policies and public finances, and more specific requirements, such as the well-known obligation to avoid excessive government spending, with the associated reference values of deficit and debt to GDP. We will not discuss here treaty

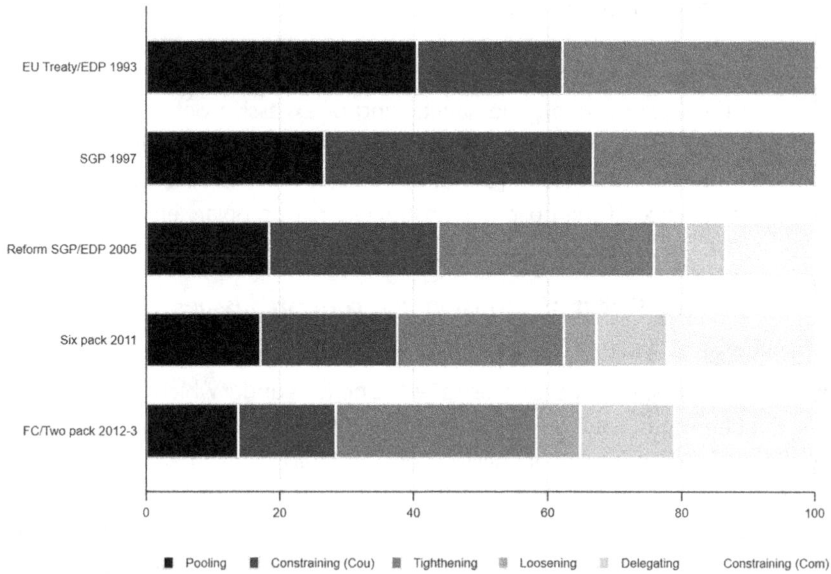


**Figure 2.** Economic governance by proportion of design provisions in force. Note: Cumulative figures. EDP: Excessive Deficit Procedure, SGP: Stability and Growth Pact, FC: Fiscal Compact, Cou: Council, Com: Commission

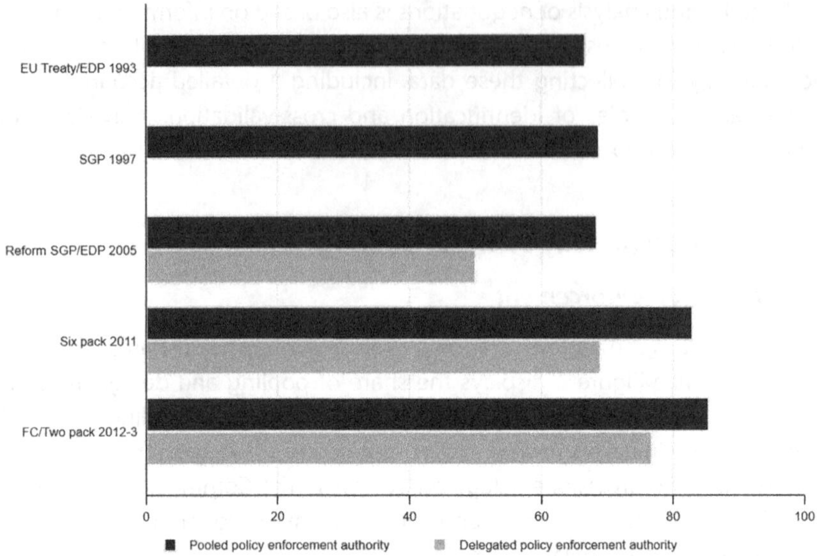


**Figure 3.** Proportion of pooling and delegating provisions related to enforcement. Note: Cumulative figures. EDP: Excessive Deficit Procedure, SGP: Stability and Growth Pact, FC: Fiscal Compact.

negotiations, but the initial design is not fully aligned with liberal intergovernmentalism. As expected, prerogatives were pooled where rules on financing, bailout, multilateral surveillance and the EDP had to be laid down, but pooling occurred also with regard to the publicity of recommendations establishing inconsistency between national measures and broad economic guidelines, and the determination and sanctioning of excessive deficits. Two-thirds of pooling provisions concerned enforcement (see Figure 3). The absence of delegation betrays a lack of concern about compliance and it is a likely indication of the unique salience of the policy, as postfunctionalist scholars emphasise.

## ***Noncompliance, threat of exclusion and contested issues***

Noncompliance as well did not have all the consequences expected by liberal intergovernmentalism. Figure 4 illustrates the periods under which governments have not been compliant with key provisions of the regime (we employ a looser benchmark for debt). Consider only the deficit criteria for the time being. By 1996, the Council established that every member state had an excessive deficit, except for Ireland and Luxembourg. As the deadline for selecting countries that would have adopted the euro was approaching and as it became clear that those with a history of fiscal profligacy, like Italy, may have been in the first wave, the German government pressed for a strengthening of the regime, under an implicit but credible threat of a smaller Eurozone.

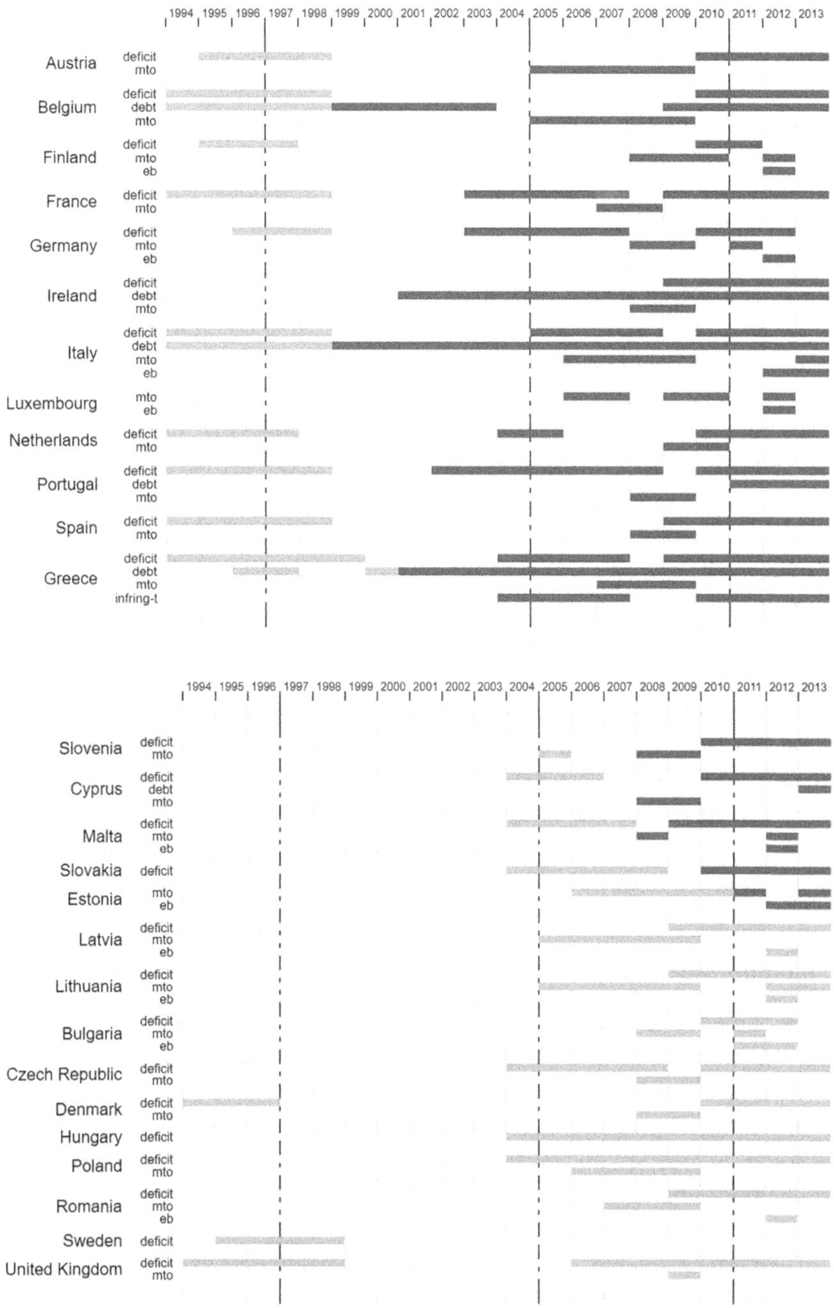


**Figure 4.** Periods of noncompliance with fiscal provisions. Note: Excessive deficit, debt greater than GDP, medium-term objective (mto), expenditure benchmark (eb), infringements. Darker bars for years with euro. Vertical lines separate reforms. See Online Appendix for more details.

Yet, delegation was barely an issue. Negotiations centred on the circumstances under which a deficit would not be considered excessive, the automaticity of the procedure and the size of the sanctions. The first two issues were about the Council's room of manoeuvre. The German and Dutch governments argued for specific thresholds (Agence Europe, 1996, p. 5) and proposed that automatic exemptions should apply only to countries experiencing an annual decline in real GDP of at least 2 per cent. The Belgian, French and Italian governments preferred keeping the Council free to determine country-specific exceptional circumstances. The 2 per cent threshold was eventually included in article 2.2 of the SGP corrective arm, but the third comma stipulated that circumstances could be exceptional also for a contraction of less than 2 per cent, '*in light of further evidence*'. It was a modest amendment. A resolution of the Amsterdam European Council summit of June 1997 further narrowed the Council's faculty to exempt noncompliant countries to cases when the reduction was more than 0.75 per cent, so-called box model. In sum, the most recalcitrant countries accepted to limit Council's powers only in case of mild recessions and this exception was not even included as a legal provision in the SGP.

In the second contested issue, the German, Danish, Finnish and Swedish governments proposed to insert the words 'the expectation is that the Council will respect the Commission's decision'. They settled for the inclusion of the words 'as a rule' in articles 2 and 11. The last contested topic concerned the deposit to be made in case of an excessive deficit. The German government argued for a fixed component of 0.25 per cent of GDP, but it had to settle with the Commission proposal of 0.2 per cent, which was supported by the majority of governments.

### ***Explaining pooling in the SGP: veto power and policy uncertainty***

Some demands for tightening were met in the SGP. The preventive measure required states to submit annual stability or convergence programmes, with an MTO of close to balance or in surplus. The need to assembly only a qualified majority in the Council for its adoption may have facilitated this outcome, as neofunctionalism suggests. On the other hand, the corrective regulation primarily circumscribed Council prerogatives by establishing conditions for an excessive deficit, deadlines and sanctions (see Figures 1 and 2). The bargaining dynamics emphasised by liberal intergovernmentalism is in clear display here. While the most recalcitrant governments caved in and agreed to revise the regime in order to defuse the threat of exclusion, these governments were empowered by the unanimity requirement. Keen to preserve Council's prerogatives, they made modest concessions to the most reformist colleagues, in order to signal commitment to fiscal stability, but avoided delegation. However, the SGP remained overall a modest reform in terms of policy design, with pooling still dominant in enforcement despite noncompliance. Two-thirds of pooled prerogatives were related to this activity (see Figure 3).

From a postfunctionalist perspective, limited tightening and no delegation stem from the unique salience of the policy. But one ingredient is missing. There is hardly evidence that the conflict surrounding these negotiations turned into mass public debates, despite raising politicisation in the 1990s (Hutter, Grande, & Kriesi, 2016). In our view, other important factors militating against delegation were the *uncertainties* surrounding these rules. This regime's primary objectives are to prevent moral hazard in public spending and to limit the negative externalities associated with the possible combination of expansionary fiscal policies and a contractionary monetary policy (the former resulting from governments' attempts to use fiscal policy to boost output and employment in the short-term at the expense of inflation, the latter from an inflation-averse common central bank). These rules should ensure sustainable public debts, allowing enough flexibility for countercyclical policies (e.g., Claeys, Darvas, & Leandro, 2016).

At the time of drafting the SGP however, these externalities were purely hypothetical consequences of establishing a monetary union. Some scholars downplayed their magnitude and questioned their direction. Buiter, Corsetti, Roubini, Repullo, and Frankel (1993) explicitly argued for the reference values to be disregarded. No bailout rules were deemed sufficient to deal with the risk of default and with financial contagion: governments would avoid excessive spending anyway, *if* the central bank is credibly inflation-averse and *if* financial markets demand higher risk premia from profligate governments (see also Buiter, 2006; Eichengreen & Wyplosz, 1998). However, the commitments to no bailout and to stable prices were obviously untested, while the prospects of countries with histories of fiscal improvidence joining the monetary union were becoming concrete.

Another concern was that these reference values could induce pernicious pro-cyclical policies since governments may have to cut spending or raise taxes during a recession (thus, undermining the credibility of financial sanctions), while they could increase spending or cut taxes during a recovery. Efficacy aside, several different combinations of debt and deficit values are fiscally sustainable, so any given set of parameters is necessarily arbitrary and it risks being excessively constraining (Pasinetti, 1998).

## The 2005 reform: Why loosening despite noncompliance?

### *Loosening and modest delegation*

This reform introduces two small but significant changes. First, four provisions (6 per cent of design provisions in force) grant member states greater flexibility. Most were inserted in the preventive SGP regulation. Article 2a replaces a common MTO (recall, the structural budget objective) with a *revisable country-specific* one, which *may* now diverge by no more than 1 per cent of GDP from a balance or surplus position. On the other hand, the EDP regulation adds new obligations about provision of statistical data, professionalism of statistics officials and assistance to Commission's inspections. Hence, about a third of the policy design still consists of tightening provisions.

The second significant change concerns six provisions in the EDP regulation conferring policy prerogatives upon the Commission (amounting to 6 per cent of design provisions). The Commission sets statistical formats, adopts data collection guidelines, and determines the implementation of accounting rules. Importantly, the supranational executive can object to the quality of reported data and amend them.

The role of the Council is unaltered, on balance. On the one hand, the definition of severe economic downturn – a key contested issue in 1997 – is relaxed. The box model is dropped, and now even a protracted period of very low *growth* can be a mitigating factor to avoid the procedure. Decisions can be revised in case of unexpected adverse events and the assessment time frame is extended.[1] On the other hand, the preventive regulation clarifies the criteria for examining structural budgets in light of the MTOs; while the corrective regulation specifies that the Council must request minimum annual improvements of the structural budget of 0.5 per cent of GDP from noncomplying states. Extensions of deadlines cannot exceed one year.

### *Consequences of EDP regulation noncompliance: tightening and delegation*

As Figure 4 illustrates, after a respite of a few years, noncompliance reappeared. In 2004, Eurostat revised upwards the Greek deficit by between 2 and 3 percentage points of GDP for the years 2000–2003 and the 2003 debt-GDP ratio by more than 7 percentage points. In December 2004, the Commission initiated an infringement procedure against Greece for failing to comply with the EDP regulation. The new design corroborates liberal intergovernmentalism. National obligations were tightened and Commission's competences expanded. Half of delegating provisions relate to enforcement, the remaining half to implementation (see Figure 3). Qualified majority may have helped addressing these demands, as neofunctionalism suggests. The most contentious issue indeed concerned Commission's prerogatives. The four largest countries opposed regular methodological inspections of national data as well as a first in-depth monitoring visit, proposed by Luxembourgish Presidency. Article 8d narrowly defines the objectives of these visits and specifies that they should take place only in case of serious problems.

This reform runs counter postfunctionalist expectations but some of their scope conditions were absent. Conflict remained circumscribed to the elite level in these negotiations. Recent works actually indicate that debates on European issues in the early 2000s were less politicised than in the previous decade (Hutter *et al.*, 2016, p. 281).

### *Consequences of SGP noncompliance: loosening, reversion point and policy uncertainty*

Governments also failed to comply with the fiscal rules. Between 2000 and 2004, four Eurozone countries, including France and Germany, had an excessive deficit, while high indebtedness persisted in some other countries. Yet, in shifting the focus from correction to prevention, the SGP loosened some national obligations and relaxed some Council constraints, while the Commission obtained no new substantive powers. Moreover, the corrective regulation pools two additional enforcement-related prerogatives concerning the revision of decisions.

This outcome is not easy to reconcile with postfunctionalism, given limited politicisation, nor with liberal intergovernmentalism, given noncompliance. A qualified majority might have been easier to assemble in the preventive arm. Indeed, the 1 per cent floor to the divergence from the MTO was inserted by the Council. But this reform of the corrective arm, which requires unanimity, is unexpected at first sight. By far the most controversial issue concerned the numerousness and specificity of mitigating factors for establishing an excessive deficit. The conflict replicated the 1997 divide, but with the German position reversed. This time chancellor Gerhard Schröder argued for more leniency and proposed a long list of factors that was viewed favourably by France and Italy. These governments either were noncompliant or risked being so. In March 2005, Luxembourgish Jean-Claude Juncker, presiding the Council, proposed a shorter list, which was criticised by both governments that wanted to add specific spending categories (the three above plus the United Kingdom) and those that considered it too long and insisted on the centrality of the reference values. The more recalcitrant Eurozone countries had a history of better compliance (except for the Netherlands). This list was eventually abandoned in favour of a somewhat fuzzy but still long enumeration of factors in article 2.3 and an invitation to a 'balanced overall assessment'. As an 'overarching principle', mitigation would be considered only if the deficit remained close to the reference value and its excess was temporary. Nevertheless, considering also the laxer criteria of protracted low growth as mitigating factor, these changes undeniably expanded Council discretion and diluted control over national authorities.

Why did recalcitrant and mostly compliant governments not veto these developments and push for delegation? Liberal intergovernmentalism proves its usefulness by directing our attention to the no agreement outcome. The reversion point of these negotiations was the suspension of the EDP – clearly an unpleasant outcome for these fiscally responsible governments. In November 2003 France and Germany managed to assemble a minority to block decisions establishing the insufficiency of their measures and demanding further action under the threat of sanctions (Heipertz & Verdun, 2010, pp. 142–154). The Council also declared that the procedure was held in abeyance. Although this latter decision was successfully challenged by the Commission before the European Court of Justice in July 2004, the Court upheld the Council's right to block decisions. It was therefore clear that there was a minority blocking *any* new Commission's recommendation – a de facto abeyance. The least reformist countries had therefore to accept a looser regime and more emphasis on preventive surveillance in exchange of resuming the procedure and stricter constraints once an excess was determined. The unpalatable consequences of no agreement defused the threats of veto and engendered a willingness to compromise.

Given several governments pushing for loosening and more Council leeway, we should hardly expect delegation. This is in line with postfunctionalism, were it not for the limited politicisation. But in our view, the prevailing reluctance to delegate may have also been motivated by the renewed emphasis on the structural budget: an unobservable quantity subject to significant estimation errors,[2] which depends on estimates of the output gap – also an unobservable quantity that in turn depends on estimates of, for instance, total factor productivity and (non-accelerating wage) rate of unemployment. Forecasting errors of output growth and inflation add further uncertainty. In sum, governments agreed to preventive surveillance based on an imprecise indicator over which they had limited control. No wonder they were not inclined to delegate.

## The euro crisis: policy failure and enforcement reform

### *Delegation and tightening*

This overhaul of economic governance was adopted in the midst of the sovereign debt crisis. In Figures 1 and 2, we distinguish between the six pack on the one side, and the two pack and fiscal compact on the other. These measures are part of the same reform, even though they span over a three-year period. As Figure 1 shows, the number of major provisions more than tripled and the main beneficiary is undoubtedly the Commission. Figure 2 reports that the share of delegating provisions has moved from 6 to 14 per cent and the share of pooling provisions are correspondingly decreased from 18 to 14 per cent. Provisions giving national authorities some leeway, mostly exemptions, have marginally increased from 5 to 7 per cent. With more powers, provisions constraining the Commission have correspondently increased from 14 to 21 per cent, while the Council share has decreased from 25 to 15 per cent. The proportion of tightening provisions has barely altered. Almost half of new ones are included in the two pack, less than a quarter in the budgetary frameworks directive and a tenth in the fiscal compact.

The reform establishes more precise assessment benchmarks: an annual real expenditure growth to assess progress toward the MTO in the preventive regulation and an annual rate of improvement of the debt-GDP ratio for countries exceeding the reference value in the corrective regulation. The fiscal compact narrows to 0.5 per cent of GDP the acceptable MTO divergence for countries exceeding the debt reference value.

The strengthening of Commission's power is both procedural and substantive and occurs primarily in four measures (adopted with the ordinary legislative procedure): the SGP preventive regulation, the new SGP enforcement regulation and the two-pack regulations (the Online Appendix summarises noteworthy delegating provisions). Notably, 77 per cent of them are enforcement related (see Figure 3). On the other side, accountability to the Parliament has been strengthened through its involvement in the economic dialogue and its oversight of Commission delegated acts.

Although the shift in policy design from pooling to delegation is clear, the triplicated pooling provisions are still predominantly enforcement related (85 per cent, see Figure 3). In the SGP enforcement regulation, sanctioning remains centred on the Council. In the two-pack surveillance regulation, this institution approves adjustment programmes, establishes noncompliance and sets conditionality requirements. A third of the new pooling provisions comes from the MIB, and the enforcement of this measure relies more on the Council than on the Commission, compared to the SGP.

## *Explaining the overhaul: noncompliance, exit cost and issue linkage*

As Figure 4 illustrates, the patterns of noncompliance leading up to this reform amounted to policy failure. The significant revisions of the Greek government deficit in late 2009 raised serious concerns about data quality and led to opening an infringement procedure. This was the proximate cause of the sovereign debt crisis but the preceding financial crisis had already put public finances under serious strain. The structural balance of every single Eurozone country, except Slovakia, intermittently diverged from the MTOs. Public indebtedness worsened. Then, in 2010, every country, except for Luxemburg, ran an excessive deficit, while Greece, Ireland and Portugal had to secure bailout loans. Negotiations were also highly mass politicised (Genschel & Jachtenfuchs, 2018; Kriesi & Grande, 2016), making this reform a sort of critical test of these theories.

Overall, liberal intergovernmentalism and neofunctionalism are more convincingly corroborated. As Schimmelfennig (2015, p. 184) aptly puts it, the ensuing bargaining dynamics took the form of a game of chicken between fiscally sound governments and those under pressure for financing their outlays. The significant risks of dissolution of the Eurozone – an exit option of vast consequences – compelled them to solve the crisis but each preferred to shift the burden of adaptation on the counterpart. The former sought commitment to fiscal discipline, the latter to bailout.[3] For instance, this *linkage* explains why the Italian and Greek governments, despite their power to veto the corrective regulation, accepted the new benchmark of a debt-GDP ratio improvement for highly indebted countries (but successfully opposed demands to narrow the mitigating factors for determining an excessive deficit).

In the other measures, the shift in policy design toward tightening and delegation (especially for noncompliance and sanctioning decisions, with the consequence of narrowing Council influence) has also been facilitated by Council qualified majority voting (and parliamentary involvement). For instance, in the preventive regulation, the discussion centred on (a) a different MTO adjustment path for highly indebted countries and (b) the consequences of budgetary deviations. The Italian government argued against a differentiated assessment and, together with the Greek government, against sanctions for deviations. The new article 5.1 instead demands the Council and the Commission to examine whether annual budgetary improvements reach at least 0.5 per cent of GDP for these countries (the Finnish, Dutch and Luxembourgish governments pressed for a more explicit requirement, which was eventually inserted in the fiscal compact). Moreover, article 5.1 not only operationalises the adjustment path through an expenditure benchmark, but the new article 6.2 also demands the Council to act within a month of a warning; and sanctions are envisioned.

Politicisation did not engender a convergence of positions over policy design. Benelux governments even proposed to extend the enhanced proposal prerogatives of the Commission to more SGP and MIB provisions. The Parliament was instead instrumental for including sanctions for manipulating statistics in the SGP enforcement regulation and for keeping Council qualified majority voting for approving adjustment programmes in the two pack, over the opposition of several ministers.

In sum, noncompliance and the pressure of securing commitment to both fiscal soundness and bailout produced a reform in the direction predicted by liberal intergovernmentalism. Additionally, as neofunctionalism expects, prohibitive exit costs limited available options and lower procedural hurdles facilitated tightening and delegation. These changes are not unexpected (cf. Bauer & Becker, 2014; Dehousse, 2016). Delegation may have been also perceived as less risky since the Commission has been building up non-trivial policy capabilities over time (Savage & Verdun, 2016). And, although uncertainties persist, the new expenditure rule is a step toward more certain and controllable performance indicators (Claeys *et al.*, 2016).

## Conclusion

We cannot rely on a single theory to understand economic governance design. Contrary to liberal intergovernmentalist expectations, enforcement has been heavily Council-centred until 2011, despite significant noncompliance, as it is in the recent two-pack surveillance regulation and MIB. As post-functionalist theories suggest (pooling aside), the salience of this policy has quite likely underlain the reluctance to tighten and delegate. But these approaches fall short in highly politicised contexts, exactly where they should do most of the explaining. In our view, the unavoidable arbitrariness and uncertainties of these rules must also have cautioned against relying on a supranational executive with limited resources.

Liberal intergovernmentalism and neofunctionalism remain valuable for explaining the overall *direction* of these reforms toward tightening, restricting Council authority and delegation – precipitated by noncompliance and characterised by commitment problems, threats of exclusion and veto, issue linkages, path dependencies and more supranational decision-making. Attention to these bargaining dynamics helps illuminating outcomes, even when loosening follows noncompliance, while functional logics, such as the need to secure credible commitments, appear unaltered.

In conclusion, policy-makers do not seem to react to mass politicisation by loosening obligations and avoiding pooling and delegation. They do not cave in and ensure that the policy remains or returns under national control. The 'new intergovernmental moment' saw a move from Council- to Commission-centred enforcement, without relying on new institutions. Tightening, pooling and delegation occurred *despite* the highly politicised negotiations of the recent reform. Response-wise, these changes indicate that, in the face of rising domestic public pressures, EU-level actors have adopted a strategy of assertive depoliticisation, although without shying away from open confrontation (Bressanelli *et al.*, 2020). Facing the serious consequences of a Eurozone break-up, this is indeed the type of reactive politicisation management ministers (and parliamentarians) would be expected to undertake, despite their electoral accountability and the domestic salience of this core state policy (Schimmelfennig, 2020). Nor should we ignore the plausible assertion that mass domestic politicisation in the latest reform was *triggered by* noncompliance and elite conflict, which may also explain why leaders have decided to assertively pursue (institutional) depoliticisation.

## Notes

1. Except perhaps for pension reforms, it is unclear whether the criteria for evaluating budgets listed in the corrective regulation allows for greater discretion.
2. Yearly revisions of the structural balance are larger than 0.5 percent of GDP, i.e. the required baseline annual adjustment (Claeys et al. 2016, p. 6).

3. For positions on capacity building measures, see Lehner and Wasserfallen (2019). As corroborating evidence, we find Germany, Finland and the Netherlands opposing article 13.4 of the SGP enforcement regulation that demands the Commission to draft a report on Eurobonds.

## Acknowledgements

We would like to thank the guest editors of the special issue, Philipp Broniecki, Frank Schimmelfennig, the anonymous reviewers and the participants at the Workshop on 'Politicising and De-Politicising the European Union' King's College London, 15–16 December 2017 and at the panel of the ECPR Standing Group on the European Union Conference, Sciences Po, Paris, 13–15 June 2018.

## Disclosure statement

No potential conflict of interest was reported by the authors.

## ORCID

*Fabio Franchino* http://orcid.org/0000-0001-8774-6494
*Camilla Mariotto* http://orcid.org/0000-0002-1116-2975

## References

Agence Europe. (1996, November 12). *Europe Daily Bullettin n.* 6851, 5.

Bauer, M. W., & Becker, S. (2014). The unexpected winner of the crisis: The European Commission's strengthened role in economic governance. *Journal of European Integration, 36*(3), 213–229.

Bickerton, C. J., Hodson, D., & Puetter, U. (2015). The new intergovernmentalism: European integration in the post-Maastricht era. *Journal of Common Market Studies, 53*(4), 703–722.

Biermann, F., Guérin, N., Jagdhuber, S., Rittberger, B., & Weiss, M. (2019). Political (non-)reform in the euro crisis and the refugee crisis: A liberal intergovernmentalist explanation. *Journal of European Public Policy, 26*(2), 246–266.

Börzel, T. A., & Risse, T. (2018). From the euro to the Schengen crises: European integration theories, politicization, and identity politics. *Journal of European Public Policy, 25*(1), 83–108.

Bressanelli, E., Koop, C. and Reh, C. (2020) 'EU actors under pressure: politicisation and depoliticisation as strategic responses', *Journal of European Public Policy, 27*(3), 329–341.

Buiter, W. H. (2006). The "sense and nonsense of Maastricht" revisited: What have we learnt about stabilization in EMU? *Journal of Common Market Studies*, *44*(4), 687–710.

Buiter, W. H., Corsetti, G., Roubini, N., Repullo, R., & Frankel, J. (1993). Excessive deficits: Sense and nonsense in the treaty of Maastricht. *Economic Policy*, *8*(16), 57.

Claeys, G., Darvas, Z., & Leandro, À. (2016). *A proposal to revive the European Fiscal Framework*. Brussels: Bruegel.

Dehousse, R. (2016). Why has EU macroeconomic governance become more supranational? *Journal of European Integration*, *38*(5), 617–631.

Eichengreen, B., & Wyplosz, C. (1998). The stability pact: More than a minor nuisance? *Economic Policy*, *13*(26), 65–113.

Fabbrini, S. (2013). Intergovernmentalism and its limits assessing the European Union's answer to the euro crisis. *Comparative Political Studies*, *46*(9), 1003–1029.

Fabbrini, S. (2016). From consensus to domination: The intergovernmental union in a crisis situation. *Journal of European Integration*, *38*(5), 587–599.

Fabbrini, S., & Puetter, U. (2016). Integration without supranationalisation: Studying the lead roles of the European Council and the Council in post-Lisbon EU politics. *Journal of European Integration*, *38*(5), 481–495.

Franchino, F. (2007) *The powers of the Union: Delegation in the EU*, Cambridge: Cambridge University Press.

Garrett, G., & Tsebelis, G. (1996). An institutional critique of intergovernmentalism. *International Organization*, *50*(2), 269–299.

Genschel, P., & Jachtenfuchs, M. (2018). From market integration to core state powers: The Eurozone crisis, the refugee crisis and integration theory. *Journal of Common Market Studies*, *56*(1), 178–196.

Heipertz, M., & Verdun, A. (2005). The stability and growth pact - theorizing a case in European integration. *Journal of Common Market Studies*, *43*(5), 985–1008.

Heipertz, M., & Verdun, A. C. (2010). *Ruling Europe: The politics of the stability and growth pact*. Cambridge: Cambridge University Press.

Hooghe, L., & Marks, G. (2009). A postfunctionalist theory of European integration: From permissive consensus to constraining dissensus. *British Journal of Political Science*, *39*(1), 1–23.

Hutter, S., Grande, E. and Kriesi, H. (2016) *Politicising Europe: Integration and mass politics*, Cambridge: Cambridge University Press.

Kriesi, H., & Grande, E. (2016). The euro crisis: A boost to the politicisation of European integration? In S. Hutter, E. Grande, & H. Kriesi (Eds.), *Politicising Europe: Integration and mass politics* (pp. 240–276). Cambridge: Cambridge University Press.

Lehner, T., & Wasserfallen, F. (2019). Political conflict in the reform of the Eurozone. *European Union Politics*, *20*(1), 45–64.

Moravcsik, A. (1998). *The choice for Europe: Social purpose and state power from Messina to Maastricht*. Ithaca, NY: Cornell University Press.

Niemann, A., & Ioannou, D. (2015). European economic integration in times of crisis: A case of neofunctionalism? *Journal of European Public Policy*, *22*(2), 196–218.

Pasinetti, L. L. (1998). The myth (or folly) of the 3% deficit/GDP Maastricht "parameter". *Cambridge Journal of Economics*, *22*(1), 103–116.

Pierson, P. (1996). The path to European integration. An historical institutionalist analysis. *Comparative Political Studies*, *29*(2), 123–163.

Puetter, U. (2012). Europe's deliberative intergovernmentalism: The role of the council and European Council in EU economic governance. *Journal of European Public Policy*, *19*(2), 161–178.

Puetter, U. (2016). The centrality of consensus and deliberation in contemporary EU politics and the new intergovernmentalism. *Journal of European Integration*, *38*(5), 601–615.

Savage, J. D., & Verdun, A. (2016). 'Strengthening the European Commission's budgetary and economic surveillance capacity since Greece and the euro area crisis: A study of five directorates-general'. *Journal of European Public Policy*, *23*(1), 101–118.

Schimmelfennig, F. (2014). European integration in the euro crisis: The limits of postfunctionalism. *Journal of European Integration*, *36*(3), 321–337.

Schimmelfennig, F. (2015). Liberal intergovernmentalism and the euro area crisis. *Journal of European Public Policy*, *22*(2), 177–195.

Schimmelfennig, F. (2020) 'Politicisation management in the European Union', *Journal of European Public Policy*, *27*(3), 342–361.

Schure, P., & Verdun, A. (2008). Legislative bargaining in the European union: The divide between large and small member states. *European Union Politics*, *9*(4), 459–486.

Segers, M., & van Esch, F. (2007). Behind the veil of budgetary discipline: The political logic of the budgetary rules in EMU and the SGP. *Journal of Common Market Studies*, *45*(5), 1089–1109.

Verdun, A. (2015). A historical institutionalist explanation of the EU's responses to the euro area financial crisis. *Journal of European Public Policy*, *22*(2), 219–237.

# The European Union's authoritarian equilibrium

R. Daniel Kelemen

**ABSTRACT**

While the European Union (EU) professes a commitment to liberal democracy, in recent years it has allowed some member governments to backslide toward competitive authoritarianism. The EU has become trapped in an 'authoritarian equilibrium' underpinned by three factors. First, the EU's half-baked system of party politics and its ingrained reluctance to interfere in the domestic politics of its member states help shield national autocrats from EU intervention. Second, funding and investment from the EU helps sustain these regimes. Third, the free movement of persons in the EU facilitates the exit of dissatisfied citizens, which depletes the opposition and generates remittances, thereby helping these regimes endure. While more fully developed democratic federations have the capacity to eventually steer autocratic member states back toward democracy, the EU appears to be stuck in an autocracy trap.

## Introduction

The EU professes a deep commitment to democracy. The first two conditions for EU membership listed in the 1993 Copenhagen Criteria are that applicants must have stable institutions guaranteeing (1) democracy and (2) rule of law. The Treaty on European Union (TEU) identifies democracy as a cornerstone of the Union, stating in Article 2 that, 'The Union is founded on the values of respect for human dignity, freedom, democracy, equality, the rule of law and respect for human rights … '. The TEU even includes a mechanism (Article 7) to sanction states that engage in a 'serious and persistent breach' of Article 2 values.

And yet, for all its stated commitment to democracy, the EU has in recent years shown itself to be a hospitable environment for the emergence of increasingly autocratic member governments. Backsliding has proceeded the furthest in Hungary, where the Orbán regime has displaced democracy with 'competitive authoritarianism' (Levitsky & Way, 2010), a hybrid regime that maintains the formal democratic institutions but fails to meet the minimal standards for democracy. Indeed, the originators of the concept of competitive authoritarianism have said that the Orbán regime is a 'prime example' (Way & Levitsky, 2019). The erosion of democracy in Hungary has been detailed by international organisations (e.g., European Parliament, 2013, 2018; Venice Commission, 2013), scholarly studies (e.g., Bozóki & Hegedüs, 2018; Krekó & Enyedi, 2018; Pech & Scheppele, 2017), and in-depth media accounts (e.g., Kingsley, 2018; The Economist, 2019). In 2018, a damning report from the European Parliament (2018) on the situation in Hungary resulted in the triggering of the first stage of TEU's Article 7 sanctioning procedure. In 2019, Hungary became the first EU member state ever to be downgraded by Freedom House to the status of only 'partly free' (Freedom House, 2019, p. 13). Describing the full story of the erosion of democracy in Hungary is beyond the scope of this article, but in short the Orbán regime has managed to consolidate control over the judiciary and most of the media, to eliminate effective checks on its power, to rig the electoral system to ensure victory, to stifle independent civil society organisations, and to seriously limit academic freedom.

Since the Law and Justice (PiS) party's election in 2015, Poland has been moving quickly in a similar direction and the Polish government is currently embroiled in an Article 7 sanctioning procedure and a series of legal battles with the EU concerning its attacks on judicial independence (Sadurski, 2019). Finally, while Hungary and Poland are the most egregious cases, democratic backsliding is also occurring in other member states (Cianetti, Dawson, & Hanley, 2018).

This situation presents an obvious puzzle: why does a political union that professes a deep commitment to democracy allow member governments to backslide toward authoritarianism? The comparative politics literature on subnational authoritarianism sheds great light on this puzzle (Kelemen 2017). That literature shows that the survival of authoritarian enclaves within large federal-type polities is common, and explains both the political dynamics that support their survival and the conditions under which they are most likely to be toppled. This article builds on a concept I introduced in my earlier work on this topic, the *authoritarian equilibrium*: a politically stable equilibrium in which the EU paradoxically supports the survival of authoritarian member governments (id.: 214). Where my earlier analysis focused specifically on the role of partisan politics, this article provides a fully elaborated theory of the authoritarian equilibrium emphasising additional factors, and it presents evidence of how these dynamics have facilitated the consolidation of authoritarian rule in Hungary.

Three factors underpin the EU's authoritarian equilibrium: partial politicisation, money and migration. The first pillar of the equilibrium stems from the half-baked character of EU-level politicisation. The EU has politicised enough that there are now strong incentives for Europarties (EU level political parties) to protect the national member parties of autocrats that deliver them votes, but it has not politicised sufficiently that autocrats' Europarty allies pay meaningful reputational costs for supporting them or that the autocrats' EU-level opponents can intervene in ways that might help dislodge them. The perverse incentives created by this half-baked politicisation are exacerbated by the dominant role national governments play in EU governance and enduring influence of sovereignty norms, both of which discourage EU intervention against backsliding regimes. Second, EU funds help sustain national autocracies. Autocratic rulers can use their control over the distribution of EU funding to help prop up their regimes. Moreover, the stamp of approval that comes with EU membership helps them attract Foreign Direct Investment that might otherwise be more concerned about the risks of investing in an authoritarian regime. Third, free movement of persons within the EU facilitates emigration by dissatisfied citizens, which tends to deplete the ranks of the domestic opposition, thereby supporting autocratic regime survival. Moreover, to the extent that emigrants send remittances to family members back at home, this may bolster the domestic economy and help sustain the incumbent regime.

In fully developed democratic polities, these three factors can support the survival of authoritarian enclaves, but under certain conditions they can also help dislodge them. The danger for the EU today is that its half-baked, semi-politicised institutional order appears to generate only the first half of the equation: it produces conditions that can support the consolidation of authoritarian member governments, but not the incentives that might eventually help displace them. To be sure, there are limits to how far a backsliding regime may go within the EU without provoking a meaningful reaction (Bozóki & Hegedüs, 2018). If a member government installed a full-blown, violent dictatorship, then the EU would likely attempt to restore democracy. However, it seems that so long as a member government limits itself to the softer, non-violent techniques of 'competitive authoritarianism' and 'autocratic legalism' (Scheppele, 2018) – such packing courts, buying and closing newspapers, and rigging elections so that are unfair but appear free – then it can persist comfortably within the EU.

The remainder of this article is divided as follows. Section 2 elaborates the theoretical arguments introduced above. Section 3 applies the three-part framework to analyze how the authoritarian equilibrium has helped sustain the EU's first competitive authoritarian regime – that of Viktor Orbán's Fidesz party in Hungary. Section 4 concludes.

## The three pillars of Europe's authoritarian equilibrium

Europe's authoritarian equilibrium rests on three pillars: partial politicisation, money, and migration. First, even as the EU becomes more politicised, its underdeveloped system of party politics and its engrained reluctance to interfere in the political affairs of its member states help shield national autocrats from EU intervention. The EU has politicised enough that it generates incentives to protect national autocrats, but not enough that it generates compensating pressures on EU leaders to dislodge them. In the EU, as in other federal-type polities (Gibson, 2012; Mickey, 2015), partisan politics at the federal (EU) level creates powerful incentives for federal parties (Europarties) to protect state-level authoritarian leaders who belong to their parties and deliver them votes in federal institutions (such as the European Parliament and the Council) (Kelemen, 2017). Ironically, as I (*ibid*) have argued previously, the incentives for Europarties to protect local autocrats increased as reformers sought to address criticisms of the EU's 'democratic deficit' by injecting more partisan contestation into EU politics. Efforts to strengthen EU-level political parties, increase the power of the European Parliament, and increase the salience of European Parliament elections, for instance through the *Spitzenkandidaten* (lead candidates) process have increased the rewards to Europarties for maximising their size, thus increasing their incentive to tolerate autocratic parties in their groups.

However, in the EU's incomplete system of politicisation, EU level partisan politics and Europarty brand identities have not developed to the point where Europarties are likely to pay a political price for supporting autocrats. The comparative politics literature emphasises that if a local autocrat's behavior becomes so egregious that it imposes significant reputational costs on its federal party, that party's leaders may withdraw their support and even press for the ouster of the autocrat (Giraudy, 2015). But in EU party politics, because few voters even realise that Europarties exist, voters are unlikely to punish them (or their national member parties) for allying with autocrats. Likewise, EU level party politics has not developed to the point where other Europarties can intervene directly in domestic politics of backsliding states to break the autocrat's 'boundary control' (Gibson, 2012) and support the local opposition with the resources they would need to compete. Such direct intervention would likely be seen as illegitimate foreign meddling and, in any case, it is illegal for Europarties or their party foundations to fund national parties.[1]

The authoritarian equilibrium is also sustained by the enduring influence of norms of national sovereignty and the intergovernmental character in much EU decision-making (Jabko, 2020). The literature on authoritarian states within federal unions emphasises that variation in the power of federal governments to intervene in state affairs influences the durability of state-level authoritarian regimes, and that autocratic states use their access to federal institutions to promote their interests (Bateman, Katznelson, & Lapinski, 2018; Gibson, 2012; Mickey, 2015). Member states play a much more powerful role in EU decision making than they do in more fully developed federations, and the EU's authority to intervene in domestic politics of its members is far more limited. Not even the most powerful upper chambers representing states in federations have anywhere near the leadership role of the European Council. Also, fully developed federal polities generally do not use decision-making procedures that require unanimity among member states, whereas the EU does on a number of important issues, including for sanctioning attacks on democratic values. Finally, EU governance is heavily influenced by norms of respect for national sovereignty, mutual trust, and the assumption that member states will respect the duty of 'sincere cooperation' (TEU, Art. 4(3)) in fulfilling their EU obligations. These factors explain why the EU's authority to intervene in autocratic member states remains limited compared to that of central governments in more developed federal systems.

The second factor supporting the authoritarian equilibrium involves funding from the center. The literature on subnational authoritarianism shows how federal funding to authoritarian member states often helps sustain them; effectively these local autocracies function as *rentier* states, where the 'rent' supporting them comes not from oil or gas revenue, but from their control of the federal funds that flow into their state. As Gervasoni (2010) notes, authoritarian enclaves often develop in states with less developed economies, and these states will tend to be major recipients of fiscal transfers in federal-type systems. Thus, local authoritarians may be able to use federal transfers to support clientelist networks that perpetuate their rule, even as they flout the federation's democratic norms. However, another lesson from the literature on such regimes is that federal governments may eventually use their control over funding to place pressure on local authoritarians.[2] So while funding may help sustain local authoritarian regimes, it may also help constrain or even dislodge them.

But in the realm of funding, as in the case of partisan politics, the EU may find itself in the worst of all worlds: Governments may receive EU subsidies as they backslide into competitive authoritarianism, but – due to the political dynamics discussed above – the EU may find itself blocked from using the threat of suspending funds as a way to pressure these governments to respect democratic values. Finally, EU membership helps autocratic regimes access financing in a more indirect sense, by encouraging the inflow of Foreign Direct Investment (FDI). A large literature on the determinants of FDI suggests that regimes attract more investment as they strengthen rule of law and democracy (Jensen, 2008). Inversely, we might expect them to lose investment if they dismantle democracy and the rule of law. However, EU membership may provide a kind of ongoing 'seal of approval' (Gray, 2009) reassuring investors and supporting the continued inflow of economically beneficial FDI that might otherwise be discouraged by the regimes' attacks on rule of law and democratic institutions.

The third factor supporting the authoritarian equilibrium involves emigration. A number of studies have explained how emigration can help autocratic regimes survive. As Hirschman (1978, p. 95) noted forty years ago, the easier it is to emigrate from an autocracy, the more likely it is that dissatisfied citizens will choose to to exit instead of remaining and exercising voice. In short, emigration can serve as a kind of pressure release valve, whereby citizens who are most dissatisfied – and most likely to mobilise to challenge the regime – can simply move away, thereby eroding the potential base of the opposition. More recently, Miller and Peters' (2018, p. 2) empirical study of the impact of emigration on autocratic survival concluded that, 'emigration can be a boon to autocratic leaders … Allowing citizens to leave can also drive out political opponents and the unemployed, leaving behind a more loyal population (*Ibid*: 7)'. With all this in mind, we can see how the free movement of persons within the EU can contribute to the authoritarian equilibrium. Citizens in autocratic member states who actively oppose their regimes or are simply dissatisfied with conditions can readily avail themselves of the freedom of movement the EU provides and emigrate to other member states. Moreover, unlike in fully developed federal polities, emigrants in the EU do not gain the right to vote in national elections in the states they move to, while autocratic regimes can make it very difficult for them to vote in elections back home, effectively depriving them of the franchise.

Emigration may have a secondary effect that serves to stabilise autocratic governments. The literature on remittances suggests that when emigrés remit money to their families, it tends to increase their support for the incumbent regime. The key driver here is the phenomenon of 'misattribution' (Tertytchnaya, De Vries, Solaz, & Doyle, 2018, pp. 758–60), whereby recipients will often (wrongly) link the improvement in their circumstances that results from remittances with some action taken by the authoritarian incumbent. Similarly, comparative studies of the political impact of remittances, show that remittances positively influence recipients' approval for incumbents (e.g., Ahmed, 2017). Given the great economic disparities between EU member states and the fact that autocratic regimes are more likely to emerge in less developed states (Gervasoni, 2010), we would expect that emigrants would often relocate to wealthier member states and send remittances to relatives back home, which would tend to increase recipients' support for the incumbent.

Taken together, the three pillars of the authoritarian equilibrium can make the EU a surprisingly hospitable environment for the consolidation of hybrid authoritarian rule.

## The authoritarian equilibrium in action

In this section, I assess the extent to which we can observe the dynamics described above playing out in the contemporary EU with respect to Hungary. An abundance of evidence suggests that all three pillars of the authoritarian equilibrium have played a role in supporting the consolidation of the EU's first non-democratic government in Hungary. There is little indication it will escape this equilibrium any time soon, and ample reason to believe these dynamics will spread to other member states.

## The politics of authoritarian protection

The EU's distinctive form of half-baked politicisation has provided a supportive environment for the consolidation of authoritarian rule in Hungary. First, just as the theory of subnational authoritarianism anticipates, the EPP has shielded Orbán because his regime delivers them seats in the European Parliament and (usually) serves as an ally of EPP governments in the Council. At the same time, because public awareness of Europarties, and of the alliances of national parties that underpin them, is so low, the EPP has paid little if any price for its association with Orbán's autocratic ruling party. The political dynamics surrounding the 2019 European Parliament election provided a kind of stress test of the resilience of the authoritarian equilibrium in the face of the increasing politicisation of the EU, and to date the equilibrium has proved stable. Second, the powerful role of national governments in EU decision-making and the enduring influence of norms of national sovereignty in the EU also shielded the Orbán regime from EU intervention – providing further support for the authoritarian equilibrium.

Partisan politics have played a key role in shielding the Orbán regime from EU intervention as it rolled back democracy (Kelemen 2017). In short, the EPP protects the Orbán regime because it delivers seats in the European Parliament that have helped the EPP remain the most powerful force in EU politics. For instance, in the last session of the European Parliament, Orbán's Fidesz party delivered twelve seats to the EPP faction (of its total of 221 seats) helping it sustain its narrow lead over the second largest party, the social democratic S&D group. Being the largest party enabled the EPP to nominate Jean-Claude Juncker as Commission President and to take a leading role in legislative processes in the Parliament. In exchange for Fidesz' loyalty, leaders of the EPP for years defended the Orbán regime against EU intervention despite its blatant violations of the EU's fundamental democratic values (Kelemen, 2017). As Meijers and van der Veer's (2019) study of roll-call votes confirms, despite some dissent within the party, most EPP MEPs have voted against censuring their Fidesz co-partisans. EPP protection extends to other institutions as well. EPP leaders in the European Council have generally resisted calls for EU action on the situation in Hungary. Finally, the political power of the EPP may also help explain why the European Commission (which has been led by EPP Presidents since Orbán took power) has been restrained in its response to developments in Hungary, not only refusing to trigger Article 7, but refusing even to launch an inquiry through the 'Rule of Law Framework'.[3]

With the EPP's relationship with Orbán attracting more scrutiny in the run-up to the 2019 European Parliament elections, there was some reason to believe the authoritarian equilibrium dynamics linking the EPP and Fidesz might break down. And indeed, there was dissent within the party about its alliance with Orbán. However, to date, the EPP has chosen to maintain its support for Orbán's regime and it has not suffered politically as a result. Quite to the contrary, the votes of Orbán's MEPs proved crucial for the EPP's eventual nominee for the Commission Presidency, the German CDU politician Ursula von der Leyen, to win confirmation in the European Parliament.

The convoluted story of Fidesz' relationship with the EPP in the 2019 election is detailed elsewhere (Kelemen, 2018, 2019), but for present purposes the following points are essential. First, in 2017 and 2018, the EPP set out several 'red lines' – for instance concerning the expulsion of the Central European University – the violation of which it promised would prompt action against the Orbán regime. The Orbán regime repeatedly crossed these red lines, and yet the EPP took no meaningful action in response (Kelemen & Pech, 2019). Matters finally came to a head in February 2019 when – as part of his European Parliament election campaign – Orbán ran advertisements promoting a conspiracy theory involving the outgoing President of the European Commission Jean-Claude Juncker (an EPP member) and George Soros (Rankin, 2019). This provocation prompted the Swedish Moderate Party and quickly a dozen other EPP member parties to call for a vote on expelling Fidesz from the EPP (de le Baume, 2019a). However, even in the face of this provocation, Manfred Weber (leader of the EPP group in the European Parliament), Joseph Daul (EPP President), and other EPP leaders refused to allow a vote on expulsion. Instead, they agreed with Fidesz that it would voluntarily 'suspend' its membership pending an investigation by a committee of EPP 'wise men' – which would only report back only after the European Parliament elections. This so-called suspension was quickly revealed to be a ruse: Most importantly, it turned out that the suspension did not apply to Orban's Fidesz MEPs in the European Parliament, and that their seats would still count towards the EPP's tally (de le Baume, 2019b).[4]

While the EPP emerged from the election as the largest party with the presumptive claim to the Commission Presidency, they needed the support of socialist and liberal Europarties to form a majority coalition. Initially, a senior MEP from Emmanuel Macron's party indicated that the liberals would not join a coalition with the EPP unless it expelled Fidesz (Simon, 2019). However, they did not stick to this demand. The socialists and liberals in Parliament did block the EPP's initial candidate Manfred Weber, but after leaders agreed to replace him with a different EPP politician (Ursula von der Leyen) the socialists and liberals supported her even though Orbán's MEPs remained in the EPP (Kelemen, 2019). Ultimately, the votes of Fidesz MEPs were instrumental in helping von der Leyen win confirmation, and Orbán eagerly claimed credit for her victory (Kelemen, 2019). Strikingly, in the aftermath of the election, the EPP rewarded Fidesz by promoting some of its MEPs for leadership positions in the Parliament, and von der Leyen gave an Orbán loyalist control of the powerful enlargement portfolio in the Commission and indicated she would try to deescalate tensions with governments in east central Europe regarding rule of law (Rettman, 2019).

In the EU's half-developed party system, it appears that the EPP paid no meaningful political price for its alliance with Orbán. Europarties like the EPP have no real 'brands' that can be tarnished by their association with autocrats. Though there is no systematic polling on voter knowledge about Europarties, clearly few voters are aware of their existence or the alliances they entail. Europarties never appear on ballots in European Parliament elections, and they are only very rarely mentioned in campaign advertisements (Alemanno, 2018). Not only is voter awareness of Europarties low, knowledge of their leaders is as well. A YouGov poll taken a month before the European elections in 2019 found that only 26 per cent of Germans knew who Manfred Weber was, even though he himself was a German and came from the most highly institutionalised Europarty (Gehrke, 2019). Likewise, a 2019 study (Grande & Vidal, 2019, p. 5) that investigated whether voters could match lead candidates to their Europarties found dismal results: on average, only 15 per cent of voters across six EU member states were able to identify that Manfred Weber was the candidate of the EPP (and results for other candidates were even lower). If very few voters know about Europarties and their leaders, then naturally fewer still must know about their alliances with autocrats. As a result, the EPP and its member parties pay a little if any political price for supporting the Orbán regime.

The EU's half-baked party system is not the only aspect of EU politics that sustains the authoritarian equilibrium; the intergovernmentalism and norms of mutual trust and deference to national sovereignty that continue to dominate politics within the European Council and the Council of Ministers (Puetter, 2014) also play a vital role. As noted above, the imposition of sanctions under the Article 7 procedure requires unanimous approval of other governments in the Council. Thus, autocratically inclined regimes can protect one another through their veto power, which is precisely what the governments of Hungary and Poland have pledged to do (Shotter & Hopkins, 2018). More generally, the European Council and Council have demonstrated a marked reluctance to take action to address democratic backsliding, thus far refusing to even vote on the initial stage of the Article 7 proceedings launched against Hungary and Poland.

## Funding autocracy

Ironically, while the EU has spent large sums promoting democracy in candidate states and in countries around the world, today it is a major funder of democratic backsliding by EU member governments. For the 2014–2020 period the total budget of the European Structural and Investment Funds (ESIFs) was €450 Billion. For those member states that are the largest net beneficiaries of EU spending, the amounts involved can be massive – amounting to between three and four per cent of GDP annually. In the last budget, Poland was the largest overall recipient, taking in 86 billion euros (European Commission, 2015, p. 45). Hungary meanwhile was the largest recipient on a per capita basis. For instance, in 2017 EU spending in Hungary amounted to over €4 billion (over €3.2 billion net accounting for Hungary's budget contributions), amounting to 3.43 per cent of gross national income. Strikingly, more than 95 per cent of all public investments in Hungary in recent years have been co-financed by the EU (Keszthely, 2017).

While EU funding is intended to serve laudable goals, it sometimes has perverse consequences. For decades scholars studying the impact of EU funds on Greece and other cohesion countries noted that these funds might act as a form of 'resource curse' fueling corruption and clientelism (Huliaras & Petropoulos, 2016). When faced with a democratic backslider, this resource curse has proven even more damaging: instead of simply funding a public sector bloated with patronage jobs, EU funds have helped prop up authoritarian member government in Hungary. As scholars such as Magyar (2016) and journalists (e.g., Dunai, 2018; Rankin, 2018) have revealed, a significant portion of the EU funding allocated to Hungary has been channeled by the Orbán government into the pockets of Fidesz cronies.[5] Incredibly, member states who benefit from EU funds have been allowed to opt-out of being subject to the scrutiny of the new European Public Prosecutor's Office, whose job it will be to combat fraud against the EU budget. Unsurprisingly, Hungary is among the six member states that have opted-out.

In a more politically developed federation, the center might use the dependence of a regime like Orbán's on its funding as a source of leverage to defend democracy. There has been recent debate about attaching more stringent rule of law conditions to EU funding, and the Commission has proposed a regulation along these lines (Bayer, 2019). However, suspending EU funding ultimately requires the political will to act, and the political dynamics discussed above continue to prevent this. In particular, other governments with grave rule of law problems oppose funding conditionality designed to address the situation in Hungary or Poland, fearing it could one day be used against them (AFP, 2018; Gotev, 2018). Given the intergovernmental character of so much EU decision-making, these governments can likely block reform along these lines.

In addition to the EU's direct funding, EU membership also makes it easier for autocratic regimes to attract international capital. EU accession provided an important seal of approval of good governance that helped new member states attract FDI (Gray, 2009). So long as these states remain EU members, they retain that seal of approval and unfettered access to the EU's single market, which should presumably reduce the risk foreign firms associate with investing in them. Developments in Hungary suggest that this has indeed occurred. Even as the Orbán regime has undermined the rule of law and democracy, Hungary continues enjoying robust inward FDI from the EU. Inward flows and stocks of FDI in Hungary were higher in 2017 than in 2010 when Orbán was first elected. Foreign owned firms remain major players in the Hungarian economy, accounting for a quarter of all jobs in the private sector (OECD, 2017, pp. 1–6) and nearly 80 per cent of all exports (*Ibid.*). For instance, a 2017 survey by the German-Hungarian Chamber of Industry and Commerce indicated that over six thousand German companies operate in Hungary, employing a total of over 300,000 people, and that more than half of these firms plan to increase their investment in the near future (Kovács, 2017). German automakers in particular maintain close relationships with the Orbán government (Klawitter, 2018) and, strikingly, in the midst of the Hungarian government's intensifying attacks on liberal democracy and just months after the European Parliament adopted the Sargentini Report calling for the invocation of Article 7 against the Orbán government, German carmaker BMW announced plans to build a new, one billion euro car factory in Hungary (Taylor & Than, 2018). In short, EU membership has helped the Orbán regime continue to fuel its economy with FDI, even as it has installed a hybrid authoritarian regime.

## Enabling exit

Has emigration helped the Orbán regime survive? While the case is not conclusive, there is substantial evidence to suggest that the easy exit option provided by EU membership is acting as a pressure release valve, encouraging hundreds of thousands dissatisfied citizens who might otherwise support local opposition parties to emigrate, and that the remittances they send home then act as an important stimulus for the local economy. Data on emigration are notoriously unreliable and tend to understate the phenomenon. The most reliable longitudinal data come from Eurostat. We can use these as a conservative gauge of emigration. Based on these data, there were 120,100 Hungarians living in other EU member states in 2010, the year that Orbán came to power. By 2018, there were 348,500. The increase in

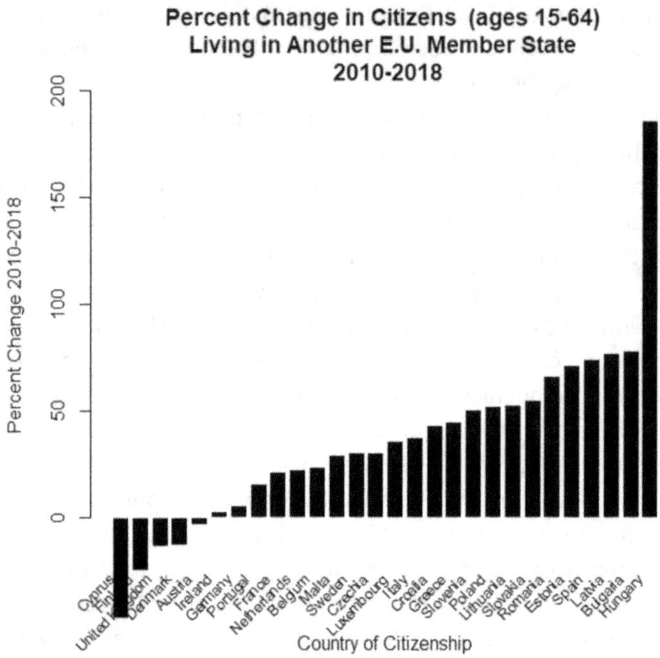


**Figure 1.** Percent Change in Citizens (ages 15–64) living in another E.U. member state 2010–2018. Source: Eurostat.

emigration from Hungary during this period (up 186 per cent) was more than double the increase from any other EU member state (the next highest being Bulgaria, which experienced a 78 per cent increase in its emigrant population). (See Figure 1) To be sure, citizens from east central European states were moving in large numbers to western member states for economic reasons long before the current democratic backsliding crisis began, and emigrants include people with a wide spectrum of political views – including supporters of authoritarian regimes. Also, Hungary by no means has the highest proportion of its population living in other EU member states. However, since Orbán came to power, emigration has clearly accelerated in Hungary far faster than it has in other EU member states, and this happened despite the fact that unemployment in Hungary was decreasing substantially (from roughly 11 per cent in 2010–3.7 per cent in 2018).

Is there reason to believe that this exodus has supported the durability of the Orbán regime? While we lack the data to reach a definitive conclusion, there is substantial circumstantial evidence to suggest that emigration does benefit the Orbán regime politically. First, we must recognise that Hungarian emigrants are substantially younger and better educated than the general population (Csipkés & Nagy, 2018), demographic attributes that make them less likely to support Fidesz than the general Hungarian population. The exodus of hundreds of thousands of voters who would disproportionately tend to favor the opposition might not matter much if they still voted once residing abroad, but in fact only a small fraction of them do. For instance, in the 2018 parliamentary elections, only 51,854 Hungarians living abroad (not just in other EU countries but across the world as a whole) voted. The low rate of electoral participation by these emigrants is no accident but is the result of deliberate policy by the Orbán regime, which suggests that the Orbán government believes that non-voting by these emigrants benefits it. Consider the contrast in the voting procedures the Orbán regime established for emigrants – whom we have strong reason to believe would disproportionately support the opposition – and the procedures it established for the nearly 400,000 ethnic Hungarians in neighboring countries whom the regime granted citizenship – and whom it expected to vote overwhelmingly for Fidesz.[6] In short, the Orbán government has made it difficult for emigrants to vote from outside the country by requiring them to vote in person at a diplomatic mission (i.e., consulate or embassy), whereas ethnic diaspora Hungarians could vote by mail. This distinction in voting procedures was criticised by OSCE election observers because it, 'challenged the principle of equal suffrage, and … the distinction was based on partisan considerations' (OSCE, 2018, p. 1).

Did this outflow of likely opposition voters influence the election outcome? Given the Orbán regime's other electoral manipulations and its large margin of victory, emigration was certainly not key to winning a majority. However, the Orbán government has placed great emphasis not simply on winning but on maintaining a two-thirds majority in Parliament, as this enables it to adopt constitutional changes. In the 2018 election, the Orbán regime hung on to its two-thirds majority by just one seat in Parliament. If the emigration of hundreds of thousands of potential voters shifted the election outcome just slightly in the government's favor – which seems very plausible – that could have given it the margin it needed to secure two-thirds.

Finally, emigration does seem to be benefiting the Orbán regime in the other, indirect way anticipated in the literature discussed above, through remittances. Not only do many likely Orbán opponents leave, they send home significant remittances, and the level of remittances being sent to Hungary has increased dramatically since Orbán took office. In that period, remittances to Hungary have increased in value from $2.16 billion to $4.6 billion (Comes, Bunduchi, Vasile, & Stefan, 2018, p. 251). As Figure 2 illustrates, remittances to Hungary have increased from 1.6 per cent of GDP in 2010 (the year Orbán was elected) to 3.5 per cent in 2018.

Of course, remittances increased across much of the region in this period with the opening up of the EU labor market to workers from accession states. However, if we compare developments in Hungary to those in the other Visegrad countries (which are its closest comparators) the rate of

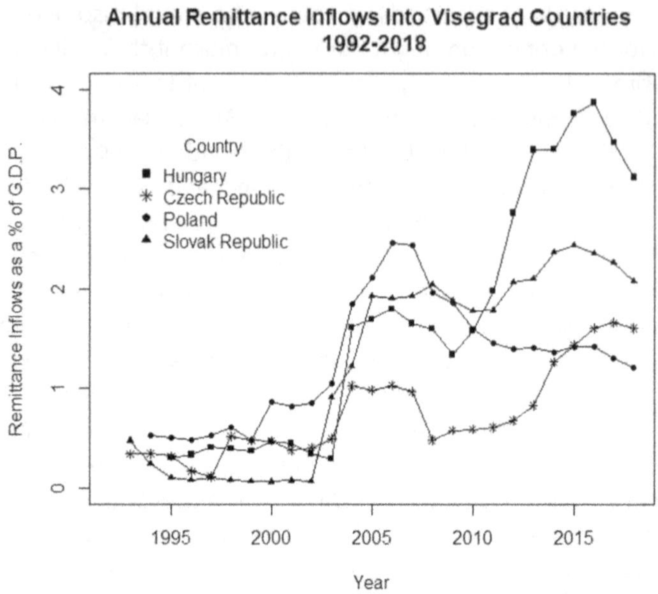


**Figure 2.** Annual remittance inflows into Visegrad countries 1992–2018. Source: Migration Policy Institute, using World Bank available here: www.worldbank.org/en/topic/migrationremittancesdiasporaissues/brief/migration-remittances-data

acceleration of remittances from Hungary is striking, and it has now become the clear leader in the region in the importance of remittances to its economy. As the literature discussed above reminds us, remittances generally lead recipients (relatives who remain in Hungary) to improve their assessments of the incumbent regime – thus providing the government another indirect benefit from the emigration of dissatisfied citizens to elsewhere in the EU. Finally, there is little reason to believe the outflow of dissatisfied Hungarians will decline in the foreseeable future: a recent survey found that 15 per cent of Hungarians – including 41 per cent of 18–29 year olds – plan to move abroad to work in the future (Flachner, 2018).

## Conclusion

This article explains how and why authoritarian member state governments may endure within the EU. It paints a bleak picture. Though the EU was intended to be a union of democracies, its half-baked institutional order is now providing a hospitable environment for aspiring autocrats. Developments in Hungary demonstrate a formula that may enable other aspiring national autocrats to consolidate power within the EU. In short, the EU appears to be stuck in an autocracy trap, and there is little reason to believe it will escape it any time soon. Quite to the contrary, worrying recent developments in Poland, Bulgaria, Malta, and elsewhere suggest that other regimes across Europe have taken note of the lesson that the EU may tolerate significant backsliding on democracy and rule of law.

Those who despair at this conclusion may perhaps find of solace in one final consideration: the literature on authoritarian states inside democratic unions suggests that these regimes tend to practice soft forms of authoritarianism – so as to avoid prompting federal intervention. While EU membership may not assure that member states remain democracies, it will likely prevent them from becoming full-blown dictatorships. And indeed, the autocratic regimes that are emerging in the EU are far milder than the dictatorships of the fascist right or communist left that existed in many European states in the past century, and also milder than the authoritarian regimes on the EU's doorstep today in Russia or Turkey. That will surely not satisfy principled democrats, but those who set their sights low enough and consider the ugly history of governance in much of Europe may still view it as modest progress.

## Notes

1. See Article 22(1) of Regulation 1141/2014 on the statute and funding of European political parties and European political foundations, 22 October 2014, OJ L 317/1.
2. For instance, the US federal government has used the threat of suspension of federal funding to pressure subnational governments to respect fundamental values such as civil rights laws.
3. Though see Closa (2019) who argues partisanship has not played a role in the Commission.
4. As this article goes to press, the EPP 'wise men' committee has yet to issue its report on Fidesz' membership, but Orbán has already indicated he is considering quitting the EPP and instead joining the European Conservatives and Reformists (ECR) - the Europarty which is home to Poland's ruling PiS party. Though protection from the powerful EPP was crucial for Orbán to consolidate his grip on power, at this point even a weaker party like the ECR could provide Orbán's regime with adequate political protection to sustain the authoritarian equilibrium.
5. A recent New York Times investigation found that the Orbán regime also uses EU agricultural subsidies to support its patronage network and punish rivals (Gebrekidan, Apuzzo, & Novak, 2019).
6. Ninety-six percent (216,561 of 225,471) of the ethnic diaspora Hungarians who voted by mail in the 2018 election voted for Fidesz. Data available from Hungary's National Election Office at https://www.valasztas.hu/levelszavazas-jegyzokonyv.

## Acknowledgements

The author thanks Sanjana Chandra and Philip Olson for their research assistance. Also he thanks the anonymous reviewers and the special issue editors as well as participants in seminars at King's College, Stanford, Harvard, LMU Munich, Johns Hopkins, Princeton and the University of Montréal for their feedback on earlier versions of the manuscript.

## Disclosure statement

No potential conflict of interest was reported by the author.

## References

Agence France Press (AFP). (2018, February 2). Romania backs Poland in rejecting EU funding conditionality. Retrieved from https://www.euractiv.com/section/eu-priorities-2020/news/romania-backs-poland-in-rejecting-eu-funding-conditionality/

Ahmed, F. (2017). Remittances and incumbency: Theory and evidence. *Economics & Politics*, *29*(1), 22–47.

Alemanno, A. (2018, February 2). Why transnational lists matter for EU democracy. *Euractiv*. Retrieved from https://www.euractiv.com/section/elections/opinion/why-transnational-lists-matter-for-eu-democracy/

Bateman, D., Katznelson, I., & Lapinski, J. (2018). *Southern nation*. Princeton: Princeton University Press.

Bayer, L. (2019, January 17). European Parliament backs plan to link EU funds to rule of law. *Politico Europe*. Retrieved from https://www.politico.eu/article/budget-hungary-poland-rule-of-law-european-parliament-backs-plan-to-link-eu-funds/

Bozóki, A., & Hegedüs, D. (2018). An externally constrained hybrid regime: Hungary in the European Union. *Democratization*, *25*(7), 1173–1189.

Cianetti, L., Dawson, J., & Hanley, S. (2018). Rethinking "democratic backsliding" in central and Eastern Europe – looking beyond Hungary and Poland. *East European Politics*, *34*(3), 243–256.

Closa, C. (2019). The politics of guarding the Treaties: Commission scrutiny of rule of law compliance. *Journal of European Public Policy*, *26*(5), 696–716.

Comes, C.-A., Bunduchi, E., Vasile, V., & Stefan, D. (2018). The impact of foreign direct investments and remittances on economic growth: A case study in central and Eastern Europe. *Sustainability*, *10*, 238–254.

Csipkés, M., & Nagy, S. (2018). Development of migration potential in Hungary from 2000 until today. *Oradea Journal of Business and Economics*, *3*(1), 32–45.

de le Baume, M. (2019a, February 22). Swedes push for Orbán's Fidesz party to be kicked out of EPP. *Politico Europe*. Retrieved from https://www.politico.eu/article/sweden-moderate-party-viktor-orban-fidesz-party-to-be-kicked-out-of-epp/

de le Baume, M. (2019b, March 26). Fidesz MEPs remain in the EPP group, for now. *Politico Europe*. Retrieved from https://www.politico.eu/article/fidesz-meps-remain-in-the-epp-group-for-now/

Dunai, M. (2018, March 15). How Viktor Orban will tap Europe's taxpayers and bankroll his friends and family. *Reuters*. Retrieved from https://www.reuters.com/investigates/special-report/hungary-orban-balaton/

*The Economist*. (2019, August 31). The entanglement of powers.

European Commission. (2015). *European structural and investment funds 2014–2020*. Brussels: Regio DG.

European Parliament. (2013). Resolution of 3 July 2013 on the situation of fundamental rights: Standards and practices in Hungary, P7_TA(2013)0315, A7-0229/2013.

European Parliament. (2018). Report on a proposal calling on the Council to determine, pursuant to Article 7(1) of the TEU, the existence of a clear risk of a serious breach by Hungary of the values on which the Union is founded, A8-0250/2018.

Flachner, B. (2018). Még mindig több mint egymillió magyar hagyná itt az országot. *Index.hu*. Retrieved from https://index.hu/gazdasag/2018/08/26/kivandorlas_politika_fidesz_publicus_politika/

Freedom House. (2019). Freedom in the World 2019. Retrieved from https://freedomhouse.org/sites/default/files/Feb2019_FH_FITW_2019_Report_ForWeb-compressed.pdf

Gebrekidan, S., Apuzzo, M., & Novak, B. (2019, November 3). The money farmers. *New York Times*. Retrieved from https://www.nytimes.com/2019/11/03/world/europe/eu-farm-subsidy-hungary.html

Gehrke, L. (2019, April 24). Only 26 percent of Germans know who Manfred Weber is. *Politico.EU*. Retrieved from https://www.politico.eu/article/manfred-weber-germans-poll/

Gervasoni, C. (2010). A rentier theory of subnational regimes: Fiscal federalism, democracy, and authoritarianism in the Argentine provinces. *World Politics*, *62*(2), 302–340.

Gibson, E. (2012). *Boundary control: Subnational authoritarianism in federal democracies*. New York: Cambridge University Press.

Giraudy, A. (2015). *Democrats and autocrats*. Oxford: Oxford University Press.

Gotev, G. (2018, May 3). Bulgaria dislikes commission plan to link EU funding to rule of law. *Euractiv*. Retrieved from https://www.euractiv.com/section/future-eu/news/bulgaria-dislikes-commission-plan-to-link-eu-funding-to-rule-of-law/

Grande, E., & Vidal, G. (2019). The EP election 2019: A vote for whom? Paper presented at the 2019 ECPR General Conference, Wrozlaw, 4–7 September 2019.

Gray, J. (2009). International organization as a seal of approval: European Union accession and investor risk. *American Journal of Political Science*, *53*(4), 931–949.

Hirschman, A. (1978). Exit, voice, and the state. *World Politics*, *31*(1), 90–107.

Huliaras, A., & Petropoulos, S. (2016). European money in Greece: In search of the real impact of EU structural funds. *JCMS: Journal of Common Market Studies*, *54*(6), 1332–1349.

Jabko, N. (2020). Sovereignty matters. *Research in Political Sociology*, forthcoming.

Jensen, N. (2008). Political risk, democratic institutions, and foreign direct investment. *The Journal of Politics*, *70*(4), 1040–1052.

Kelemen, R. D. (2017). Europe's other democratic deficit: National authoritarianism in Europe's democratic union. *Government and Opposition*, *52*(2), 211–238.

Kelemen, R. D. (2018, November 12). The rot on Europe's right. *Euronews*. Retrieved from https://www.euronews.com/2018/11/12/the-rot-on-europe-s-right-view

Kelemen, R. D. (2019, July 17). This is how Europe got its new President. *Washington Post*. Retrieved from https://www.washingtonpost.com/politics/2019/07/17/this-is-how-europe-got-its-new-president-it-wasnt-pretty-process/

Kelemen, R. D., & Pech, L. (2019, March 15). Of red lines and red herring. *Verfassungsblog*. Retrieved from https://verfassungsblog.de/of-red-lines-and-red-herring-the-epps-delusions-about-restraining-orban/

Keszthely, C. (2017, March 30). Hungary's economy heavily depends on EU funds, study finds. *Budapest Business Journal*. Retrieved from https://bbj.hu/economy/hungarys-economy-heavily-depends-on-eu-funds-study-finds_130880

Kingsley, P. (2018, February 10). A west fears rise of autocrats, Hungary shows what is possible. *New York Times*.

Klawitter, N. (2018, October 5). Warum Audi und Daimler mit Orbán bestens zurechtkommen. *Spiegel Online*. Retrieved from https://www.spiegel.de/plus/warum-deutsche-unternehmen-in-ungarn-so-gut-zurecht-kommen-a-00000000-0002-0001-0000-000159786792

Kovács, Z. (2017, November 3). Hungarian FM: Record many German companies plan to increase investment in Hungary. *Daily News Hungary*. Retrieved from https://dailynewshungary.com/hungarian-fm-record-many-german-companies-plan-increase-investment-hungary/

Krekó, P., & Enyedi, Z. (2018). Orbán's laboratory of illiberalism. *Journal of Democracy*, *29* (3), 39–51.

Levitsky, S., & Way, L. (2010). *Competitive authoritarianism*. Cambridge: Cambridge University Press.

Magyar, B. (2016). *The post-communist Mafia state: The case of Hungary*. Budapest: CEU Press.

Meijers, M., & van der Veer, H. (2019). MEP responses to democratic backsliding in Hungary and Poland. An analysis of agenda-setting and voting behaviour. *JCMS: Journal of Common Market Studies*, *57*(4), 838–856.

Mickey, R. (2015). *Paths out of Dixie*. Princeton: Princeton University Press.

Miller, M., & Peters, M. (2018). Restraining the huddled masses: Migration policy and autocratic survival. *British Journal of Political Science*. Advance online publication. doi:10.1017/S0007123417000680

OECD. (2017). *Hungary: Trade and investment statistical note*. Paris: OECD.

OSCE (Organization for Security and Cooperation in Europe). (2018). Hungary: Parliamentary elections 8 April 2018, office for democratic institutions and human rights, limited election observation mission final report. OSCE: Warsaw.

Pech, L., & Scheppele, K. L. (2017). Illiberalism within: Rule of law backsliding in the EU. *Cambridge Yearbook of European Legal Studies*, *19*, 3–47.

Puetter, U. (2014). *The European council and the council*. Oxford: Oxford University Press.

Rankin, J. (2018, February 12). How Hungarian PM's supporters profit from EU-backed projects. *The Guardian*, 12 February.

Rankin, J. (2019, February 19). Brussels accuses Orbán of peddling conspiracy theory with Juncker poster. *The Guardian*.

Rettman, A. (2019, July 19). Von der Leyen signals soft touch on migrants, rule of law. *EU Observer*. Retrieved from https://euobserver.com/news/145504

Sadurski, W. (2019). *Poland's constitutional breakdown*. Oxford: Oxford University Press.

Scheppele, K. (2018). Autocratic legalism. *University of Chicago Law Review*, *85*(2), 545–583.

Shotter, J., & Hopkins, V. (2018, September 12). Poland pledges to veto sanctions against Hungary. *Financial Times*.

Simon, Z. (2019, May 28). Europe's eastern nationalists brace for backlash after big EU election wins. *Bloomberg*. Retrieved from https://www.bloomberg.com/news/articles/2019-05-28/europe-s-eastern-illiberals-brace-for-backlash-after-big-ep-wins

Taylor, E., & Than, K. (2018, July 31). BMW to build 1 billion euro car factory in Hungary. *Reuters*. Retrieved from https://www.reuters.com/article/us-bmw-production-factory/bmw-to-build-1-billion-euro-car-factory-in-hungary-idUSKBN1KL12X

Tertytchnaya, K., De Vries, C., Solaz, H., & Doyle, D. (2018). When the money stops: Fluctuations in financial remittances and incumbent approval in central Eastern Europe, the Caucasus and Central Asia. *American Political Science Review*, *112*(4), 758–774.

Venice Commission. (2013). Opinion on the fourth amendment to the fundamental law of Hungary, Opinion 720/2013, 14–15 June.

Way, L., & Levitsky, S. (2019, January 4). How autocrats can rig the game and damage democracy. *Washington Post*.

# Index

Note: **Bold** page numbers refer to tables; *italic* page numbers refer to figures and page numbers followed by "n" denote endnotes.

www.ingramcontent.com/pod-product-compliance
Lightning Source LLC
LaVergne TN
LVHW011133300926
849160LV00008B/632
* 9 7 8 0 3 6 7 7 4 0 8 0 1 *